KU-502-431

WORLDS APART

A Memoir

DAVID PLANTE

BLOOMSBURY
LONDON · OXFORD · NEW YORK · NEW DELHI · SYDNEY

Bloomsbury Paperbacks
An imprint of Bloomsbury Publishing Plc

50 Bedford Square
London
WC1B 3DP
UK

1385 Broadway
New York
NY 10018
USA

www.bloomsbury.com

BLOOMSBURY and the Diana logo are trademarks of Bloomsbury Publishing Plc

First published in Great Britain 2015
This paperback edition first published in 2016

© David Plante, 2015

David Plante has asserted his right under the Copyright, Designs and
Patents Act, 1988, to be identified as Author of this work.

Every reasonable effort has been made to trace copyright holders of
material reproduced in this book, but if any have been inadvertently
overlooked the publishers would be glad to hear from them.

All rights reserved. No part of this publication may be reproduced or
transmitted in any form or by any means, electronic or mechanical,
including photocopying, recording, or any information storage or retrieval
system, without prior permission in writing from the publishers.

No responsibility for loss caused to any individual or organization
acting on or refraining from action as a result of the material in this
publication can be accepted by Bloomsbury or the author.

British Library Cataloguing-in-Publication Data
A catalogue record for this book is available from the British Library.

ISBN: HB: 978-1-4088-5480-8
PB: 978-1-4088-5405-1
ePub: 978-1-4088-5394-8

2 4 6 8 10 9 7 5 3 1

Typeset by Newgen Knowledge Works (P) Ltd., Chennai, India
Printed and bound in Great Britain by CPI Group (UK) Ltd, Croydon CR0 4YY

MIX
Paper from
responsible sources
FSC
www.fsc.org FSC® C020471

To find out more about our authors and books visit www.bloomsbury.com.
Here you will find extracts, author interviews, details of forthcoming
events and the option to sign up for our newsletters.

ΝΙΚΟΣ ΣΤΑΝΓΟΣ

Author's Note

I met Nikos on June 28, at 5.00 p.m., 1966, and I saw him breathe out but not breathe in and felt his body go quickly cold at 10.00 a.m. on April 16, 2004. Those were the years of my life, and it was during those years with him that this book has most meaning. I loved him and he loved me, loved me more than I did him, and I have, since he died, perhaps made of him more of a lover than he might have been.

I would like here to write about the love between Nikos and me, and the life – not lives, but life – we built together, from our first buying two little yellow ceramic pots that started our life as lived in the world outside ourselves, and, too, in our collecting books, pictures, plants, records, and, because we were the same size, the clothes we bought together.

And so the acute sensation of our being together when we listened to music, or hung a picture we had just enough money to buy, or cooked, or watered the plants, or when we wore each other's clothes.

We were fortunate that our world was made interesting by friends whose different worlds – as known as a well-known writer and as unknown as an Italian peasant – made our lives interesting; for, again, we lived in the world together.

But what most united us was something difficult to make sensible, as when we sat on the sofa to listen to music, or did our grocery shopping, or did the washing-up after dinner guests had left: the stillness of the most powerful world apart from us, and we were most in love with each other when we gave in to it, the stillness of something great, grand, sublime.

I sense that stillness now, at its most expansive, in his death.

I dedicate the book to his memory:

ΝΙΚΟΣ ΣΤΑΝΓΟΣ

———————

Considering the diary to be lived experience, I have chosen from that lived experience people and events that interconnect and form a narrative that is meant to sustain itself. In effect, I have written a contained memoir extracted from the uncontainable mass of the diary.

London

Every single event in a person's life refers to that person's entire life, past, present, future. Every single person is at the centre of history.

———

I received a letter from Öçi informing me that he has become an American citizen, and has settled in New York with a job. If I want to come to New York and stay with him I am welcome. He signed it *agape*, 'love' in Greek. When I showed this letter to Nikos, he smiled and said, 'Your first love.'

———

I have been very upset since my aunt Belle's letter about my mother. I wept when I read it. I must go to Providence. I rang. Momma was home from the hospital just five minutes before and I spoke with her. She, weeping, said, 'Oh, I'm fine. I'm really fine. I'm a tough old woman, you know.' I said, 'I'm coming home to see for myself.'

What greater violation can there be than that one's mother has had her breasts cut from her body?

———

The night before I left, Nikos and I, sleeping together, dreamed about one another – he that I come home from a party and refuse to talk to him; I that he has asked another young man to bed with him and I, sobbing, plead with him not to, because whoever he is will replace me when I am gone.

I said to Nikos straightforwardly – as if by my being straightforward he had no reason to object – 'Look, I'd like to see Öçi again when I'm in New York.'

He said, 'Of course you must see Öçi again.'

Providence

In the train station in Providence, I telephoned my brother Donald to tell him I'd arrived; he said he'd be there to pick me up in his car in fifteen minutes, and, wandering about the station as I waited, I did not, I found, have to make an effort not to remember – though I did not want to remember – that I'd left from here, my parents and brothers watching me from the platform, on my way to Europe when I was nineteen years old, which Europe has since become where I grew into maturity and where I live my life.

My parents looked old, my mother thin and pale. From time to time she would get up from where she, my father, my brother and I sat at the kitchen table with cups of tea and go into her room, closing the door behind her, to do the stretching exercises she was told by her doctor she had to do. While my father and brother and I sat in silence we listened to her whimper.

She would come out of her room and join us at the kitchen table and ask me to tell her more about my life in London. My life, as recounted, left Nikos out, though leaving Nikos out was as if my mother and father, in speaking about their lives, left each other out. They had – I wrote 'had' as if they no longer are – lived together for more than fifty years.

My mother went to bed early in what, all the while I had lived at home, had been hers and my father's room, where they had, all their married lives, slept in the same bed; but when, shortly after, my father said he'd go to bed, he went into another bedroom. I was shocked, and I asked my bachelor brother Donald, 'Don't Momma and Dad sleep together any more?'

'No,' he said.

I didn't understand. Some bond had come undone between my mother and father that I had taken for granted would last all their lives, and, as if by some retroactive belief in what I once but no longer believed, even beyond their lives: that they would remain bonded in their deaths. Why were my mother and father not sleeping in the same bed?

I too went to bed, and I lay awake longing for Nikos.

I have spent two weeks in Providence, and with each day I have asked myself: is it just for his indulgence of my selfishness that I long so much for Nikos? I ask myself further: he, who sees me more clearly than I see myself, has to see the selfishness in me. And why would he, who does see the selfishness in me, indulge me in it if there were nothing more to be seen in me but selfishness?

A warm Sunday afternoon, my brother drove my mother and father and me out to the house in the country. The house was closed up, and no one, now, spends summers there. While my brother went about the house to check if everything was all right, I sat on the screened-in porch with my parents and with them looked out over the lake. I was struck not only that no longer did they sleep together, but that they no longer seemed to have anything to say to each other.

As we looked over the lake, one long, dark cloud rose from behind the pine trees on the other shore and covered the sun, so light shone above and below the cloud, a clear but flat light that made everything on the lake and the woods surrounding us go still, as if the air itself was aware of a sudden event that would change everything; the picnic table on the overgrown lawn, the pines and oaks and maples, the small waves on the lake that seemed, themselves, to have become arrested in their movement, all appeared to be back-lit and, themselves shadowed, emitted fine rays. Just outside the screened-in porch on the ground among pine needles stood a chipmunk, raised on its back legs, its forelegs hanging limply, and staring out at the lake as we did, stopped in its tracks by its sudden attention to what was about to occur. The cloud rose above the sun and in the light of the sun everything became rounded and familiar, and the chipmunk hopped away.

And I recalled that summer when I was seventeen and I sat with my mother on the glider, rocking back and forth. She was agitated, not now rocking in slow rhythm with me, but herself impelling the rhythm in quick jerks with her feet on the floor, as if she were keening in quick jerks of her body. I became rigid, the soles of my bare feet rising to the heels, which scraped against the cement, then my soles falling flat, over and over.

I didn't want to sit there, didn't want to listen; I didn't want to be her favourite son, but wanted to get up, go out, run along the dirt road out to the main road and – what? – hitch a ride to anywhere.

She went on and on: I was her favourite son, I was, because she had made such a sacrifice to have me, and I must know that, know the sacrifice she made to have me there, there, sitting next to her, listening to her patiently, she thanking me over and over for being so patient, I must know how much she loved me—

I couldn't, I couldn't any longer bear it – she was broken and I would break too.

I stopped the jerking swing of the glider by slamming down my feet and I said, in a flash of anger: 'I didn't ask to be born.'

And the only time in all my life, my mother hit me across the face.

———

During the weeks I shopped for my parents, prepared meals for them, even did the laundry and cleaned the house for them, which allowed my brother time off.

When, at the end of my stay, I kissed my mother goodbye, she said quietly, 'Don't think I don't love your father. I do. He's been so kind to us all our married lives.'

She had sensed that I'd wondered what had come between them that they no longer slept together, no longer talked to each other.

She said, 'I just needed, after so long, to be a little on my own.'

'Yes,' I said.

My father, hearing this, stood apart. I put my arms about him, perhaps the first time I had done this, and for a moment embraced him.

Whatever world I live in, my parents are my primary world, and their primary world is the world of their love for each other, the love of more than fifty years. Why does that world of love fill me with grief?

How I long for Nikos!

———

The God of the religion I was born and brought up in, our Franco-American religion, commanded us to long for nothing but eternity. This was the lesson imposed on all the students of the parish by the Mères de Jésus-Marie who taught us and Monsieur le Curé who preached to us every Sunday morning: we live to die to be with God in eternity. Even had I been able to say, as I do say now, 'I no longer believe in God,' the darkness of eternity would have remained, and does remain. The darkness was – is – more powerful than God.

I write as if surrounded by darkness, and the truth of my writing – the spiritual truth for which I write – is all in that darkness, and, like eternity, there is no seeing to the end of it.

———

I have a recurring nightmare that I am in America and can't get back to England and to Nikos.

I have begun to think that Nikos doesn't really exist, and that I'll never return to London.

I *would* die if I had to stay here, and only the thought of Nikos makes it possible for me to bear it, if Nikos does really exist.

On Train to New York

Someone once said to me, 'New York is the place you go to to flunk out.'

I lived in New York for just a couple of years before going to London, and, yes, those were years in which I flunked out.

Nikos' love for me assures me that I am not a failure, and I will never, ever allow myself in New York to feel I am a failure, will not allow anyone to make me feel I am a failure. Again, Nikos assures me that I am not, though he does tell me not to disappoint him.

The friends I want to see in New York come from friendships made in London, American friends whom I met in London but who live in New York, English friends whom I knew in London who have moved to New York.

Having come from my parents, I think of them, newly wed, on their honeymoon in New York, two young people who had never been outside the parish. My mother had no idea about what would happen to her on her honeymoon, and I suspect my father would have hardly known more. I know nothing about my mother and father in New York. It is as if they are there, in a hotel room, young and beautiful, and I can only hope that what they discover in their love is a joy to them.

New York

With my valise, I went immediately from Penn Station to Jennifer Bartlett's opening at Paula Cooper Gallery, the white walls as if given deeper dimension by juxtaposed white-enamelled plates on which the multi-coloured dots appear to float in space. She was not there.

There I saw the British artists Mario Dubsky and Mark Lancaster and Keith Milow and Julian Lethbridge, all London friends, and all tremendously friendly in greeting me. I felt close to everyone, I loved everyone. Jennifer Bartlett hadn't known I was coming. She shouted when she saw me, threw her arms around me, and we laughed and laughed. All of us, a group, went to dinner together.

I stayed with Mark at the Bank. The Bank was once a functioning bank that Jasper Johns bought and converted into a living space, a vast living space; but Jasper doesn't live there since someone was killed at night in the recessed entrance and before the bronze door, though Mark, Jasper's assistant, does. There is a big John Chamberlain piece of crushed cars, a site-specific lead piece on a floor thrown by Richard Serra, and, in a glass or Perspex case, three nails with which Chris Burden had had himself nailed to a car that was then driven through the streets of Los Angeles. The Bank has its original vault. One wall of the vast space is hung with Mark's paintings, inspired by the paintings of Duncan Grant, for

Mark, who has given up London for New York, is still in the thrall of Bloomsbury.

———

I had forgotten my valise at the Paula Cooper Gallery, and the next day went to fetch it, and then went to Keith's loft in Broome Street to see his latest work, crosses, which he calls a cross between painting and sculpture.

I was wearing a tweed jacket and carrying my valise. Keith took me to a leather bar on the Hudson River front but, outside, said I might not be allowed in, wearing what I was wearing, but we entered and the men there stared at me as if I was wearing the kinkiest get-up known. Men in black leather and chains were kissing one another and drinking beer. I was both fascinated and bored. Then Keith took me to Christopher Street, which was crowded with older queer men, then into a bar on Christopher Street packed with young queer men. We looked and looked, until we had scrutinized everyone, and I said, 'Let's go.'

We went to meet Öçi, who had told us to meet him at the apartment of a friend of his in the Village. Seeing Öçi after some years, I noted he has aged, his nose large with oily pores, and he has a thick moustache that curves round his lips, and his sideburns are long and his black hair is almost to his shoulders. A long, narrow silk scarf tied around his neck is left to float about him as he moves. Öçi's friend, as all of Öçi's friends, was very beautiful.

Mario was there also, he too having moved to New York, where he hoped to make it in a bigger way than he had in London, but he complained that his reception in New York was less than in London, where I had often heard him complain he had no reception at all. So, Mario, Mark, Keith, and Julian left London to make it bigger in New York. I did not say what someone had told me: that New York is where one goes to flunk out.

We all more or less stood about, not settling, talking at cross-purposes. It occurred to me that there were sexual connections among us, though perhaps leaving Öçi's beautiful friend aside: that

Keith and Mario and I had, separately, been lovers of some kind with Öçi, making Keith and me related through Öçi, and that Keith and Mario had been lovers of some kind, so that Mario was related to me at one remove. Are we brought together in ways that bond us? And what was Öçi's bonding relationship with his beautiful friend, to whom he seemed to pay more attention than to me, to whom he had written he longed to see?

In New York, I was more aware of the wonder of sex than in London with Nikos.

Again with my valise, I left after a short while to go to Jennifer's loft in Lafayette Street. I had sent her *Preface*, my piece of abstract writing which is based on geometrical figures, to read, and we talked about that. I had read parts of her *History of the Universe*, which is based on concrete mundane details, and we talked about that. I like the flat declarative way she writes, which comes across as funny:

'You won't be able to have intercourse for two weeks.'
   'OK.'
   Across the surface of the desk the doctor said, 'My patients have two reactions to that: "Oh no!" and "Thank God."'

At about 1:30, we went out to the Spring Street restaurant, and talked and talked about our mutual friends – Julian Lethbridge and the artists Jan Hashey and Michael Craig-Martin – and who was having an affair with whom. We saw a rat run across the floor of the restaurant, empty but for us. She insisted on paying the bill, which I thought she did to let me know she has much more money than I do, and we left. It was 3:00 a.m.

We were walking together, silent, and I remembered my valise, which I had left in her loft. I heard my name called out from the window of a taxi, turned to see who it was, and, the taxi stopped at a red light, I saw Keith, completely dressed in black leather, get out. He had been to a bar, and was going home alone. Jennifer and I went up to her loft, from where I rang Mark to say I was on my way to him (he wasn't feeling well), and he said I should be very careful about getting to the Bank at that hour, and that I shouldn't carry my valise. Jennifer said, 'Well, stay here,' and I told Mark I'd see him in the morning. Jennifer said (and I imagined it was the thing to say when someone was staying over), 'I can make up the couch for you to sleep on or you can sleep with me in my bed,' and I said, 'I wouldn't mind sleeping with you in your bed.'

I felt a spasm in the small of my back I had not experienced before in making love.

She said, 'But you're supposed to be gay.' I said, 'I am. I don't know what's happening. I suppose I should be confused, but I'm not. I'm not going to think about it.' 'No, don't,' she said. 'But I know I'm happy,' I said. In the morning, we lay in bed a long while, and now and then we'd laugh, or we'd kiss.

Jennifer has told everyone we spent the night making love, which I don't mind, but I don't want Nikos to know until I tell him. She was on the telephone more than she was with me. I think she can read, write, paint while on the telephone. We talked a little about our night together. I said, 'I think it has to do with my dying parents,' and she said, 'I think so too.' We were sitting together on the couch and began to make love; I had dates to see other people – my publisher – and I wanted to go, yet I wanted to stay. Jennifer wanted me to stay, and said, 'You've turned my whole world upside down.' I kissed her and said, 'I'm suddenly anxious,' and she, 'Then you'd better go. You're programmed to do other things. You can't stop them.' A sadness settled over me leaving her, the sadness, perhaps, of leaving her to do the things I was programmed to do, whatever they were, but which kept me from her.

I got into a taxi to go uptown to Öçi's flat, and I remember that taxi ride, and believe I will always remember it, as one of the happiest experiences of my life. I knew I was loved, and I knew I loved, and I felt all the love fountaining and fountaining in me.

Öçi lives on the Upper West Side in a brownstone on 76th Street that is owned by two male lovers. Hanging on the walls are framed fragments of textiles: a Coptic weaving, early Venetian velvet, an Ottoman embroidery of tulips.

Alone together, we embraced and laughed, though as ever I was not quite sure what Öçi was laughing at, except that, whatever, his laughter made it absurd. Öçi does have a great appreciation of the absurd, one of his richest sources of amusement. To him, something about our being together in New York was absurd, and very funny. Not knowing why, I took it as funny too.

He said he was having an affair with someone named Olivia, but I didn't ask about her.

He made tea, from time to time flicking his silk scarf over a shoulder, and he described his becoming an American: he had stood among a group of people gathered before the American flag – he the only Occidental person there, as vaguely Occidental as he was – to pledge allegiance to the United States of America.

'There were people there,' he said, 'from countries I – can you imagine? I – had never even heard of, of colours and shapes of eyes I'd never before seen.'

I said, 'It's strange to me, your becoming an American and living in America and my living in England. We've changed places.'

'You must know that I always wanted to become American,' he said.

'And you feel that you are American?'

'In a way I could never have become British. In America, a foreigner can become American just by, like other Americans, making a life of his own as an individual. In Britain, yes, you can become Islamic British or West Indian British or Hong Kong British, but you remain in your group. I never belonged enough to one group in Britain. In America, I feel I don't have to belong to any group, but can make it on my own. Which I've done. I'll show you the textile gallery I've opened with friends, a Russian and a Swede.'

I had thought Öçi was more original than he showed himself to be, mouthing what I, as an American, considered banalities about America. All I asked was, 'How difficult was it to get American citizenship?'

Öçi smiled by pursing his lips under his large Turkish moustache. 'Not if you have a lawyer with mafia connections.'

He has always been, in his subtle way, lawless.

After a cup of tea in his living room, I said, 'It doesn't matter if I
don't ring Nikos,' because I still did not want him to think I was so
committed to Nikos that I had any strict duty towards him, though,
in fact, I wanted very much to ring him, very much wanted to let
him know I had arrived safely. I looked at my watch. 'Five hours
ahead, he'll probably be in bed by now.'

'I'm sure it does matter,' Öçi said. 'Ring him.'

I did, and hearing Nikos' voice from across the Atlantic Ocean
a sudden, sharp longing came over me to be back with him, to get
into bed with him for the night. I hadn't, in the many years we'd
been together, felt so separated from him. It was only at my distance
from him that I heard his soft but precise accent, which seemed to
put him at an even greater distance than across the Atlantic Ocean.

As much to reassure him about me – I was always trying to
reassure Nikos about me – as to make him hear me over the bad
line, I shouted, 'Don't worry, everything will be all right, I'm here
with Öçi.'

Nikos didn't respond and I realized that what I'd meant to be
reassuring – that I was safe with Öçi – came out as anything but
reassuring. I glanced over at Öçi, putting the tea things on a tray,
and he looked towards me and smiled a knowing smile: he thought
I was telling Nikos not to worry because I didn't want Nikos to
suspect that, in fact, I wasn't safe with him and that he did have
reason to worry. The more Öçi pursed his smile the more knowing
it became.

Before I hung up on Nikos, confused by and anxious about
what I'd communicated to him that I had not meant to communicate, Öçi said, '*Filakia* to him.'

I said, 'Öçi sends kisses.'

'Oh?' Nikos said.

Never before had Öçi expressed any affection towards Nikos,
and now he was sending kisses, which I thought was intended to

suggest to Nikos that if he felt free to send him kisses, it was because
he felt even freer with me.

Nikos said to me, 'Well, give Öçi my best.'

But after I, reluctantly, hung up, I said to Öçi, 'And *filakia* to you
from Nikos.'

Nikos assumed I'd come to New York to be with Öçi because I
was, after all, still desperate for him. But when Öçi asked me if I was
too tired to walk in Central Park I said, with over-enthusiasm, I'd
love to go. I didn't want him to think I was confused and anxious.

We walked along a narrow, winding path through an area in the
park of small hills and valleys with jagged rock ledges and trees,
where men stood at distances from one another and stared at one
another.

'What are they doing?' I asked Öçi.

'You must know. They're picking one another up.'

He held out his hand, in the way a gamekeeper might hold out
his hand both to stop a visitor and silently call his attention to a
deer in the woods, and we paused in our walk to watch a guy in
tight jeans all at once start towards another guy in tight jeans, say
something to him, and go off, down a curving path among trees,
with him.

Out of the park, we walked down town.

Öçi is, linguistically, the personification of New York, where
he obviously feels very much at home, for when we went into a
Hungarian shop he spoke in Hungarian, in a Puerto Rican shop
he spoke in Spanish, in a Greek shop he spoke in Greek. In one
shop I heard him speak what I was sure was Yiddish, and when
we came out I asked, 'Are you Jewish as well as everything else?'
He said, 'Enough.'

Öçi and I walked along the Hudson, down to the wharves.
Öçi told me he thought I'd be amused to see what the wharves,
some listing and rotting, were used for. A high wind was blowing
off the river, and, even at this early hour, men were cruising one
another, their hair and beards – most had beards – and clothes
blown about by the wind. Among the men was a tall, thin, bony,

black woman with a long skirt and very high-heeled shoes, her hair teased up into a mass and held in place against the wind by a tight red kerchief. She was reading out loud from a book, as if to the men about her, who, however, paid her no attention. The book was the Bible.

Öçi asked, 'You see that woman?'

'I see her.'

'She's a man.'

We had lunch in a Chinese Cuban restaurant, where Öçi spoke to the Chinese waiter in Spanish.

I said, 'I expected to find you changed, but at least in one essential way you haven't.'

'How's that?'

'The way you're amused by things happening.'

'I have to be amused,' he said, 'and I hope I will always be amused.'

'You never let on about the rough times you've had.'

'I wouldn't find it amusing to let on.'

'Who is Olivia?' I asked.

'She is Olivia,' he answered.

'What do you do, then, if you want some amusement apart from her?'

'Whenever I need that amusement,' he said, 'I go to the baths.'

'Oh.'

'You've never been to the baths?'

'No.'

'I'll take you. It's a part of your culture. We'll go tonight.'

Öçi took me to a Turkish restaurant for dinner, and there he spoke Turkish to the waiter. He taught me some words to repeat to the waiter, who laughed. The words, I knew, had to do with sex.

When I asked Öçi what time we'd go to the baths, his sense of fun seemed to become all the more acute for my anticipated fun. We were giving ourselves up to spirited pleasure, which Öçi had always inspired in me.

On the way by subway downtown, to the Lower East Side from the Upper West Side, Öçi said, 'If I were you, I wouldn't tell Nikos about this.'

'He won't mind,' I said, because, once again and more than ever, I did not want Öçi to presume that whatever I did with him, whatever he drew me into giving in to, could have any influence on my relationship with Nikos. And I myself believed it couldn't.

'I think he'd mind,' Öçi said, and I suddenly felt that Öçi was taking me to the baths with the idea that Nikos would find out and that he would mind. Öçi did not like Nikos, and especially didn't like my living, day after day, with Nikos.

'Follow me,' Öçi said, and as I followed him into the Saint Mark's Baths I began to get an erection.

Inside, I said to Öçi, 'Tell me exactly what to do.'

We paid, signed a register, using invented names, and we were each given a key. I followed closely behind Öçi along dim, carpeted corridors lined with metal cubicles and brushed against men walking up and down the corridors silently, naked but for towels wrapped about their waists. Öçi showed me to my cubicle, and left me to go to his. Inside, I undressed, and, naked, took a towel laid out on the narrow bed and wrapped it about my waist and went to find Öçi in his cubicle, passing men who glanced at me.

I followed Öçi round and round the corridors and past the cubicles, many with their metal doors open, which I looked into at what, in the soft dimness and the deep silence, appeared to be dream images: a thin young very black man lying naked on his back and slowly stroking his big erection, the back and bucking ass of a white man fucking another white man, a man sitting cross-legged on his bed and masturbating as he stared out at men passing, the large buttocks of a man who was on his knees and bent forward so his head was on the bed and his ass was raised in a position of Oriental supplication. I found this amusing because Öçi did. He found everything amusing which I, alone, would have found intimidating, if not frightening.

He went to his cubicle and I continued to wander about on my own. In the maze of corridors, I became disoriented, and was surprised to pass Öçi's cubicle, so that he appeared for an instant to be someone I didn't know. He was sitting on his bed, his towel now loosely thrown over his groin. His moustached face appeared crude, his eyebrows as thick and wild as his moustache, but his body was thin and taut. He told me to come in, and I sat beside him on his bed.

I asked him what he would do if someone came into the cubicle he didn't want to have sex with, and he said, 'I say I'm resting.'

I went out. I looked into cubicles. I saw no one I wanted to have sex with. But, I thought, you're here to have sex. The door to a cubicle was open and a beautiful young man, his body smooth and slender, was in it sitting on his bed, but when I stopped at the door he said, 'I'm just resting.'

All at once, I wanted to leave.

I didn't think of Nikos. I was calm, light spirited, even light bodied, and the sight of a man coming out of a toilet carrying the red rubber bulb and the tube and the long black nozzle of an enema apparatus made me smile.

I went back to Öçi's cubicle, but the metal door was shut. From inside, I heard groans I recognized came from Öçi. I returned to my cubicle and closed myself in and sat on the edge of my bed to wait. I heard hard slaps and just-suppressed groans of pain from a nearby cubicle.

After half an hour, Öçi knocked on my door and called, 'David?' and I opened to him.

'How are you?' he asked.

'I'm fine,' I answered.

'Did anything happen?'

I said, 'Things happened.'

He said, 'And did things ever happen to me. My God, it was wonderful. I had a big, beautiful black man.'

I quickly embraced Öçi, whose eyes were glazed from his continuing pleasure.

With our towels, we went down to the basement where we sat together in a round wooden tub of very hot swirling water. From time to time, Öçi would close his eyes and smile and sigh.

Upstairs again, dressed to go, he encountered a big, beautiful black man with a towel round his waist still wandering the corridors, and he and Öçi hugged and kissed quickly, then, laughing, said so long to one another.

Leaving, Öçi asked me what things happened.

'What happened,' I said, taking on his way of speaking in paradoxes, 'was that nothing happened.'

'Nothing?'

I said, 'I'll tell Nikos the truth: nothing happened.'

'You were too intimidated.'

'No,' I said, 'no, I wasn't intimidated. I guess I need to know someone for things to happen between us.'

I was somewhat embarrassed to say this in case it sounded as though I was bettering him, for in fact I admire Öçi for his open sensual life, so I did not say that this was what Nikos felt, what, it came to me, Nikos has made me feel.

I kissed Öçi goodnight on his forehead.

I felt very free.

But, thinking back, I sense there was another reason for not participating in the sex: I was frightened of it all, and I recall the moment of most fear when Öçi took me into a room with what looked like a wide playpen covered with red plastic where, he said, orgies took place, and I hurried through.

———

It is as though I am at a distance from myself, and at that distance I'm aware of myself, and that awareness is filled with wonder.

I want to shout out, as I suddenly imagine Jack Kerouac, that other Canuck American, shouting out, Wow! Wow! Wow! for the mysterious, the miraculous, the divine wonder of everything.

Oh, and my love for Nikos!

———

Αγάπη μου!

After what seems a lifetime away, soon I'll be back with you! I will arrive at dawn, and I will find you in bed still, and I will get into bed with you and we'll make wonderful love!

Αγάπη σου!

With Jennifer, I feel sure of being, in myself, someone she is attracted to, and with whom I feel sure of being, in myself, attracted to her, making love with her.

And we do laugh a lot together.

I told her about my adventure in the baths, and she laughed the laugh I have become familiar with, a laugh that seems to come from her abdomen and that rises into something of a knowing shrug that shrugs off anything but what she finds funny, even, she will say, weird. Her comment about my going to the baths was a shrugging dismissal and 'weird', and a half-laugh.

The fact is I do love Jennifer. And I love her as Jennifer, Jennifer in the character of Jennifer, which character so defines her as a person I almost see her as having her own sex, not so much the sex of a woman but the sex of Jennifer Bartlett, and this draws me to her to hold her and kiss her and make love with her. And, yes, I want it to be known that I have made love with Jennifer Bartlett.

As if we were now known as a couple, we were invited together by Jan Hashey, who now lives with a Japanese man, Yasuo, to a grand Japanese restaurant where the slivers of beef from cattle washed with sake are cooked over a white-hot stone placed in the middle of the table, served by geisha girls.

When Jennifer left to go to the loo, Jan said she was annoyed with her for appropriating as a subject for painting simple brown bowls, which is Jan's subject, and she had told Jennifer as much.

Jennifer asked me how I will react to being back in London, meaning back with Nikos, though neither of us refer directly to him.

I said, 'I don't know.'

'You don't think you'll see it all differently?'

'I'll see it all more clearly than ever that London is my home.'

We talked about when we might see each other again.

I thought with guilt, I've touched Jennifer, and she doesn't know what to expect from me.

I didn't see my current paperback publisher, Avon Books. I thought it didn't matter, as I felt I didn't matter much to the publisher.

Providence

The taxi driver from the Providence train station to Lynch Street said, 'I don't know what's happening to this country. No one does. Everyone is depressed. Everyone you talk to – other taxi drivers, fares, friends, even policemen – everyone is depressed. It's a sad sad country.' Then he said, 'Maybe we think that we always have to be happy.'

Momma greeted me at the door with a warm kiss.

I dreamed a lot about Nikos. The dreams were filled with anxiety, and I woke with the worry of how he will react to what I have done.

Jennifer rang in the morning. She was disappointed that I missed her birthday. I felt more guilt. I said, 'I missed my mother's birthday when I was in New York,' and I said, 'Maybe there's a lot to be said about my missing both your birthday and my mother's.' She told me the gifts she was given for her birthday, and I felt guiltier and guiltier.

It was very strange to have talked with Jennifer with my mother listening.

I must think how Jennifer can become a part of my life with Nikos, because she is a part of my life with him. He must see that.

I realize the greatest risk I've taken is not in reliving my past with my mother and father, but in undoing my present life with Jennifer. If Nikos reacts against my love for Jennifer, I'm dead.

Next day –

Again, I didn't sleep well, thinking of Nikos, wondering if I should ring him. In the morning, I did. I needed to hear his voice. He said we have been away from each other for too long.

And even stranger that I should be talking with Nikos while my mother could hear.

In Ireland with our Dear Friend
Anne Wollheim

Αγάπη μου! Αγάπη μου!

How I love you!

And how jealous I am of you. I never thought I would be so jealous of you.

You have every reason to be jealous of me, but you are not a jealous person, and I am, as you know, and, oh, I try to get over my jealousy of you here in Ireland with Anne.

It is so beautiful here. I keep telling myself how you would love being here, would love being here with ecstasy, because it is all, I know, what most raises your spirits: rolling rocky mountains, bright green fields, a dramatic yet delicate sea, clear warm light, and so calm, so calm, with no noises but the singing of birds and now and then the mooing of a cow, and all so pure. When I see a whitewashed house on a rocky promontory over the sea, I think of Greece.

What I thought would take so long to settle between us in London would here go quickly. You said we needed to be separated for a while, for me to settle, but together, walking, collecting mussels, fetching fresh milk, or simply sitting in the cottage sitting room, all the windows and doors open to the sunlight, we would be at peace.

Yes, as I told you, my jealousy of you and the unknown Paul is completely out of proportion with what happened between Jennifer and me. I know, I know. You are not a jealous person. I wish I were not, and that what you told me about Paul and the expression of affection you and he had for each other was just that, an expression of affection, which I should be able to accommodate, as you have accommodated what I feel for Jennifer, but I can't, I can't.

In two weeks, I'll come home to you to loving you.

And I pray you don't decide that you're a fool for loving me.

Anne is wonderful. She bakes bread and scones and pies. We've had fresh fish, sea salmon and prawns and mussels, and grilled meat over the fire. She cooks, I do the washing up. In the evening we play Scrabble, and she always wins. Yesterday we took a very long walk to a spot called Three Castles, where the ruins of a medieval castle stand at the edge of a mountain lake, other mountains rising beyond, and beyond them the sea – a place where, it seemed to me, Tristan, ill, would have lain waiting for Isolde's ship to come round a rocky headland out in the sea. Anne climbed over stone walls, crawled under fences, slogged through bogs, pressed on through heather and gorse, climbed mountain after mountain, and, when we got lost, led the way.

When Anne and I were coming through Irish customs in her car, a customs officer stopped us and asked, 'Do you have any drugs or guns?' and when Anne said, 'No,' he said, 'Then you can go right on through.'

Αγάπη σου.

London

Stephen and Natasha Spender came to dinner with Nikos and me, and Stephen was effusively kind, attentive, loving to Nikos and me, which seemed to amuse Natasha.

Always, I think of the dimension of the love Stephen and Nikos and I have for one another, love from years past when I met Nikos, who worried what Stephen's reaction would be to Nikos and me becoming lovers, Stephen's reaction so movingly expressed in a letter that Nikos showed me at the time, a passage of which I copied out.

> I love the idea of David and you and me. In fact it makes me extremely happy. In each of your letters I seem to be measuring your happiness, and in this last one I feel you have achieved something that was potential in them all. It is quite marvellous that you have found David, and that doing so does not exclude me. Perhaps my one virtue is that I am able to have relations with people in which I wish them to be happy, and feel that their being so will not make me lose them . . .

During the evening, Stephen, giggling of course, described a pantomime he had been to, *Flowers*, in which a young actor appears naked, then, suddenly looking guilty, he said to Natasha, 'You were away.' She, laughing, said, 'Natch.' I said, 'Oh, Natasha, Stephen is in very safe hands when he's with us.'

I wonder if Stephen and Natasha's being so loving towards Nikos and me has to do with some accord they have reached between them about us.

———

Jennifer is in Italy for the first time, in Genoa, where a gallery is showing her work. Before she left New York she rang me. Our conversation was light and bright and jokey, then she said she wanted to come to London. I, wanting to see her but mostly not wanting. I found myself as if split into two people, one saying, 'Come!', the other saying, 'That's not what you really want to say, what you really want to say is, "Don't come."' I said, 'Nikos will be away in Athens and I'll be alone. So why don't you come to London and stay with me?' and the other side said, 'No, no, no!' She said, 'So we can be together.' 'If that's what you want,' one part of me heard the other part say in a low voice, and the part listening said, 'It's not what you want.' I felt physically split after I hung up. As I often do when I am split in two, I retreated from both parts into a vague sense that, after all, everything would work out, and no one would mind that I'd made promises I didn't at all intend to keep.

I didn't tell Nikos. The day after his birthday (he was very depressed on the day of his birthday) a letter from Jennifer arrived which Nikos opened before I woke, as I want him to do, and as I do his post. He burst into the bedroom so the door slammed against the wall, very angry, and said he was going away, that he wasn't going to tolerate lies from me or intrigues behind his back which made a fool of him in everyone's eyes, because he was sure that everyone knew what was going on between Jennifer and me but him; that I must make up my mind if it was Jennifer I wanted, and that I should do what I wanted, but that I should leave him out of it. He left, slamming the door shut, without saying goodbye for the first time in all our relationship. I was frightened. I got up, dressed, walked about the flat from room to room, and after a while

I rang him at his office. I said, 'It's all my fault, not Jennifer's.' He said, 'You must do what you want, I don't want to restrict you, you're free. On the way to the office I thought that perhaps it's wrong of me to object: you should do what you want, and if you're attracted to Jennifer, you should live with her.' 'I don't want to live with her,' I said. He said, 'Then you must make love with her if you want.' I said, 'I don't want to make love with her or anyone else but you.' His voice was calm. He said, 'I won't tell you what you should or shouldn't do. You must do as you want.'

I rang Keith, now in London, to tell him what had happened, and he suggested that Jennifer stay with the architect Max Gordon. I rang Max, got no reply, but decided I must write to Jennifer in any case and tell her she couldn't stay with me. Writing the letter took the whole morning. I rang Nikos and read the letter to him. Again, he simply said, 'You must do as you think best.' I went out and posted the letter, and immediately I felt relieved. That afternoon Max rang, and I asked him if Jennifer could stay with him. He said, 'I saw Jennifer two weeks ago in New York and told her that if she was coming to London she was going to stay with me – I told her she wasn't to stay with you under any circumstances. We all know your weakness for, even willing intimidation by, strong neurotic women, Jennifer herself knows it, and we've got to protect you from your weakness, your intimidation. And it's very unfair to Nikos. I told her that as well.'

Jennifer rang me from Genoa; she wasn't enjoying Italy very much (she said she was having an 'attack of xenophobia'), her show had been put off, and she thought she might go back to New York.

At a seminar given by Stephen and the academic Keith Walker in Stephen's study with students from U.C.L. The students sat about on the arms of chairs and on the floor, gathered around Stephen and Keith. The seminar was about Keats. I leaned on a doorjamb, listening.

Then everyone went into the sitting room for wine.

Nikos arrived.

Then Angus Wilson.

Natasha and Keith sat at the piano to play a Schubert duet, and everyone stopped talking to listen. I had been talking to Angus Wilson – I sitting on the arm of the sofa he was sitting in – and when we stopped talking to listen, I thought, Now this would make an interesting scene, everyone suddenly silent, the music the common element of communication, all outside of everyone; and while thinking this I saw Angus take from the inside pocket of his jacket a little notebook and open it and write what I imagined he noted about the scene.

The students left, and the guests who stayed on – Angus and Keith and Nikos and me – went down to the dining room for a supper prepared by Natasha, Stephen presiding.

Nikos and I sat on either side of Angus, who, constantly shifting his head from side to side, talked to both of us at the same time about his partner Tony Garrett, who is also a writer, but being the partner of Angus Wilson is not an advantage for publication. He chuckled and said being Angus Wilson is not an advantage for publication.

———

Sometimes, at my desk writing, the image comes to me of Nikos and this unknown Paul, and I have to stare through it, out of the window to trees and clouds and sky.

———

Jennifer is coming to London. I told Nikos I would treat her warmly, but I won't make love with her. He said that he doesn't care, and, once again, that I should do as I want, but he does care, because during the night, knowing Jennifer would be in London, he couldn't sleep – he couldn't dispense with her as he has been able to with anyone else I have made love with, because she's an unknown to him, not only as a person but as a woman. He can't see my relationship with her in terms of relationships he knows. He said, 'I don't want to see Jennifer, but I'll have to, and I'll have to be nice to her, or she'll think I care about what happened, and I don't care, really, I don't.' Then he said, 'Why don't you marry her, that'd solve your problem?' I said, 'I don't have a problem. There isn't any problem. I swear.' But of course there is – and I don't want to face it, tell myself it isn't important; it is as important, however, as all my relationships with women, and in moments of honesty I realize that my relationship with Jennifer is testing all my relationships with women. Nikos is half aware of this. He said, 'I limit you.' 'No, no, you don't,' I insisted, and he doesn't, because he *is* everything to me. I said, 'But I want to know women, want to be close to them, because they do make up half the world.'

Nikos, a director at Thames & Hudson, proposed doing a book of Stephen's photographs, of which he has many, all in old, busting cardboard boxes in a room in the basement called by Natasha 'the bottomless pit'. After dinner, in the sitting room, Stephen and Natasha opened box after box to sort out the ones that might be used for the book. Photograph after photograph was held up for Nikos to see and he often identified who was photographed. 'Jean-Paul Sartre', or, 'Auden, looking so young, his face so white and smooth you'd never think it could wrinkle.' Nikos would from time to time pick up a photograph and ask, 'Who is this?' and Stephen or Natasha would say, looking closely, 'Oh, that's Bernard Berenson,' or, 'That's Frieda Lawrence.' Everything went well as long as the photographs were of famous people, or of Matthew and Lizzie Spender as children, but there were moments when Nikos or I would ask about a photograph of a young man studying a classical statue, meant to compare the two, and Natasha couldn't answer, as if she became deaf and blind. More and more of these photographs of boys appeared, some naked standing by a lake and pitching stones over the water or lying on a flat rock, and Natasha became restless. She would say, flipping quickly past a photograph of a boy, 'That was before my time,' and she began to object to the photographs leaving the house. Nikos was getting annoyed. Natasha picked up a photograph of Stephen with his arm about the shoulders of a German youth, and Natasha, turning it over, said, 'I think that's Stephen with his first wife Inez,' but whatever was written on the back made her put the photograph quickly back into the box. I thought she felt more and more out of control, of not only her life, but Stephen's as well, and, I could sense, wanted to put the boxes away. She had seconded Stephen in wanting the book published, and Nikos was frustrated, but said nothing. Stephen was anxious. He kept saying, 'We'll do it another day.' Nikos insisted, 'It's up to you if you want the book.'

The next day Nikos sent Natasha a letter to let her know he didn't want her to feel she was being invaded by snoopers, and she rang early the following day to say, no, everything was fine – perhaps, alone, she had sorted through the photographs she wanted used. The next day, Stephen rang to say that, as Natasha was out, he was going to send a mass of photographs to Nikos at his office, but Nikos must not tell Natasha he had.

Often, when I think of Nikos in the publishing house, I imagine him encountering the Paul, the unknown Paul, he made love with, and a spasm of jealousy shoots through all my nerves, and I try, I try, I try to steady myself by insisting I have no reason to be jealous.

———

Keith is having a show of his crosses in the Round House in London, and, as Keith will do, he insisted that I go, and it always seems to me that I do what Keith insists I do, but he never does what I would like him to do, such as read my books. I don't mind, as I, myself, prefer looking at works of art than reading. I went. The show of many crosses, all constructed at various angles, are hung in the gallery around the top of the Round House, so I had to walk round to see them all, appearing and then disappearing. Keith insists that his crosses do not refer to religion, but he uses the elemental shape – as he does the tondo, the wedge, some architectural features, and all in elemental media, such as resin, cement, copper, lead – to inspire the variation. He was angry when he heard that one of his crosses is in the foyer of a church in New York, with a pot of white geraniums set before it. As I walked around, I became aware of the shadows the crosses cast on the walls, and, too, I became aware of the outlines of the shadows, which, in turn, made me aware of the crosses.

Yes, I can see behind Keith's work layers of the work of artists of another generation: van Doesburg, Mondrian, Lissitsky, Rietveld, but when I saw Keith later I told him I thought his work has to do with the awareness of edge, an edge that is between the work and something more than the work. There is a lot to expand upon in his work in the word: *between*. Whatever that something is, he would never talk about it; the work makes its own expansions.

He more than dislikes my using the word 'spiritual', which flattens the work. But it always happens that my appreciation of an artist's work is to the artist too obvious, and does not apply.

———

Jennifer rang to ask me if I would meet her at Victoria Station, on her way from Gatwick airport. We took a taxi to Max's, and on the way I said, 'I've been feeling as anxious as a freshman waiting for his date to come for the weekend.' 'With her strapless in a plastic bag?' she asked. She brought American college dating back to me: the guy waiting on the train platform for the gal to arrive for the prom, her strapless gown in a plastic bag, which Nikos would not have understood, and which made me feel Jennifer and I did understand each other for being Americans. I had a drink with her and Max, then left, and I wondered if she thought I should have stayed, as she had come to London to see me. She rang in the morning, and I went to Max's flat (he was at work), and we had a long lunch together.

I tried ringing Nikos in his office before leaving Jennifer, but he was in a meeting, and I left a message. When I got home I rang again, and this time I was told he had already gone. Something has gone terribly wrong, for we speak to each other every afternoon, a vital part of the day, he from his office, I at home.

Jennifer rang shortly after. She said, 'I felt a strain for the first time we were together.' I said, 'You see, I think of Nikos all the time, and feel that I'm being unfair to him – and I'm being unfair to you as well.' She said, 'We won't expect anything from one another, all right?' 'Yes,' I said, 'we won't.'

———

Nikos did ring. He hadn't left his office, but was hours at a meeting, and was very tired, feeling unwell, and thought he wouldn't go to dinner at the Flanagans', as we'd planned. I thought he meant this as a complaint that I had spent half the day with Jennifer. I went first to the Flanagans'. Barry was very silent, Sue bright but occasionally a tic made her cheek or eye shudder, the girls, Samantha and Tara, spirited. Tara held two little teddy bears with their arms about each other, and when I asked, 'Who's the boy and who's the girl,' she answered, 'No. they're like you and Nikos, they're both lesbians.' Nikos came about 8:30, and was very warm towards the Flanagans, but he ate little and only just kept up the talk, though he usually initiates the talk and carries on, sometimes aggressively, discussions about art, writing, politics. At 10:30 we left, and climbing the stairs to our flat he appeared to be descending into darkness. Again, I thought, he is this way because of Jennifer, but he won't say, as he had said everything in saying I must do what I want. I felt helpless and maybe annoyed, because he should have trusted me that I would not make love with Jennifer. In bed, he twisted and turned, couldn't sleep, then he suddenly jumped up, ran to the bathroom and toilet, and vomited. Everything in me gave way to him. I, by him, tried to comfort him, stayed with him until he finished vomiting, washed him, got him back into bed, cleaned the toilet and floor. In the morning I told him to stay in bed, but he got up quickly, as I know he doesn't like staying in bed, but he did say he would only go to work in the afternoon.

The telephone rang. Nikos answered. Jennifer was calling. I heard Nikos laugh, then he passed the receiver to me, making a funny face, and I thought he had decided to treat the whole situation lightly, if not with ridicule, and I was relieved. Jennifer asked if both of us would come to Max's that evening for drinks so that she could see that we were human beings, not just ideas, but I said we would both be too busy. She said, all right, but she was angry. Nikos left for work.

Nikos told me that Natasha, confronting Stephen about the absence of photographs, rang him at his office and asked for them back, and he sent them, including negatives, by courier.

In the evening, I went with Nikos to David Hockney's studio. David said, 'I'm so bored by parties and society, I'd rather be in a gay bar.'

And then we went together to Keith's, where Jennifer was sitting in a big brown armchair. She was very drunk. I leaned over and kissed her, and I said to Nikos, 'You remember Jennifer.' He smiled and shook her hand, and they talked a little, I standing by. I had no idea what state she was in, what she was thinking; she never left the big brown armchair. She asked me to sit with her. I sat with her. She put her arms around me and kissed me on the face, leaned her head on my shoulder, touched my chin and lips. I sweated, knowing Nikos, among others who came in, saw us, but I was frightened of Jennifer, and I was frightened of Nikos, of what they would both do. She said, 'I was so angry with you this morning. I made a big effort to invite you and Nikos together for drinks. It wasn't even my idea, it was Max's. And you turned me down.' I said nothing. She said, 'I came to London only for you, no other reason. Are you avoiding me? What do you think of me? Don't you like me?' I hugged her and said, 'I'm terrified of you.' Her voice seemed to burst from her: 'Oh, I'm terrified of *you*! What's going to happen? I think it's going to be a disaster.' I was trembling. I said, 'Perhaps, but I don't want it to be.' Nikos' back was turned towards us.

Nikos, I thought, was flirting with a very attractive young man. Aren't we too old for this?

The artist Sylvia Guirey came in. I asked her what she thought of Jennifer and she shrugged her shoulders and said, 'She's okay,' and she went to speak to Keith, who came to me to say that Sylvia had the feeling that Nikos and I are about to break up, and already, in a way, had. 'Because of Jennifer?' I asked, and Keith nodded, and I said, 'That's not possible.' Keith said, 'You'd be a fool if you did break up from Nikos because of her.'

Jennifer was still in the big brown chair. I said goodnight to her, and Nikos and I left. In bed, I asked him what I should do. He hugged me. He said, 'You're creating problems – you and Jennifer are. You both talk too much. It's all literature to you, and you like living the drama of literature.' I said, 'Yes, I do.' He said, 'Go to sleep.' But I wanted to make love with him, and we did make love, and then we fell asleep together.

———

There are moments when my religion comes back to me – as a dark space all around me.

Even as an adolescent – especially as an adolescent – I would think that the dark was more essential, for there was, as we all know, darkness before light was created. This is a distinction as old as religion, and in philosophy the distinction between essence and accident, a concept that is not only one with my religion but one with my philosophical scholastic training at the Jesuit Boston College.

The concept informs all my books, in which I try, try, try to go down to what I believe is the deepest, and what to me is the deepest is the deepest dark, and so the darkness of my books.

Friends ask me how it can be that I seem to be so spirited when my books are so dispiriting – though they don't use that word – and I have no answer, for how can I explain to them a vision that is my vision of the universe? And if I tried to explain, now to explain to them my religion, and, expanding on my religion, the concept of what is essential, which essential is to me the darkness of God?

And so my prayers, which come to me in French, the language of my religion.

Si je prie à Dieu de m'aider dans mon désespoir, ça ne veut pas dire que je crois en Dieu. Mais je prie: Dieu, Dieu, soyez mon désespoir.

Chaque matin, je me reveille dans le noir qui ne me promet rien que le noir. Je l'accepterais comme un fait de ma vie, comme j'accepte chaque jour la nuit, si je ne savais pas que ce noir c'est l'absence de Dieu, si je n'avais jamais cru que Dieu est mon matin, que Dieu est la lumière de ma vie.

Pour la grâce de votre lumière, Dieu, dois-je prier que votre obscurité soit encore plus obscure qu'elle soit assez obscure que je puisse voire votre lumière briller? Votre noir, ô mon Dieu, n'est il pas déjà assez noir?

Que le monde existe m'étonne, qu'une chaise, une table, un verre d'eau existent m'étonne. D'où vient cet étonnement qui n'a pas de sens dans son existence? Et comment est-ce que l'existence de Dieu m'étonne quand Dieu n'existe pas?

Dieu, Dieu, donnez-moi la foi de croire en Dieu même s'il n'y a pas un Dieu. Etonnez-moi.

Qu'est ce que ça me peut faire de prier à Dieu si Dieu ne me peut rien faire? Rien? Mais je prie à ce Dieu qui ne me peut rien faire, je prie en dépit de ce Dieu qui ne me peut rien faire.

Je prie pour rien, je prie pour rien, je prie pour rien que de crier: Dieu, Dieu.

Est-ce que c'est à Dieu que je prie quand je ferme mes yeux et prie de ne rien voir quand j'ouvre mes yeux, de ne rien voir que le noir?

I pray to God though I don't believe in God.

God frightens me, and I draw back from God. When I told Nikos that I was taught by nuns in my parochial school to offer up all suffering to God for my salvation, as an aunt who offered up to God her cancer, he replied, 'Why would God want to be offered a cancer? God wants flowers, incense, music.'

Once, I said to him that we should talk about what Jennifer means to both of us, and he said, starkly, no, he would not, he would not indulge me in my American introspection, and it occurred to me that we have never discussed any problems that have risen between us, that whenever I have even suggested we do he has said I should know he loves me, and there was nothing to discuss.

But then he will, without my asking, make observations about me that have the effect in me of stark self-awareness. He said to me as we lay in bed, 'You're enjoying the drama of your relationship with Jennifer,' and I listened with a little shock when he added, 'And enjoying bringing me into the drama, as though my love for you isn't drama enough for you.'

I sensed a little buzz of attention in my head. I asked, 'You think I'm being false?'

And he said, 'You are false.'

I said, 'Not with you.'

'No, not with me, because I understand what makes you false, and you know I understand.'

'What makes me false?' I asked.

He said, 'Let's sleep,' and he put an arm over me.

I want to die, and Nikos knows I do, and he understands that I'm frightened of this longing, and that my strained attempts to be spirited among friends, to want to meet people, to want to have supper parties, to invite and be invited, to be at the openings of exhibitions, to be noted as a known writer, to gossip, all this is forced, is false, because accidental to the truth of my essential spiritual longing. And I think this longing most informs my novels, about which I write so little in my diary. In my diary I try, try, try to be vivid about everything that most makes me false, about my being spirited among friends, about meeting people, about supper parties, about inviting and being invited, about openings of exhibitions, about being noted as a writer, about gossip. And so my novels represent me.

Again, Nikos knows this longing in me.

He sometimes tells me to become Orthodox, to believe in the God of Orthodoxy, but I tell him I don't believe in any God.

––––––––––

Nikos is in Athens to be with his mother. (He needed a rest from his work, though he was reassured in his position as director at Thames & Hudson by a rise long before he expected it, and about twice what he expected. Yet, he treats money with disdain, gives a third of his salary to charities, mainly for cats. But he is also reassured, made content, even happy when he knows he has a hundred pounds to spend, and will say, 'Now I'm going to buy lots and lots of things.') As he was leaving for Athens, I said, 'You have nothing to worry about, nothing.'

I didn't want to see Jennifer. I rang her and asked if we would have tea together instead of dinner. She said, curtly, 'All right.' I was too tired to talk, talk, talk. I went to Max's for tea, he in Egypt. More talk. She: 'What are the possibilities of our relationship?'

I held her and kissed her. She said, 'I'm terrified of sex with you.' I said, 'You know, I'm not. I wasn't in New York, and I'm not now. That's curious, isn't it, because I should be.' She asked, 'Won't you spend the night?' 'No,' I said, 'I have to go home.' She said, 'You're at least partly responsible for my being here, you know. Your letters were so warm.' I said, 'I am responsible, yes. The fact is, I want to be with you, like being with you, am attracted to you, and we do have wonderful times together.' 'But?' she asked. I said, 'I'm deeply married.'

London

I saw my friend the writer Bernice Rubens. Bernice said, 'You lead women on, David. You're a cunt-teaser. You flirt and then step back. It's wrong. You flirted with me. It's only thanks to my thinking it doesn't matter that we're still friends. You *have* to accept the fact that you're a homosexual.' I said, 'But I like women. I like being with women. I like being close to women, like touching them, like holding and cuddling them, like being intimate with them in the most personal talk. Should I not have anything at all to do with them?' Bernice didn't know what to answer.

Bernice is the first writer to win the Booker Prize for her novel *The Elected Member*.

Nikos rang from Athens. He said that he was having a good time, but there was darkness in his voice. He then said he had been reading old letters sent to him, and they depressed him – letters from old friends, school mates, some of whom he'd been in love with, and they all repeated, over and over, that he complained too much, he was too demanding, he was cruel. He asked, 'How do you put up with me?'

I had lunch with Stephen Spender and I told him about what Nikos had said to me over the telephone. Stephen told me that when he was in Washington, at the Library of Congress, he sent Nikos letters he thought warm, loving and intimate, and in response received letters from Nikos in which he accused Stephen of being cold, distant, unloving, which were puzzling, and made Stephen feel guilty and think that perhaps he was cold, distant, unloving. He had even thought that when he returned to London he would stop seeing Nikos, but I came along.

———

Jennifer and I out to dinner out with Max, he back from Egypt and eloquently enthusiastic about the country. He said his whole life has changed, and he wants to go back, wants, now, to take great risks with his life.

Max said he was going to stop going out, was, as soon as possible, going to go back to the village where he had spent five days. He asked, 'Why should I, a Jew, so love an Arab country?' I couldn't drink more than I had at dinner but they had brandy back in Max's sitting room. Max went to bed. Jennifer and I sat on the floor. I asked her why, as she had herself said, she was so grouchy. She said, 'Because I don't know what I'm going away with. You mean more to me than anyone else, and I feel I have nothing from you.' I said, 'I'm not going to give you any statement to take away. If you don't feel what I feel, what I know I feel without analysing it, then I suppose I have given you nothing. But I feel I have given you a lot, that you have given me a lot.' She said, 'I want you to stop me from thinking so much.' She hugged me. I said, 'I feel so well, I feel I've accomplished so much, and I feel that I do love you.' She held me more closely. I said, 'I think I know more about love than you do.' She said, 'You probably do.' After a short while, we were joking and laughing with each other. I felt large and calm when I left, about 5:00 a.m.

Max drove her to the airport, I in the back seat. Jennifer was terrified of getting into the airplane. A strange sadness came over me when I saw her go through passport control and out of sight.

In the car back to London, I said to Max, 'Well, I survived that,' and he burst out laughing. He said, 'It's good to have your life rearranged now and then, especially you, whose life is your work. You'll find you'll be much closer to Nikos when he comes back.'

I said, 'He'll say, "Drama! Banal drama!" And I'll say, "Yes, yes, it is."'

But Jennifer did once say to me that she likes the way I dramatize.

———

Nikos is home. The flat is filled with life, even with him sleeping.

I gave him my diary of the days he was away to read, and he said, with a flat, matter-of-fact voice, that what I wrote is embarrassing.

———

One night, Nikos and I were talking about his life. Going to Athens had been to go back into his past, which he hasn't dealt with (as I suppose I haven't dealt with my past, whatever dealing with one's past can mean), and he'd felt that he'd failed in everything, and he feels that now. 'That's not true,' I said, 'and you know it isn't,' and I told him that the reason why he thinks he's failed is because he applies such impossibly ultimate standards to everything he does. I said he has in himself a built-in destructiveness, which only requires him to ask himself, what's the point? for the destructiveness to take over, and makes him feel that everything he does has no point, and is at best a temporary endeavour. He said, 'I've always thought that everything I do, every place I've lived in, every relationship I've had, was temporary.' I said, 'Deep down, you think that, even after many years of our being together, I'm temporary, don't you?' 'Yes,' he said. I said, 'Well, I'm not.' He said, 'I know this – that my love for you is not temporary. I may ask myself, what's the point? and though I can't find an answer, I know there is a point. I love you very much.'

———

Stephen to us for dinner, after which he asked me to read from my diary, as if to make sure that I do keep up my diary, perhaps because he thinks I will be more open in what I write than he can be.

I read from the time when Nikos and I were staying in San Andrea di Rovereto, on the Ligurian coast, and Stephen came to visit:

Today it is raining, so Nikos and I stayed in, reading and writing letters. The little whitewashed house on the high steep slope of the Ligurian coast is enveloped in cloud, pouring down over the mountain ridge above us; there is a smell of mint everywhere. We've been here four days.

Stephen stayed at a hotel down the road for three days.

He left yesterday to go to Paris, where he'll meet Natasha. His trip to Italy is a secret from her. He said, 'She's suffered so much from my friends in the past, I don't want her to suffer any more.' Another time, he said, 'Natasha despises weak people. I'm weak. I don't understand why she doesn't despise me.'

The three days with him were beautiful. We took a long walk up the mountain and snapped many photographs. Stephen was filled with anecdotes. About John Lehmann: 'Rosamond and Beatrix and John were waiting together as their mother was dying. After some time, John took out his watch and asked, "How long will this take? I have many things to do."' About Auden: 'Wystan said he would write a poem for my birthday. I thought, How nice, a poem for my birthday. Then he said, "I didn't have time to write a poem, so I sent a letter to the *Guardian*." But the letter didn't appear, and Wystan told me they must have lost it.' Talking about poetry, he said, a very revealing thing about Auden's poetry is that it completely lacks mystery. The same applies to Isherwood's prose. He thought that mystery is what his own poetry is essentially about.

The hour after he left seemed vacant. I said to Nikos, 'It is so mysterious when people leave: I can't really imagine Stephen now on the same train we saw him off on, settling into his compartment and reading his newspapers. Separation is incomprehensible.'

'I hate it,' Nikos said.

Stephen blinked a lot while I was reading, and after seemed for a moment to be thoughtful, then he said, 'Yes, that's good,' and I knew he meant it, meant that I should write whatever I want about him and that he would approve, even if about him and Natasha, who would not approve.

Nikos became nostalgic for that time in the little Italian village on a mountainside, the house we rented for five shillings a day with a view over the sea. Nikos is nostalgic in a way I am not, but I am moved by his longing for a past that he imagines was better than the present; and that past in our lives together in the village was perhaps better than our time in the present, because then we were getting to know each other as we were getting to know Italy, and we are, I think, more engaged in the world around us than engaged directly with each other's self.

———

Stephen confided in us – and made us promise not to tell anyone else, as it would be a family disaster if Natasha found out – that he is in love with a student he met when he was teaching at the University of Florida in Gainesville. The student is Bryan Obst, who is eighteen to Stephen's sixty-eight.

He repeated, 'It could be a disaster.'

———

From time to time at a party, I see the party as if I am out in the universe and looking down on the world and the people in the world whom I have known – my parents and brothers, my friends in my parish school, then friends in high school, then friends away at college; and, too, the people I pass in the street, people I sit next to on buses, people I wait next to in post offices; people I share train compartments with in foreign countries, stand with to look at pictures in museums, eat next to in cheap restaurants – and at those times I am more aware of the world than I am of myself.

———

Frank Kermode invited me to high table at King's College, Cambridge, and Bernard Williams, the provost, asked me to sit next to him.

I know him – as I know Frank and almost everyone else I have met – through Nikos, these people known by Nikos not only as a publisher who is attentive to people he considers to be at the level of intelligence and culture he most admires and whom he may approach for a book – and, oh, the list of such people is long, many of them dedicating their award-winning books to him for his commitment, his concern for their problems, and, always, his taking their sides at editorial meetings against the commercial mandates of Thames & Hudson, though the fact is the director Thomas Neurath admires Nikos for his commitment to his authors – but Nikos is also known as someone equal to them for his own level of intelligence and culture. And yet, Nikos shies away from thanks, and will say to me not to thank him, he does for me what he does without expecting, or even wanting, thanks. It is as though he keeps himself at a distance from his authors' having any responsibility towards him, the responsibility all his towards them. And the same can be said about our relationship: his responsibility is towards me, and he does not expect, or even want, me to be responsible towards him.

At high table at King's, I wish I had had the presence of mind to ask Bernard, there sitting next to him, questions about what moral philosophy can be.

My 'sense' of philosophy is of 'essence' as distinct from 'accidents' – so shouldn't moral philosophy deal with morality as an essence, as a universal, though it appears that morality as lived is lived in the particulars, in the day to day relative behaviour among people in different places and at different times? Really, can there be a moral universal to which all the diverse, even contradictory, acts of all the people of all the world refer? I think that Bernard would find this a fundamental question.

So –

My own 'sense' of morality – and I use the word 'sense' as more potent, more overwhelmingly inclusive, more universal than 'understood' – is that there *is* an essential morality, and that this morality comes to us not from within, but as a universal outside of us that we – what? – 'apprehend', yes, 'apprehend', in the way I imagine Plato's universal forms of morality are 'apprehended'. This 'sense' is as old as philosophy, and I like to think the 'sense' is *the* essential from which all philosophy is derived into its various accidentals of truthfulness, of justice, of charity, of beauty, of love –

And what do I imagine that 'sense' to be at its most essential? A 'sense' of making connections, a 'sense', as Frank Kermode might call it in his own use of the word, of 'divination', by which we 'divine' parts into a whole.

And it is fundamental to me, to my philosophy, that what we 'divine' – to use the word much more expansively than Frank would allow, however much I wonder at his perhaps ironical use of the word – comes to us from the Platonic form of the one great whole Sphere revolving at the centre of the universe.

That 'divination' perhaps occurs most potently when we put words together to interconnect and form a sentence, far beyond our understanding of how we do this, but which is happening now, right now, as I write, the very fact of writing and in writing making connections an essential moral act. And, as we know, writing is a gift from God.

Whenever Nikos talks about the publishing house, I can't help but wonder if he meets, in passageways, on the stairs, in the little cubby holes where the makings of coffee are kept, the still unknown Paul, who works there.

Nikos, Keith, Stephen, I to lunch at Bianchi's restaurant. Stephen was marvellous – so funny, so bright, so loveable. He said, 'My trouble is that I lose my interest in someone when he loses his looks; my interest in you three must mean you are all still beautiful.' 'Oh, no,' Nikos and Keith and I said together, 'you're the one who's beautiful.'

He said, 'All my life I wanted to be beautiful. It was only when I was old that people told me that when I was young I was beautiful.'

Stephen has asked Nikos and me to be the poste restante for letters from Bryan Obst to him. Stephen comes alone to supper, goes into a room and closes the door, and having read the letter, gives it to us for safekeeping. He doesn't want to hurt Natasha by having her find a letter left hanging about, as he would be likely to do. Bryan Obst's handwriting so clear, and the impression is of an eighteen-year-old, if that is his age, so clear-minded:

Dearest Stephen,

I hope that all is well with you and your family. I am writing this from Gainesville, having just returned from Jacksonville, where I spent the Thanksgiving holiday. My weekend consisted of eating lots of turkey, cranberry sauce, etc. and visiting with my myriad relatives as well as my brother's fiancée's relatives, all of which made me groggy. The only redeeming element of my visits to home is that I can contact friends of mine who still live there, and go out bird watching or play music with them (depending on whether they are musicians or bird watchers).

A rather unusual thing happened to me this weekend which I thought you would like to know about. I went to sleep on Friday night thinking about you, and I may have dreamed about you later that night (I can't remember definitely). Anyway, when I woke up on Saturday morning, I reached for a literature text which I had been reading the night before (I habitually leave books and papers lying on the bed, along with my old shirts and dirty socks), and found a little paperback book which I had never seen before. It looked interesting, so I read it a while, perhaps half an hour, and then I suddenly discovered that you had written (edited) it. It was a book about Goethe, the title of which I can't now recall. Anyway, this seemed rather strange since I hadn't bought the book or even seen it before. Then, when I went to put the book away on a shelf in the hall, I discovered that another copy of the same book was already on the shelf, which, in my early-morning stupor, nearly overwhelmed me.

As it turns out, my father had bought both books at a used-paperback sale when he saw them in a stack and noticed your name on the jackets. He did not, however, put one on my bed or even in my room. So although the story has a partial explanation there is still something mysterious about it.

The most amazing part of the story, however, and the part which I hesitate to tell you, is that the last thing I read Friday night, just before I went to sleep, was a poem called 'Lullaby,' written by your friend Wystan, and that the book I was reading was still on my bed, opened to that poem, and next to your Goethe book when I woke up on Saturday morning.

Perhaps I am just exaggerating its strangeness, but this incident seems very peculiar to me. It seems almost beyond coincidence that the particular poem involved, 'Lullaby,' should begin

'Lay your sleeping head, my love,
Human on my faithless arm,'

and that it should go on to say

'Soul and body have no bounds
To lovers as they lie . . .'

At any rate, I think the poem is very beautiful, and it was this poem that made me think of you lovingly as I was falling asleep . . .

I just realized that although I have written two pages I haven't yet said that I love you, which, of course, I do. No matter what else my letters might say, I hope you realize that the message that they are meant to carry to you is that I do love you, dearest Stephen. I think that you probably do know that very well and that perhaps that is why you tell me just to write anything at all to you, and you will be satisfied. Still, I feel that somehow you need reassuring now and then, so I hope you won't think it tedious of me if I say it occasionally. I love you, Stephen.

When Nikos is discontent, I think, Well, a change will open up possibilities for him to be content. He perhaps thinks the same. But the changes don't make him content, and he remains as complaining as ever. He has been saying for a long while that he felt a migraine coming on. Every morning, he complains, 'We're running out of clean socks. I don't have anything to wear. I've put on so much weight. My hair is horrible. I look dreadful. I'll be late. I've got so much work to do, how will I ever get it done? I've got to have lunch with an author, what a bore, I hate having lunch out. One of the kitties was sick in the bathroom. The cat litter needs changing, it smells terribly. The flat is filthy, we live in squalor. Our house cleaner isn't any good, I find dust everywhere.' I wonder how anyone who complains so of the physical world – and, by complaining is so *present* in the physical world – be, in fact, more content in the world than I am?

I sometimes wonder if he wants me to be financially dependent on him. He once said to me, 'I want to take care of you. I want always to make you well. When you say your stomach is upset, I think that you may be reverting to the state you were in when we first met. I don't want you to go back to that.'

But when he is ill, I become impatient, and I think his illness is really hypochondria. He will say, 'No one pays any attention to me. I might as well be by myself in a hotel room.' As much as I do do for him, he complains that the bedclothes are not neatly arranged and that I've spilled the orange juice handing it to him. I never feel that I have done enough, and it *is* never enough, not for him and not for me to feel that I have ever done enough for him, however impatient I become, however much I think he suffers hypochondria and not real illness.

He came home with pains in his back. We had dinner, after which the pains were worse. I suggested he get into a hot bath. 'A hot bath after dinner!' he said. I said, 'Why not?' He said, 'In Greece, they say it's very very bad for one to have a hot bath after dinner.' I said, 'Well, we're in England.' He is now soaking in a hot bath, and says he feels a little better.

Italy

Nikos and I are staying with Joe and Jos Tilson in their house among chestnut trees high on the side of a deep valley outside of Cortona. Joe is making, as works of art, ladders with elemental words branded on the rungs and Jos is making pots out of clay dug up from a stream and fired in a wood fire.

Joe and Jos have become friendly with local peasants and invite them for meals at a long wooden table outside under a pergola. Perhaps Joe mentioned to one of them that Nikos and I are looking for a house, or perhaps they simply knew, as they have their own ways of knowing what is going on among us *stranieri*, for someone named Massimo, missing a thumb and wearing a sweat-stained felt fedora, arrived to say that if anyone was interested in buying a house he would be able to help. He opened his arms wide and said of course without any self-interest.

Nikos and I walked across the valley with Massimo to an abandoned stone house where an elegant man, wearing a straw fedora but not sweat stained and a neat jacket, Signor Virginio Mammoli was waiting for us. He is middle aged, with dark circles about his eyes. He was deferentially polite to Nikos and me, though I wondered what he could make of two young men from far different places wanting to buy a house in this remote place. He had a Cinquecento automobile and asked us if we minded getting in, as though we were used to a chauffeur-driven car, but as we said we didn't mind he opened the doors and we got in the back, and Massimo in the front with Signor Mammoli, who drove us up and up and up along a dirt road, up into chestnut forest where great trunks of trees were piled by the sides of the road.

The road, now level and smooth, curved along the far edge of the valley, and ahead we saw what appeared to be a mountain hamlet, but as the little car approached the buildings of the hamlet revolved slowly and separated into a big, half-ruined villa, a chapel, a walled-in garden, a long, stone, two-storey house, stables, outhouses tangled in vines, and, beyond, chestnut forest. The passages among the buildings were paved in flat stones, weeds growing between them. All about, bushes of flowering yellow broom shook in the mountain wind.

We got out, and if the fantasy was not Nikos' it was mine that we, two of us equal to the task, would live here, and friends would come to stay and all together we would have drinks in the walled-in garden once the walls were reconstructed and the fountain in the middle made to flow and the fruit trees in the garden were pruned. Nikos, as is his way, said nothing as Signor Mammoli showed us about, indicating the coats of arms carved into lintels from the twelfth century, when the whole complex, called Montemaggio, was a convent.

He was particularly excited by the possibility that buried in the earth floor of the chapel, which had no roof, was treasure from the time when nuns lived in the convent and had to hide the treasure when threatened by a marauding gang.

Half of the main building had fallen apart, and though the other half had cracks in its walls it was solid enough that Signor Mammoli, his face twitching, showed us in to the ground floor where old farming tools and wine-making presses were covered in webs, and up a flight of stairs, delicate frescoes of flowers on blue background on the walls and ceiling, to the floor above with large fireplaces, and up again to smaller rooms, and yet up again to a floor where the floorboards were covered with rotting apples. I kept saying how beautiful everything was, but, again, Nikos said nothing.

Signor Mammoli showed us the outbuildings, including a *casa colonica* that he said could easily be made habitable.

His face kept twitching.

London

I suppose Nikos thought that by now I would have accepted his
past with Paul, so much past that it would no longer be of relevance to his seeing Paul, so when he mentioned, as if in passing,
that he had had lunch with Paul, still unknown to me, a rage came
over me that was totally inordinate. I knew it was inordinate, and
said nothing, telling myself to let it go, let it go; but when we were
in bed together *it* wouldn't let me go, and it would not allow me
to sleep, and if I was not allowed to sleep I would not allow Nikos
to sleep.

But then, as always, always, always, one of us reached out and
placed an arm about the other, and a great letting go of our separate selves into each other occurred and we fell asleep.

Jennifer rang me from New York. She said she has decided to have
a baby, and I am on her list of potential fathers. I asked her who else
is on the list, and she said, laughing, 'No one else.' She said she'd
gone to a gynaecologist in New York who said she is in perfect
condition to have a baby, and when she asked about the dangers
of inheriting depression, having my mother in mind for I had told
her a lot about my mother's depression, the doctor said that could
be tested in the potential father. I was left feeling that I was already
a father.

I told Nikos. He said, sharply, 'Well, have the baby, but I refuse to be godfather, and it won't inherit from me.'

I kept thinking, not of Jennifer, but of the baby.

I had a fantasy that was strange to me but, I suppose, not original to fathers: I saw myself as a luminous link in a long long chain which diminished into infinity behind me and before me, and I felt it was being a father which would make me a link in the chain. I felt infinitely extended into the past and into the future.

———

John Fleming and Hugh Honour, James Joll and John Golding came to dinner that evening – two male couples, and I thought, looking at them at our small table: well, there is something a little creepy about male sexual couples. Is there anything creepy about Nikos and me?

———

Stephen and Natasha and Anne Wollheim and Angus Wilson and Tony Garrett (they for the first time) came to supper. Angus and Tony were very warm, and, I felt, were immediately comfortable. Five minutes after they arrived, I asked Angus, 'When are you going?' and he looked a little startled and asked, 'Going? We just arrived.' I laughed, but was embarrassed. 'I mean,' I said, 'to Spain or Ceylon or wherever you said you were going the last time we met.' He laughed and said, 'Oh, I like a good joke,' and stuck his tongue in his cheek.

At the table, we talked about other people being one's conscience.

I said, 'Nikos is my conscience.'

'Oh, I know,' Anne said, 'and I think for me, too, and a rather demanding one.'

'One never quite meets the standard he sets for one,' I said.

Nikos blushed.

Stephen said, 'Angus, you're a conscience to us all.'

'Yes, yes, I'm afraid I am,' Angus said. 'It's my schoolmistress side. There it is. I can't help it.'

On the Plane back to London from Rome

I'm on my way back from staying with Signor Mammoli in his house in Umbertide, where he is bailiff for the local count, and, clearly, respected by the men he overlooks in the fields. I thought what a special life he leads when he said that the work that most pleases him is pruning fruit trees. He lives in a house in the town, the house with a garden and a rabbit hutch.

He showed me about the house, up to the top floor, a storage space, from the beams of which hung large bunches of grapes left to become raisins, the raisins then squeezed to make vinsanto, of which there were little wooden casks on the floor.

Massimo, without a thumb and wearing his sweat stained fedora, came shortly after I arrived, and as he went with Virginio outside I followed too. I hadn't known that Virginio would take a rabbit from the hutch and holding it by the ears quickly kill it with a blow to its neck, and this shocked me so a little gasp rose from me. Massimo, rough Massimo, put a hand on my shoulder and said he too was always upset when he had to kill a rabbit. I was surprised at how quickly Virginio stripped the skin off the rabbit and disembowelled it.

A woman, Letitia, prepared the meal, and I imagined she was Virginio's wife, but after the slices of bread with liver paté and the pasta and the roast rabbit and potatoes, with wine all throughout, and cake with vinsanto, she left.

A young man named Luciano arrived, fleshy, with large dark sad eyes, but eyes that were aware of their sadness in such a way that they wanted everyone to know the person looking was a sad person. He was languorous. Virginio introduced him as his nephew, his *nepote*, which I understood could mean any kind of relationship. He works in the post office, and that day had sent a parcel off to America. Virginio said he must be very tired then. Luciano looked sadder. Virginio, Luciano and Massimo taught me various words for kitchen utensils: *pentola, metsolo, mortaio* and *pestello*. Luciano and Mario left.

I sat alone with Virginio at the large round dining table, and, not knowing what else to talk about, recounted a dream I had had. He went for a book which he opened onto the table and in it found interpretations of the dream images. One was the image of briars, but I don't recall the interpretation, though I suspect whatever the meaning it did not bode well. Suddenly, Virginio slammed the book shut and reached out to grab me, and I, startled, stood. He stood. Half of me at a distance and looking on and the other half there, I saw from the distance myself run round the table with Virginio after me, I exclaiming, *Non sono così*, and Virginio insisting, *Sì, sei così*. Two minutes in bed, he said, two minutes, and Montemaggio would be mine. I stopped and, facing him, said that I was very tired and had to go to bed, and he demurred.

Worried, he asked me, please, not to denounce him to the police, and I told him that sentiments of affection are never criminal.

He showed me to my room, the heavy bedclothes risen into a mound by, he showed me, a wooden frame from the centre of which hung, in a little pot, embers to heat the bed, the contraption called *un prete*, a priest, but he said this as if embarrassed, without smiling. On the tile floor was a round pan of glistening ember to heat the chilly room. I said good night to Virginio and kissed him on both cheeks, and he said goodnight.

I think that we will not buy Montemaggio, that it was a fantasy, and any attempt to turn that fantasy into a reality would ruin us.

This morning, on leaving him, Virginio asked me if I would come to his funeral when he dies.

———

I see that Nikos has a lot to complain about when he comes in late, having stayed in his office when everyone else has gone so he, undisturbed, can finish a project, and deeply tired.

And I see this about Nikos: that, though he is considered to have a privileged position as a director at Thames & Hudson, a distinguished publishing house, and though he commissions books from the very best art historians that win prizes, and though he is very supportive of the authors and rings them to ask if he can help in any way, he feels that something is wrong, and the culture he is trying to sustain by his books, culture he believes in, is a commodity, and there is nothing he can do to change this. It is as though Nikos were working in a system that he must work in because that is the system, but always aware that the system falsifies his work as he believes it should be, and this tires him more than the work itself, tires him morally, spiritually.

I think of getting Nikos away to Italy for a holiday, there where he comes alive, and where I come alive with him.

San Leo Bastia

So Nikos and I have bought an old mill, Il Molino, in Umbria, about an hour's drive through mountains from Cortona, where I am now, here to make sure work is done. Of course we didn't buy Montemaggio, but we were shown other possible houses, and Nikos liked this, which is on two floors, has sloping fields down to a poplar-lined river beyond which are mountains, and behind a wood, a wood with a field hidden in it. I discovered the field wandering through the wood, abandoned, the grass high, and floating above it a fluttering cloud of white butterflies. I am just able to live in the house, where curious locals come to chat. The wife of the blacksmith across the valley said she would ask her husband to forge us a set of andirons, which he did, old-fashioned andirons used in the wide stone fireplace we have, the andirons with rings at the top of each on which pots can be placed for cooking. And Nikos and I, in Cortona, bought some pieces of furniture: what are called *madie*, peasant chests, an elegant table, a cherrywood desk, and best of all a large chestnut cupboard, then old-fashioned iron bedsteads, the mattresses filled with straw, and sheets and blankets and pillows and towels, and, too, a set of heavy white plates and bowls and platters that are used in *trattorias*.

The people who come round to visit do not like to be called *contadini*, but *coltivatori diretti*. They earn their living from the land, but the land, they say, *non renda*.

When I think of the stories I have heard:

About the war and the German occupation, Bruno told me this: One day, a German came to the valley with his family and asked the whereabouts of a certain house, and was told, everyone knowing that the house had belonged to a farmer whose horse had been taken away from him by the Germans, but he, needing his horse, took it back, the punishment for which was his entire family was rounded up and locked into the house and a bomb thrown through a window. The troops of Moroccans were worse.

Massimo, who often gave us pecorino cheese, at the time of the war one night when drunk enough placed his thumb on a block and had it chopped off so he would not have to serve in the military.

Massimo had had a daughter. The midwife of the valley, Anna, told me that his daughter had been made pregnant by Massimo, and when the baby was born it was smothered and buried, and the daughter disappeared.

I once went to Anna because of a cut that had become infected, and when she said the alcohol would burn and I said it wouldn't matter, she said, yes, it mattered, there was too much pain in the world to add to it.

I heard she was a morphine addict, and procured the morphine from a hospital in Città di Castello.

Massimo beat his wife, and called his sensitive son, who was close to his mother, a male whore.

I heard many stories from him when he came in the evening. During the hard time, one of them wore the shoes of another, either too big or too small, to walk to the market in Cortona to sell an egg. They lived on chestnuts.

On a certain day, chicks were taken from nests to roast them, which was illegal, and all the locals knew it was, so when I entered a kitchen and saw the little creatures with claws on a spit over the embers of a fire I sensed the embarrassment of the locals at being found out, and I too was embarrassed at finding them out; all they could do was ask me if I would like to try one and all I could do was say I would, and I was given a little crunchy body with his claws and beak and, oh, it was delicious.

Too much, too much.

———

After two weeks at Il Molino, Nikos has left. I saw him off at the train station in Camucia, the modern town below medieval Cortona on a mountainside. I feel he had the time here that he had wanted to have, which was mostly to rest.

As if this gave him a sense of personalizing the furniture we bought, he polished everything with odorous beeswax, rubbing the wax into the wood until the wood shone. Yes, that's it: we both wanted to personalize the furniture, the house, the land, the valley.

We shopped in the hamlet, San Leo Bastia, with its sole shop, and once when we asked if a chicken was available we were given a live chicken in a sack, but the shop owner, seeing the consterna-tion on our faces, laughed and took the sack back and told us to return the next day for a dead, plucked chicken. We also bought a demijohn of wine from a farmer, and in our kitchen amused ourselves siphoning off the wine into bottles, sealing each bottle, as we were told to do by the farmer, with a little olive oil, so, as we had seen the locals do, we would jerk the bottle for the oil and a little wine to spurt out onto the ground before pouring the wine into glasses. In these small ways, these gestures, we liked to think we were entering into the world of the locals. For example, I noted the way a loaf of bread is cut, held to the chest and sliced inwardly towards the chest, a gesture I imagine has its long history, but this history I was reluctant to make part of mine. I did borrow a copper tank to strap it onto my back and spray our grapevine blue, and this made me feel, oh, authentic, though the farmer from whom I borrowed the outfit clearly saw that I was doing it all wrong.

How very often Nikos' words come to me from when we first started to live together: We are, as always, making our lives together.

Nikos and I helped the widow and sons across the valley with making a huge stack of sheaves of wheat from stooks, in preparation to be threshed.

The discussion among us was whether the world is round and turns round or is flat. The widow said she didn't believe the world is round and goes round, for if so we'd fall off. In fact, I said, I often wonder why, when I jump up, I land in the same place, for if the world were round and turned round I would land in a different place. The widow said to her sons that they should listen to me, I knew, and the boys jumped up and down to experiment. Nikos was smiling.

The widow gave us lunch in her kitchen, and I noted that her and her sons' pronunciation is particular, substituting 'e' for 'a', so 'chese' for *casa*, 'italieno' for *italiano*, 'demeni' for *domani*, and sometimes they eliminate the final vowels so the words sound French with a strong accent.

Some days, Nikos and I walked through the valley to Joe and Jos Tilson's house for a meal under their pergola, or they would come to us, either on their way to or on their way back from shopping.

Once, we arrived up from the olive trees below the Tilson house, Casa Cardeto, to find Germaine Greer with Joe and Jos, the three under the pergola drinking wine.

Germaine has a house on the other side of the mountain that separates our valley from her valley. As always, whenever I see her, no matter where, she never appears to be surprised, but appears to assume that meeting people in unexpected places is what happens in the world.

London

As if in a distracted way, Natasha will recount her memory of playing the piano to the inmates of the liberated concentration camp, Belsen, her playing an excited reminder to them of civilization, and I write 'distracted' as if she is at the same time preoccupied by something else, and the distraction makes her face blank, her eyes unfocused. When these moments occur, I wonder if not only Belsen is too much to recollect, but more, a lifetime of events too much to recollect. Her forehead becomes tense with the preoccupation, and then all she can concentrate on enough to whisper is, 'The olives at Saint Jerome need picking,' but even this sounds a distraction from the constant preoccupation that is the overwhelming too much she can hardly bear. At these moments I have a deep sense of her isolation, her vulnerability, her innocence, and also, strangely, her beauty. When she becomes aware of me, she smiles, and she may say, though rarely, 'Darling David, where was I?'

———

Jennifer rings often. I try to control our relationship, even from a distance, by talking about anything but us. I've told her about the old mill Nikos and I have bought, which I like to think she understands is an architectural confirmation of our lasting relationship. I bring up Nikos whenever I can in our long talks, which she is paying for from her end, though I like her extravagance, as I have always liked her extravagance. Nikos, hearing, tells me after, 'You want everything, and you think you can have everything by some kind of compromise between Jennifer and me.'

I said to Max, 'I had hoped Jennifer would let things between us go.'

Laughing, Max said, 'Jennifer let things go? You don't know Jennifer. She's been very polite with you up till now. Wait till she starts putting on the pressure. I know a former lover of hers who said he had to get out of it before it broke him.'

———

Stephen is in Gainesville, Florida, I presume to be with Bryan Obst. I went to see Natasha in Loudoun Road. The house, she said, will be taken over by workmen and she had no idea where she would stay while Stephen would be away. I asked her to stay with Nikos and me, thinking, really, she would never want to, and she became thoughtful, as if the possibility had not occurred to her, then she said, 'Well, that would be nice.'

I said to Nikos, 'It's odd – Natasha and Stephen have so many grand acquaintances they will break a date with us to be with, and yet when it comes down to it they have few friends really. In a way I like the fact that we are such friends that they can stay with us.' He was unsure about her staying; they're never at ease with each other. He said, 'We've got to buy a lot of toilet paper. Women use a lot of toilet paper.'

She arrived on a Sunday afternoon with many suitcases and bags of books. She slept and worked in my study, I worked in the kitchen. We came together for lunch.

———

Knowing that Natasha is staying with Nikos and me, Stephen sends her letters from Gainesville. She becomes very excited when in the morning she finds a letter from him. One morning, she said, 'You know, when Stephen is with me he doesn't show me much affection, but his letters are so affectionate.' I said, 'I think you love each other very much, you know.' She stared at me for a moment but didn't answer. Another morning, at breakfast, she said, 'I can love anyone who loves Stephen. I can see the point of anyone who sees the point of Stephen. He has hurt me often, so deeply I've wondered how I could survive. Even now, when I look through our photographs and see endless pictures of young men I don't know, my heart crashes to my feet. He is not a malicious person, never never never means to hurt, and I know that, and I accept that.'

And what would she say of Nikos and me if she knew that in our flat, in a drawer we presume she would not open, are letters from a young man Stephen may now be with?

———

Philip Roth rang. He said, 'I can't face the desk today. Do you want to have lunch?'

I met him at one o'clock at Luigi's in Covent Garden.

'I can't think of anything I want to write,' he said. 'I don't know if this is because of the reception of my last book. I don't really know. Maybe. Or maybe I don't have anything more to say about what I've written about. I've written about sex, about women, about being a Jew. I want some new subject.'

He talked a lot about Claire Bloom, with whom he is living in London; she is also demoralized. He talked on and on.

'We have meals together at which we're totally silent. Or she says about something or other, just to break the silence, "Look at that, isn't that pretty?" I say, "Don't do that, don't use those meaningless words."'

He said, 'I will never leave her. Never. If I left her, she would kill herself. She may kill herself while with me, but that I could face, because I know I do everything I can to support her. It's difficult, because as I'm holding up one wall another wall is collapsing. If I left her, and she collapsed, I wouldn't recover. Also, I love her.'

I asked him why he was first attracted to her.

He thought for a long while, his fingers kneading his chin, then, dropping his hand, said, 'Her aura.'

'Oh yes,' I said, 'she has an aura, a deeply beautiful aura.'

'That, and because she is a famous actress, because I'd seen her in *Limelight* and fallen in love with her years before, because she was connected to what I thought was interesting work in an interesting world.'

I said, 'I can understand that,' and thought, as I often do about Philip, of how honest he is. He will admit anything about himself, admit it, perhaps, as he's doing it, however crude he is in the self-exposure. And there is nothing self-aggrandizing in the self-exposure: it is simple, stark admission.

There are moments when I sense in Philip – especially when he talks about Claire – a compassionate sense for helplessness in people (whatever, he would ask, *that* is?) which to me rarely, if ever, comes through in his books. Philip's characters do not give way to *helpless* feelings, feelings that make the characters vulnerable to more than what the writer intends their feelings to be; the feelings of his characters are in Philip's control. This may be why so many people say all Philip can write about is himself, because of that control. I sometimes think about Philip's novels that the driving force he impels in them is to break out of the control he imposes on them, so he makes the driving force extreme in the actions of his characters, but this is deliberate and the characters, however extreme, are in his control and do not break out. He said to me once, 'I can only write about people in extreme situations. Nothing else interests me.' In person, Philip gives way to helpless feelings.

I said to him, 'You've had a lot of analysis, haven't you?'

'Yes,' he answered, 'a lot.'

I said, 'I've never had even therapy. I don't know what it's meant to do for one.'

He stared at me.

'What did it do for you?' I asked.

'It kept me from killing my first wife.'

Then he told me about the women in his life, all, he said, without fathers as it turned out, and he tried, for a time, to play the part of a father to each of them.

'But shouldn't analysis have made you aware that you were entering relationships with women who wanted fathers?'

'The fact is, they were all very different women, really. It was only after a while that I found out they didn't have fathers.'

He told me about a past depression following the abrupt end of a long love affair, so severe he crawled to the bathroom in the morning, unable to stand. His eyes wide and laughing his light laugh, as if light with surprise at what he so improbably once did, he told me how, in great pain, he struggled to put his shoes on and then saw he had forgotten to put socks on first. Philip began to enjoy recounting this, and his laughter rose higher with the wonder of what he had done. 'I just about managed, then I stood and lifted my pants' legs and saw that my ankles were bare.'

He asked, 'Well, what should I do, doctor?'

I said, 'I'm more worried about Claire than about you. You'll be all right. You'll wake up in the morning and you'll know what you want to write. But Claire—'

I walked with him to Moss Bros, for him to collect a tuxedo for the evening, some theatre event he didn't want to go to, and we walked about the show room among the dummies wearing formal clothes, and joking.

What else did Philip say when we had lunch? We spoke about writing from experience. He said there was about a ten-year gap between his life and his writing; with Updike, there was less than a twenty-four-hour gap.

We laughed a lot.

He talked about the British attitude towards Jews; he said, the English were embarrassed when he said 'Jew' instead of 'Jewish'.

It interested me that the people he grew up with, his family and relatives, were in no way as intelligent and open and sensitive as he makes them in his writing; they were uneducated, closed, bigoted, so, in his writing, he had to elevate them.

I said I worry about writing directly from life in my novels, and think I should be more inventive about my life; I think that writing directly from my life is a cheat, because it's not really writing. He said, 'You're using words, sentences, paragraphs, aren't you?' I said, 'I guess.'

I have become used to Natasha ringing. She asked to see me. I worked most of the day and went to Loudoun Road in the late afternoon. I went by Underground, and felt I had been dragged bodily through a dark dirty cold rough cement tunnel. Stephen was out. Natasha was very upset, but did say she did not want to burden Stephen with her being so upset. She showed me the proofs of a biography of Raymond Chandler which had been sent to her and in which is a long passage about her based on quotations from Chandler's letters of an affair with Natasha, such as, more or less, 'she wept in bed; she said she had no one to love her and she had no money,' and the biographer's suggestion that Chandler was giving her the only sexual satisfaction she'd had in years married to a queer. Natasha insisted: all of this was totally, totally untrue. She said, 'If this biography is printed as is, I'll kill myself, I really will.' I tried to reassure her, insisted that she should get a solicitor at once to defend her and that, above all, she shouldn't worry that anyone would take seriously the raving fantasies of an alcoholic. But I couldn't hold her back, I quickly saw, from becoming, there before me, obsessed. The more I tried to reassure her the less attentive she was, her eyes unfocused, and when, from time to time, she did focus – 'They can't print anything about you that is personal that you disapprove of' – she said, 'But they *can*,' and a moment later a vagueness would come to her eyes.

Once again, I strained to be clear and rational, thinking, well, she does have a clear and rational mind (Stephen has often said she is much more intelligent than he is, and I have often been deeply impressed by her clarity and rationality hearing her speak about music or the functions of the brain according to Piaget); I tried, for a while, to reassure her by being as objective, as objectively truthful as possible. I would say, 'I'm not sure what the libel laws are about quotations from letters, so you really must get a solicitor to inform you, though I should think that quotations from letters in a biography can be considered libellous,' and, well, on and on, my sentences convoluted in my attempt to be objective and objectively truthful, and yet to take Natasha's part. But I soon realized that I was wrong; I shouldn't have tried, in no matter how convoluted a way, to be objective as a disinterested outsider, because that was not what Natasha wanted from me. She suddenly focused on me and snapped, 'You're not comforting me,' and I, stunned, bit the cuticles of my index finger, and she snapped again, 'Don't bite your finger!' I thought: Now I'm in for it. I had wanted to help as a disinterested outsider, and she pulled me inside. I became weak and wanted to leave. It was an effort to speak, and the more I did speak – now, simply, to comfort her, not at all to help her see clearly and rationally – the more uncertain she became, and the more uncertain the more I felt I had to reassure her. I left very tired.

She rang in the afternoon. She was crying. She said she'd just finished the book, and she couldn't bear it, especially the death of Chandler. His wife was Cissy, who was eighteen years older than he and whom he married on the death of his mother and with whom he lived for forty-six years.

In the evening I met Nikos at David Hockney's. Peter Schlesinger and Eric Boman were there. David made a stew. It's almost impossible to have a conversation with David. He speaks with all the impersonality of the famous, and usually about figurative art against abstract art. But the very impersonality of his talk was to me a great freedom from my talk with Natasha.

With David I relaxed, I drank a lot. David's talk became less academic, and we all talked about sex, joking, telling stories. We looked through the albums of David's photographs. Leaning together over an open album on a table, Peter and Eric looked so beautiful.

David showed us a stack of naked young men – Americans, he
said; they're always the best. He had taken the photographs in
Paris when he'd lived there for a while, mostly of the young men
in the bathtub, their smooth erotic bodies wet, shiny. I said, 'My
God, how beautiful!' David opened a cupboard and took out a big
cardboard box of American magazines of young men engaged in
sex and we sat in a circle and passed the magazines from one to
the other and I thought: Oh, the body! The body! I wanted to
make love with all the young men in the magazines, wanted to be
engaged in sex with them all, there, right there, fantasizing their
emerging from the pages full bodied into the room. Peter and Eric
left to go off together, then Nikos and I. It was late. I thought of
David alone with his pornographic magazines.

Nikos and I were filled with the 'sense' of the evening – the
'sense' comforting and very sensual, and, in bed making love with
each other, I imagined us making love with hundreds of young men,
whose beauty – because in photographs it was only the beauty which
could attract erotically – was the impulse of our love making.

In the morning, in the bath, I thought: the degree to which I
can be obsessed and excited by pictures of beautiful young men –
pictures that depersonalize the obsession and the excitement is the
degree to which sex can be a depersonalized fantasy, and, oh, how
wonderful that fantasy can be.

The telephone rang, and I, wet and dripping, got out of the bath
to answer. It was Natasha. She asked if I could go to Loudoun Road
to type out what she had written. I said I would in the afternoon.
She opened the door, more gaunt, more tired, and she was hardly
able to concentrate, or she concentrated on one thing so deeply she
couldn't concentrate on anything else. Opening one or two drawers,
she said, 'We don't seem to have any paper.' I went out to a shop for
paper. She said, when I came back, 'Now we've got to look for a
typewriter.' We went down to the bottomless pit, so heaped up with
boxes, books, broken lamps, frames, old radios, that I didn't dare
touch anything, imagining the great heap would collapse on us. She
reached in and pulled out a typewriter. She said, 'Come upstairs to

my study to type, next to my room. I've been so lonely, and while I lie on my bed we can commune while you type.' I carried the typewriter up to the desk in her study, but found it didn't work. 'It must be broken,' Natasha said; 'well, you can use Stephen's electric in his study.' I went down to Stephen's study, figured out how to use the electric typewriter, but the ribbon was so worn it didn't print on the paper. I went up to Natasha, who was lying on her bed in the midst of papers on which she had been writing. She appeared not quite to hear me. She said, 'Well, maybe Lizzie knows where there's another one around the house.' I rang Lizzie; she was in bed with a cold. She said, 'I could never understand, ever, how, when I went into my father's study and found heaps of typewritten and handwritten pages on his desk, I could never, ever find a typewriter or even a pencil stub in the *entire* house.' She didn't know of another typewriter. She said, 'Poor David.' By now, the problem was mine. I again went to Natasha's room, where, on her bed, she was lost in correcting the pages she wanted me to type. With some of the pages, I went down to Stephen's study and his electric typewriter and rolled into it two sheets of paper with a carbon paper between the two, hoping the carbon copy would be clear, for, of course, I couldn't see what I was typing. After a while, the type on the top sheet became visible, but the capital 'I' didn't print.

I managed to type what she wanted typed, though on watching her reading the typescript, I saw her eyes focusing not so much on it but so much beyond it into some grim grey doubt about it all.

———

On a walk, Natasha and I passed a house with a large lighted window, an old man, dressed in a dark-brown suit and waistcoat, standing at the window and looking out, and Natasha whispered, as though the man might hear, 'You see that man? He used to be one of the world's great pianists – Solomon – who has been a complete recluse for the past twenty-five years.'

———

A drinks party at Keith's. Max came in. He had been to New York, staying with Jennifer. He said Jennifer sends me love. 'Is she all right?' I asked. 'Oh yes,' Max said, 'She's in love.' 'Who with?' 'With a very small and very beautiful Japanese.' 'And is she working?' 'Yes, very hard. Her father died a short time ago, leaving debts of more than half a million, so that has her worried. She's very very worried about money. But otherwise she's very very well.' And I felt disappointed that she had got over me, and, too, was jealous of the very small and very beautiful Japanese.

Spent all afternoon with Natasha. She had rung me to ask me to come over to go on typing. She kept giving me sheets of paper, with lots of crossings-out, the pages out of order. From time to time she'd say, 'It's useless – they'll publish the book – and I'll be known forever as Raymond Chandler's mistress.' I realized it was no use protesting against her obsession, which is greater than any obsession I or Stephen or any solicitor could deal with. I was typing in Stephen's study; for long stretches I had nothing to type, Natasha up in her study writing, and I would look through Stephen's books. On his desk was a *Who's Who*. I opened the cover and found this written: Raymond Chandler, London, 1956. When Natasha came down I asked her if she had known that Chandler had signed the book; she stared at the signature, stunned. She had been writing on slips of paper that were all in disorder, so I suggested we do a paste-up, and for hours she handed me the little slips of paper which I pasted, in order, on sheets of paper.

Now that Natasha has sent off to the writer of the biographer of Raymond Chandler all her objections and lengthy corrections, she has shifted her obsession from the book to what people are saying about her. She has asked me on the telephone, again and again, not to spread the story around, as I do know of it, and though I reassure her again and again that I haven't and won't, she is not reassured. She said, 'I've got to go out. People will become very suspicious if they think I'm in all the time. I'm going to make the effort to go out to dinner tonight. Then Stephen will be home soon. He needs taking care of. I've got to get myself active.'

———

Stephen talked to us about Bryan, as if he was talking not only of a person but of a world in which a flute player attracts birds to flutter about him, which Bryan does, but a world so far away from him now he, in the world of his life with Natasha, may never be able to return to it. He stops talking and a look of forced resignation comes to his face.

He says Natasha will never recover from her obsession. Some days she seems to have a sudden recovery and he would think everything would be better, but of course it never was. He said, 'Maybe I should give it two years to work itself out.'

After lunch at Bianchi's, Nikos returned to his office and Stephen and I, as we used to do at the time we were getting to know each other, went from gallery to gallery in Cork Street, looking at pictures.

———

Stephen asked Keith to give him a birthday party, as Natasha was not up to it. Keith said yes, and I said I would help. While Keith and I were preparing, Stephen arrived, very animated. He said, 'A miracle has happened. This morning, because I couldn't work, I thought I'd clear out the bottomless pit. Natasha helped me. I had to leave for a while and when I got back I found Natasha *completely* changed – she had discovered about a hundred letters from Raymond which prove everything she's been saying, letters that show Raymond up as a hypocrite, a liar, an obscene boaster. It *really* is a miracle!'

———

There are two telephones in the Spender house. Stephen, talking
to me on one telephone receiver, seems always aware that Natasha
may pick up the other receiver, as when he talks about Bryan, so
often stops talking to ask, 'Natasha, Natasha, are you listening?'
I heard a voice, Natasha's, say, 'Yes.' I said, 'How marvellous that
you found those letters.' In a low voice, she said, 'Oh yes?' Stephen
quickly said, 'I told David, Natasha. But you don't think it's so
private, do you?' 'Well,' she said, 'yes, I do,' in a doubtful way. My
spirits sank. I said, 'Natasha, the only person I've told is Nikos.'
'Please don't tell anyone else,' she said, and I answered, 'No, no.'

But Stephen has told Keith.

Keith said Natasha had rung him to thank him for the party,
and he had said how marvellous that she had discovered the letters.
She asked him who had told her and, in total innocence because
he couldn't imagine why it should be a secret, said I had. But, I
exclaimed, Stephen had told us both! Keith seemed not to remember this, but said that Natasha was trying to contact me. She had
rung Nikos. Back home, I told Nikos, and, angry, said I would ring
Natasha and tell her that Stephen had told both Keith and me. He
said not to, but I did, and to take the guilt from Stephen I apologized. Natasha said she understood, but hoped I hadn't told anyone
else. I swore that I hadn't. My guilt made me imagine I had told
any number of people.

————

Natasha's intelligence – Nikos and I happened to turn on the radio
just when an announcer said Natasha was going to speak on absolute pitch, and she did, for half an hour, brilliantly.

————

Dinner at Richard and Mary Day Wollheim's: Stephen and
Natasha, R.B. Kitaj and his lover Sandra Fisher, James Joll (John in
the country), Nikos and me.

Towards the end of the evening, Natasha left the table to go
upstairs, she said, to rest a little. Stephen and R.B. were talking

at one end of the table, and I was at the other end with Mary Day and James. Richard and Nikos were in Richard's study to discuss a book by Richard that Nikos would like to publish. I heard Stephen say to R.B., 'Well, I suppose Rothko is like Whistler, a kind of mood painter,' and R.B. said, 'Yes, that's it, that's just what I think – Rothko is like Whistler.' Suddenly James turned to both R.B. and Stephen with the quick, spasmodic way he has of turning, and said, 'That's nonsense. Rothko is one of the very greatest painters of all time.' R.B. said, slowly, 'I have to accept that many people think that – people I do respect very much – but for me the figure is essential. I can only react to paintings that are referential.' A flame shot up in James' face and his voice rose. 'It's exactly your attitude that is now making figurative painting fashionable, abstract art unfashionable.' R.B. was stunned, but his voice, too, took on an edge, and I thought: whose anger is more intimidating, that of R.B. or James? He said, 'I didn't say that abstract art is unfashionable – but I think it is academic.' Mary Day got up from the table and went out to bring Richard back. Stephen and I were silent. 'No,' James said, 'you, and your influence on David Hockney, on him and on others, have made abstract art unfashionable, and figurative art fashionable, and abstract art is suffering as a result.' James' voice took on a tremor and I was frightened that he would shout, and was more frightened that R.B. would shout. R.B. asked, 'What abstract art have I made unfashionable?' James said, 'You kept John out of the Milan Exhibition.' 'Now wait a minute,' R.B. said, 'we've got to get something straight.' 'Yes,' James said, 'I'm an historian, and I want the facts. I want to know the date when John was dropped from the exhibition, when you were put in because David Hockney said he wouldn't show unless you were shown as well. I'm not implying you shouldn't have been in the exhibition because you're American—' R.B. interrupted James with 'I'm School of London. How many painters who belonged to the School of Paris were French?' 'Yes, quite,' James said, 'but the fact remains that some abstract artists were dropped from the Milan Exhibition for figurative artists because Hockney said he would not show unless they were included.' R.B. said, 'David gave me half his space. I didn't take anyone else's space.' 'That very well may be the case,' James said, 'but I'd like to have the facts.' R.B., embattling himself, said, 'I'll get you the facts.'

Richard and Nikos came back to the table with Mary Day. Stephen said he would go find Natasha, but didn't come down for a long while. We wondered what had happened to them. Richard said, 'Maybe they have both gone to sleep.' Mary Day went upstairs, came down, and said, 'I didn't want to go into the room, the door is shut, but I did call and there was no answer.' Richard went up, came down, and said, 'They've gone.' He had found on a table in the hall a bit of cardboard with a message written in lipstick: 'THANK YOU DEARS WE'VE GONE.' R.B. and Sandra James were silent while Richard and Mary Day and Nikos and I talked about Stephen and Natasha, believing that Natasha is having a breakdown, all of us worried as much about Stephen as about her.

R.B., on the way to his and Sandra's, left Nikos and me off. He said, 'I almost walked out.' He snapped his fingers. 'And that would have been the end of James Joll, John Golding, and abstraction.'

He asked Nikos and me not to talk about it.

So much not to talk about, but no one tells me not to write about it all.

———

The next day, over the telephone, Stephen told me that Natasha, back in Loudoun Road, had disappeared for a weekend. She told him she had packed a bag, had gone to Victoria Station, had taken the next train out, which was to Eastbourne, had asked a taxi driver to take her to a modest hotel on the seafront. Stephen hadn't known where she'd been.

———

Nikos is in New York, at an annual conference, the College Arts Association.

Stephen and Natasha were going to come to lunch, but when the chicken was already roasted in the oven Stephen rang to say that only he would be coming as Natasha was going to stay in bed. I suggested that I take the chicken out of the oven and I go to them. Natasha, who was on the other telephone, said, 'Oh that would be lovely.' Stephen came in the car to fetch me.

In the car, he said, 'I was very upset when Natasha left and I didn't know where she had gone. She wouldn't have tolerated my doing that. So much of what I do she won't tolerate, and the rest, it seems, she's not interested in. Well, I honestly don't expect my family to be interested in my work. But I'd like to get on with it, and I can't. Raymond Chandler is like a ghost who's come back to stop me from working. The letters haven't changed anything. Natasha sometimes accuses me of ruining her career by not having encouraged her. I can't say she encourages me very much. But I don't mind about that. Anyway, I was very upset, and I wanted to see someone, and, really, the only people I could think of were you and Nikos. And, of course, Bryan, who is 4,000 miles away.'

We had lunch in Natasha's room.

After lunch, Natasha read to me what she has written about Raymond Chandler, which she hopes to have published. Stephen left the room.

I could never go on living if I didn't know that Nikos would come home.

A letter from my mother, her handwriting very frail. Again, alone, and again I revert – if that is the word – to a world that is distant but that is in fact the world I most relevantly live in.

Dear Son David,

Have you given up on me? I would not blame you if you did.

I have a confession to make. As time went on and on since my operation, I got stronger, but I was wrong. I had a check-up at the hospital and two cardiograms were taken. The doctor found I have mild heart trouble and needed a lot of rest. Well, I had my rest and am now active around the house doing light work, such as drying dishes, setting the table, etc., and your Dad does the heavy work.

I told him not to let you know as I feared you would worry and that I did not want, you being so far away.

Now I feel that you should have been told, as every other member of our family was. Please forgive me, David, for that mistake. I'll never forget your patience and kindness with me when I needed it most. You are in my thoughts quite often, believe me.

How is everything coming along concerning the house in Italy? It sounds great.

Always stay happy and content, doing what you like.

Our seven sons are our pride and joy. God, we are so very fortunate.

It's time to stop writing and save some for the next time, which I hope will be sooner than the time it took to get in touch with you.

God bless you, David, and you know our love for you is now, and will be always.

Momma and Dad

I have written to her that I live with Nikos, that he and I have bought Il Molino together, but she leaves him out. I don't mind, nor does he mind that he is left out. He said to me, with understanding that mitigates any offence, 'Your poor Mother.'

She remembers the time when I, still a teenager, spent a summer at the lake house with her when she had a breakdown, and I sat with her on the glider on the screened-in porch and we rocked back and forth, back and forth, she almost chanting, 'My son, my son, my son, help me,' and I didn't really help her, not any more than I can help her now, but she wants me to believe I did help her.

The fact is, I feel guilty towards my mother for not helping her even now, for not going back to the parish, to what I imagine the parish to be in winter gloom, and the house in deeper winter gloom, and my mother in a large armchair, her eyes shut, silent, and I unable to say anything to make her open her eyes and respond.

Oh yes, she would have her rosary beads, of large wooden beads, on her lap.

––––––

Again, why should I be so drawn to God as a darkness that does not care about me, does not care about my love for Nikos and his for me, does not care that I write, does not care about anything, not even religion? And yet, that God is the God of my greatest awareness.

Il Molino

Waiting for Nikos to come, I have been preparing the old, stone mill.

As Nikos looked about the rooms, I looked at him with the wonder of how he appeared to be totally at home, a cultured Greek who could only have imagined living among Umbrian peasants but who seemed to understand them in a way that imagination wouldn't have supplied him.

We have an idea of living here, if we can only find the way of doing so. The peasants tell us that there is no way of earning a living by farming.

The doors to the outside were open to fireflies in the elder bushes, and the son of the widow above us appeared in a doorway carrying a weighted, knotted bandana which he held up and said his mother sent us some eggs.

Nikos asked him in, and the boy placed the bundle on a table and untied it to reveal, on the blue and white cloth, ten white eggs.

In the morning I heard, from outside, my name called. Nikos was asleep beside me in the bed with a high iron bedstead, and I thought that it would not have surprised any of the farmers that we two males slept together, usual among them, or so I imagined.

Giuseppe once told me that his mother had said to him that he could no longer sleep with her, he was now thirteen, and this frightened him.

I got out of bed and crossed the redbrick floor to the shutters and opened them to Giuseppe, below, standing in the dawn mist. He said his mother wanted to speak to me. I asked if it was grave, and he hunched his shoulders and said, no, not grave. Woken, Nikos asked what was going on, and when I said the boy's mother wanted to speak to me, he, frowning, asked about what, and I said I didn't know. Nikos was annoyed, and I thought he couldn't really be one of them by saying that they think that because they get up at dawn everyone does. I told Giuseppe I'd be down. As I dressed, Nikos said I would let the widow take advantage of me again, as I always do; he knows what they are like and they know what I'm like. I said I wanted to know what she had to say.

The valley was filled with mist which appeared to drift, and the white sun appeared to drift with it. I followed Giuseppe through the terraced fields, along a path; on either side of the path, in the broom, webs drooped heavy with dew. My espadrilles became wet.

I thought: how beautiful, how beautiful.

Giuseppe asked me: do I have cows down there in London?

I said, yes.

And pigs – do I have pigs down there?

Yes.

And sheep?

Yes.

Then, he said, it must be just like here.

A fire of twigs was burning in the large kitchen fireplace, and beside the stone hearth sat the widow's mother on a low chair, an old woman in black, a black kerchief tied about her skull-like head. She tried to stand when I came in, but couldn't, and sat back. A dirty handkerchief, with weeds stuffed under it, was knotted around the swollen calf of her leg. She leaned over and held her leg and moaned.

As she could not speak Italian, but only her Umbrian dialect, I hardly understood her, but I knew she was apologizing for not being able to stand to greet me.

I asked, with a loud voice, what was wrong with her leg, and I
did understand her saying it was infected.

The widow came in from a back room. She is thin, gaunt, also
wearing black mourning. She prepared coffee in a little pot over
the coals in the fireplace. The kitchen was hot. Flies flew about and
settled, flew about and settled on the table, on the yellow-brown
walls, on the black hams hanging from a beam.

I said to the widow that *la Nonna*'s leg looked bad.

Yes, she said; she wasn't able to work.

Shouldn't she see a doctor?

The widow said they never go to a doctor.

Barefoot and arms folded, she stood before me as I, sitting in a
chair by the fire, drank the thick coffee from a small white cup.

She asked me if I'd eaten.

I said I'd just got out of bed.

She would give me something to eat.

No, I couldn't eat at this hour.

She would give me something to eat.

She lifted the lid of a chest and took out a cloth, spread it over
the end of the table; she placed on it a glass, a knife, a loaf of
bread, a round sheep's cheese, a bottle of wine, and a ham from
which meat had been cut to the bone. She told me to bring my
chair to the table, which I did. She poured out wine, sliced bread
(holding the loaf against her breasts and cutting the slice towards
her), and on the slice placed ham and cheese. While I ate, she sat
on a bench; her elbows were on the table and she held her jaw in
her hands.

She said there was a lot of work to do that day.

I said, yes, there must be.

She didn't know how they were going to do it. The tobacco
had to be picked and taken to the cooperative tobacco drying plant
by that night, or the whole picking would be lost. This is what I
understood, though I wasn't sure. She had her four sons to help,
her brother-in-law, and herself. Her mother couldn't help. She was
worried that they wouldn't be able to do it.

I chewed a dry piece of bread and cheese and ham and swallowed it and said I would help.

No, no, no, she didn't ask me over to help.

I said I'd help, and I'd ask Nikos to help too.

No, no.

Yes, of course.

She would pay us.

Nikos and I would not want money.

I found him at a stone table outside the house, drinking coffee.

I told him that I had promised the widow that we would help with picking the tobacco.

He complained: he had come here to rest.

What could I do? I asked.

By a field at the river, we joined the widow, her young sons, Giuseppe among them, and the old brother-in-law, who had one tooth and wore a sweat-stained black fedora. The work was, crouching low, to snap off the bottom leaves of the tall tobacco plants and place them one on another until each of us had a thick sheaf, which sheaves were then taken to the widow's youngest son, Candido, a pale six-year-old, who placed them, one upon another, in a metal frame by the riverbank, there where there were a number of frames. Nikos and I were separated.

I heard the widow shout at Nikos that if there wasn't room at the cooperative for tobacco brought in too late, the tobacco was thrown out. Did he think that was fair?

Why didn't she do something about this?

She stood and with the back of her hand wiped her sweating forehead. She shouted from deep in her throat, what could she do?

Nikos shouted, as if they would not otherwise be able to hear each other, she should go to a Communist cooperative.

It is a Communist cooperative, she yelled.

Her eldest son, Ulderico, shouted that he was a Fascist. He worked his way picking tobacco leaves along a line between the tall pink-blossoming plants. He had a large brown body.

The old brother-in-law laughed.

My shirt and trousers were sticking to me not only with sweat but with the resin of the tobacco leaves; when I made a fist, my fingers adhered to one another.

Another son, Matteo, came along a line of plants with a clean glass, a bottle of red wine, and a bottle of well water. He handed each of us in turn the glass, then poured in a little water, used to rinse the glass, and then filled the glass halfway with water, the rest of the way with wine. The glass was sticky with resin when it came to me.

My back, arm and legs ached when the widow yelled that it was, in dialect, *è ora de magnà*.

We all went to the river. The bar of soap was not passed around one to another but placed on a stone after each one had used it. We tried to wash the black gum from our hands and arms. As we washed, we tried to swat away the horseflies.

Ulderico jumped into the water with the soap, sank in up to his neck, rose, lathered his chest, sank in again, splashing; he emerged dripping and crouched on the bank where his three brothers rubbed his body with thin towels, and he laughed. He had a front tooth missing. Laughing, he hit his brothers' heads, and they hit his chest, legs, arms.

The widow shouted for them to stop.

From plastic bags, she placed food out on a cloth under poplar trees along the river: bread, cheese, ham, and salad in a large white bowl which we ate with forks.

The widow said, wasn't it true that a person who works hard should be paid for the work? We work, we work, and what are we paid? What do we work for? To die? No. The more we work the better we should live. She was indignant, and tapped her chest and said that's what she believed.

So would any good Communist, Nikos said.

She asked if he is a Communist.

He said he is.

Her husband was a Communist. She clasped her hands and shook them. But does being a Communist mean your work has more value than if you were anything else? They say yes, yes, yes, but what difference does being a Communist make to what she earns?

Nikos lowered his head to eat a piece of bread and cheese.

Ulderico asked him when he became a Communist.

When he was a young man in Athens.

The brother-in-law said about Nikos that he was not old, but he wasn't so young that he didn't know the hard times.

I did not know what hard times the old man referred to, and I wondered if the old man was assuming hard times for everyone in the world.

I know that when Nikos was at Athens College as a student, he used to lock himself in an office late at night and on a mimeograph machine make copies of Communist propaganda, which he then took out to cinemas the next day under his shirt to throw the sheets from the top balconies, and then run.

What the farmers listening to him understood of what Nikos meant by being a Communist, I could only wonder. What they understood of Nikos as Greek and me as Anglo-American, I can only wonder. Perhaps we are too foreign for them to imagine we can be different from them, because they can't imagine such difference.

Once, walking through the valley on my way to visit the Tilsons, I met an old woman, who asked me where I was from, always the first question when I meet a local, and when I said London she looked at me for a long time as if to take in what someone from London could look like, then she nodded and said, well, after all we are all Christians.

Never before had I heard Nikos expound on being a Communist as now, among people who were Communists but who complained about being Communists.

The brother-in-law, whose face was all small, dirty wrinkles, his eyes round and sharp, asked Nikos why he became a Communist.

Nikos said that Communism gives our work meaning in the world.

The old man pointed at himself and asked, what does Communism do for him? Last year, he earned two hundred thousand lire for his pigs. Two hundred thousand lire for a year's work. Can a man live on that? What meaning does Communism give to work in the world if you can't live on what you earn in your own world?

Yes, Nikos said, he knew.

The old man rolled up his shirtsleeves over the sleeves of his thick, long underwear. Did Nicola really know?

No, Nikos said, he didn't know.

The old man lowered his head and said, the world is big.

All of us barefoot, we filed back to the blazing field, where the tobacco plants shimmered in the rising heat waves. We picked silently, line after line, dripping sweat.

Ulderico left and returned with a tractor, and he, Nikos and I lifted the heavy tobacco-laden metal frames, one after another, onto the trailer. When they were stacked, I said to the widow, who was collecting leaves that had fallen from the frames, and I said that they'd finished in lots of time to get the tobacco to the cooperative.

Pointing with a big leaf, she said there was the field on the terrace above.

We worked, snapping the big sticky pale-green leaves from stalks as the sun moved across the valley. No one spoke, not even when we hefted the heavy frames onto the trailer as the sun set. When Ulderico put on a shirt and drove the tractor, the frames of tobacco stacked on the trailer behind, off to the cooperative, no one said anything to him. We all stood in a line at the edge of a field, all of us, I thought, motionless because we could not move our stiff bodies. When I raised a hand to scratch a cheek, a spasm of pain passed down my back to my buttocks.

The brother-in-law went into the field to disconnect and heft onto his shoulder a long irrigation pipe. He carried it to another part of the field, dropped it, and came for another to heft it and carry it to that other part of the field, where he dropped it. The widow joined him, and when she raised a pipe onto her shoulder I went to her to take it from her, but she walked off with it. I reached down for a pipe, but it was so heavy I dropped it. The boys, their faces streaked with resin, watched me. Nikos was behind them, he also watching me. I again reached down, hefted the pipe up to my waist, and almost lost my balance as I hefted it higher to a shoulder; I had not balanced it in the middle and the unequal weight of either side again threw me off and I staggered backwards. The boys laughed. I found the fulcrum and walked across the field, passing the old man and the widow on their way back for more pipes; and when I went back for another pipe I met Nikos carrying a long pipe. We had, too, to change the pipes in the field above.

The widow invited us to supper.

No, no, I said.

Nikos said to me in English that we had to go, she had to feed us for the work we'd done for her.

Giuseppe took Nikos' hand as we all plodded up the long path, through moonlit bushes, to the widow's house.

La Nonna was sitting in the dark by the fireplace, the fire out, and she was moaning. The widow turned on the small electric light hanging from a beam among the hams. She asked her mother how her leg was. Bad, *la Nonna* said. You let the fire go out, the widow said.

Draped over the back of a wooden chair were many strands of yellow pasta. The widow washed her hands at the low shallow stone sink in the kitchen. Then, when the men and the boys washed, she started the fire with a heap of broom, and while the men and the boys sat on chairs and the bench and watched her, she heated the water to boiling in the pot hanging over the fire, and gathered the pasta from the back of the chair and threw the pasta into the water.

She prepared pasta with oil and garlic, and as we others ate this she fried, over the fire, pigs' livers, which she took from a big oil-filled jar with a fork. She did not sit with us but ate bits of liver on bread, standing.

Before Nikos and I left, she asked us if we'd like to see her cows. We followed her slowly, stiffly and step by step, down the stone stairs to the stables below. She opened a large wooden door into darkness and a hot sweet smell, and she went in and lit a dim electric light and three grand white cows appeared, tethered by chains to a stone wall; they turned their large heads to us and stared with wet, black eyes. The widow picked up from the floor a broom made of twigs to clean the dung from the stone-paved floor.

Nikos and I walked along a path in the moonlight. I was drunk. He told me to watch out, we were coming to a ditch with a plank over it, and I took his arm.

Nikos with the widow and two of her sons

Jerusalem

When Philip and I left Claire in London this morning, she, at the doorway in her dressing gown, shouted out to us in the taxi, 'What a pair of comedians.'

Philip shouted back to her through the open window, 'So which one of us is the straight man?'

She couldn't come to Israel because she has an acting job. Philip asked me instead.

On the way to the airport, Philip told me, with wide-eyed astonishment in the way he often recounts what has happened, that his elder brother Sandy has just had an emergency heart-bypass operation in Chicago. This shook Philip. Perhaps he should be going to Chicago to see his brother rather than to Israel. It has occurred again and again in their lives, he said, that when Sandy became sick, Philip came down with the same sickness. Maybe he should have his heart tested. He would be worried all the while he was in Israel about his brother, and, thinking that what has happened to his brother will happen to him, about himself.

As the plane was about to take off, he, sensing I'd become tense, said he, too, used to be frightened of flying, but he'd managed to get over it. 'I learned to enjoy it, especially the take-off, the most dangerous part. What you do is slump back and you open your legs wide and you fantasize the plane is between your legs and you're riding it as you rise higher and higher into the sky.' I said I'd try, and as the plane took off did try, my eyes closed. When we were airborne, he asked me how my fantasy had been. I said, 'You've really taught me something that will change my life.' He said, 'But I have no fantasies for you about coming down.'

I wondered why he'd asked me to come to Israel with him.

He said, 'Now look, you've never been to Israel before. You may find the people in the street a little rude, a little brutal, a little pushy. They don't respect lines there. Jews can be an aggressive lot, you know, just a little. You may have heard.'

I said, 'Someone in New York once told me, a long time ago.'

'I'm just warning you so you won't be offended,' he said. 'It's not meant for you, the aggressiveness, just because you're a goy. Goys they treat well. You'll see how they treat one another.'

I said, 'I thought Jews always help one another.'

'Sure.' Then Philip said, 'You may wonder why I've asked you to come with me.'

'I did wonder.'

'I want to go to Israel with a non-Jew to compare my own reactions to the place with those of a non-Jew.' Then he confided, 'This is just between you and your diary.' He was having difficulty with the novel he was working on, he said. He'd finished two chapters, but he didn't know how to develop it further. His main character was a goy, and he thought he'd bring his goy to Israel to react as a goy to the country. He wanted his goy character to meet, not the fair-minded, intelligent, humanist, cultured, middle-class people he, Philip, already knew in Israel, the left-wing ones who want to make peace by returning the West Bank to Jordan, but the narrow-minded people, the fanatics, the unprincipled, the rough and aggressive, who are on the right and refuse to have the West Bank returned, and who are settling it in small colonies which they believe will be the pioneering beginning of annexation to Israel.

I thought: I've got to react to all those people for Philip.

Philip said, 'You know what I'm going to do to you? I'm going to turn you into an anti-Semite. After a week, you won't be able to stand even the word Jew.'

I tried to laugh. Philip really has a way, I thought, of making me feel self-conscious. And why do I like it?

He referred often to his brother in Chicago.

From the taxi, on the way from the airport near Tel Aviv up to Jerusalem, Philip pointed out the rusted and twisted chassis of military vehicles on the banks on either side of the highway left from the Six-Day War.

We are staying at Mishkenot Shananim, the row of guest houses overlooking the walls of Jerusalem for visitors provided by the city council. By the time we settled in, it was dark. We had a light supper in a restaurant, then, back in our house, Philip said he'd go to bed. From my room, I heard him telephone, maybe for information about his brother Sandy. Now, writing this, I imagine he is asleep.

As a boy, and a believer, I had a favorite rosary with a wooden crucifix on it on the back of which was a tiny, narrow panel which could be removed by turning a screw to reveal, in a twist of paper, sand from the Holy Land, the very sand into which the blood of my Saviour, the Saviour of all mankind, had flowed. Israel and the Holy Land were, to me, different places, and yet, because I have been invited by Philip, who is an entirely secular Jew, they are the same place.

———

When I came out of my room this morning, Philip was eating cereal at the dining-room table. I prepared myself some cereal and milk also, a little confused by the labels on the cupboards distinguishing milk and meat dishes, and wondering, were I to mix them up, if they'd have to be buried. I sat with Philip.

Even early in the morning, he could joke. 'I heard you last night,' he said, 'shoving furniture against the door so I wouldn't be able to come in.'

Never before have I felt so accepted for my own homosexuality by a heterosexual.

I asked about his brother, and Philip told me he would be all right, but I could see his worry in his eyes.

We went out. Philip said he'd show me some sites. What first struck me was the number of soldiers, men and women, in what appeared to be their own individual, scruffy versions of combat fatigues, carrying their carbines and rifles around in the streets. And then I saw a tank with a blue Star of David on its side.

The first place Philip said he'd bring me that morning was the Church of the Holy Sepulcher.

In the church, Philip let me wander about, and he followed, smiling a little, I felt, with the awareness of bringing me to the very centre of my religion. I never know if his smile is ironical or not. He was, I thought, letting me see my Holy Land first, and then he would show me Israel.

I looked at cracked slabs of pink marble, raw holes in the brownish, crumbling masonry, smoke-black icons and hanging oil lamps, and it seemed to me this old building was returning to nature, that all its walls were exuding the same brownish calcium that produces stalactites in a grotto, so I expected everything to drip water. Philip didn't follow me into the tomb itself; I got in line to enter the small, airless, crowded space, in which a Greek priest opened a little wooden shutter in a marble wall to show the original stone wall beneath.

I did not believe that any of what I saw was what it was meant to be, nor did I feel I was capable of any kind of veneration inspired by my past religion, which, more than my nationality, my class, my sex, I imagine made me what I am. And yet I felt something come over me in the tomb, and I wanted to be able to account for it to Philip, who had taken me there. It was important to me that something should come over me and that I should tell Philip what it was. I felt he expected it of me. But, really, what I felt was that I was in a place that had nothing to do with my parish church, as though I had grown up in a religion that was so much itself, evolving generation after generation in the forests of North America, that it was as if a bird that was native to the forests; we in our religion were native to the forests.

Philip was waiting for me when I left the tomb. I said to him, 'I don't know what it means,' and tears rose into my eyes. He put an arm over my shoulders for a moment and smiled. I half expected him to make a joke, wanted him to make a joke, but he didn't.

The tomb from which Jesus Christ rose from the dead was at the very centre of the Christian belief, but I had entered into and come out from that centre believing more than ever that the Christian God, of whom my Canuck God was some manifestation, was as arbitrary as any historical God. The tomb was to me incidental to some high absolute dark God beyond God in whom there was no Christian light, or the light of any religion, or of any human-ity. How explain to Philip that what moved me to tears was the pathetic human devotion to the lower God who, believers believe, loves us with a glorifying love that forgives us all our sins for being merely humans, who out of that love suffered and died as a human to sanctify our own human suffering and deaths with the divine suffering of a God, who when we die our temporal deaths will raise us into eternal life with God, the God whom the believers call Christ in the name of their religion? How could I not weep with pity for that tragic religion?

We walked about the church, and found ourselves on the roof, where Egyptian Copts live in little cement sheds with tiny windows, and down stone steps into a chapel where, behind a grill painted green and silver, a service was being held, and Philip and I sat on a bench against a wall and watched. It was a Coptic service. Within the grilled enclosure, where dark men in black robes and round, black hats and holding staffs sat on benches, and women, almost completely enveloped in black robes from which only a tattooed hand protruded to hold veils close about their faces, sat behind. They were all facing the altar screen, through the open main gate of which the priests in the sanctuary, in long, white, gold and green robes were moving about with Coptic gold crosses on long staffs, chanting, one swinging a censer of smoking incense. Beside Philip and me, on the stone bench outside the grill, were three women in white robes, their veils close about their faces. When the priests came out of the sanctuary everyone in the congregation, includ-ing the three women in white by Philip and me, knelt, way over, touching foreheads to the stone floor. Philip and I stood. One of the priests carrying a golden cross on a staff came out of the grilled enclosure towards us, smiled at us, then turned round to face the altar. For a moment Philip and I were standing in the folds of his wide robe. He chanted, in the language the Egyptian pharaohs wouldn't have found unfamiliar. When he went back to the altar, Philip and I left.

His eyes wide behind his gold-rimmed glasses, Philip said, 'Amazing,' and shook his head.

I thought, The people in that chapel, who were the most exotic to me in the world, were Christians, as I. But I had only as much to do with them as did Philip.

As we left the church, we saw, standing in the forecourt, a long-haired and bearded man in a long brown robe and wearing sandals and carrying a rough wooden staff and shouting out in an American accent that everyone around him was a sinner, and that the destruction of the Temple was upon us. He frowned so his thick eyebrows overhung his eyes and he stared at Philip and me, then, with a look of disgust, turned, using his staff as a pivot, and walked away, his shoulders hunched.

I said to Philip, 'He seems like a pretty narrow-minded, rough and aggressive fanatic to me. Maybe we should go talk with him.'

Philip didn't find this funny. He said, 'He's a nut.'

We walked down the Via Dolorosa, taking the opposite direction Christ took, and we stopped to look in at various chapels. A sense of detachment had come over me, and I wasn't taking anything in; perhaps there was too much to take in, not only of what was there but what it all meant. I remarked that there were no great works of art, as I might have expected, equal to the importance of the sites to the religion, as there would have been in Europe, but that the chapels were filled with the kinds of cheap devotional pictures and chalk statues I recalled from my parish church in America. We went into the Chapel of the Flagellation, where Philip stared for a long time at a chalk, multi-colored statue of the scourged, thorn-crowned, red-robed, suffering Jesus Christ. It was the kind of statue

I had in my parish made the sign of the cross and prayed before. If I had had any sense that a visit to the Holy Land would revive in me, not nostalgia, as I have no nostalgia for anything, but an affinity with my past religion, I didn't find it. What I saw in terms of my religion was all too familiar to me, and what I had wanted was a difference. I found myself wondering, not what it meant to me, but what the statue of Jesus Christ meant to Philip. He didn't say anything.

At the bottom of the Via Dolorosa, as if he had shown me everything there was to be seen of Christian Jerusalem, he said he'd take me now to the Wailing Wall.

In the large, open square before the Wall were wooden enclosures, one for the men and another for the women, and before we went into the men's enclosure we put on paper skullcaps supplied in a big box at the entrance. I had never seen Philip wearing a yarmulke before. Worried that it would drop off, I held mine on. We walked together to the high Wall made of different-sized blocks of stone, with, high up, caper plants and birds in wide cracks.

Facing all along the wall, men were, while rocking back and forth, praying. Some hit their foreheads against the stone, in the cracks of which were bits of rolled-up paper inscribed, Philip said, with requests for God's help. Not far from us was a man in a business suit, a briefcase on the ground by his side, praying. Philip was explaining everything to me, as if now he could, as if he wanted me to learn. I felt he wanted the Wailing Wall to mean something to me and that he would give me the meaning. To the left of the Wall, we entered into what looked like the great, groined, ancient remains of underground vaults, where there was more intense praying, men rocking back and forth, about a large wooden cupboard with a velvet curtain in which, Philip said, there was an especially venerated Torah. Chanting their prayers, the men, almost all Hasidim, rocked not only back and forth but from side to side, and, at what I thought moments of greatest intensity, turned round, still chanting, to see who else was there. Some of the Hasidim were talking to one another, not necessarily about religion, Philip said, and most likely about business. 'For Jews, business is holy,' Philip said, and I felt by his joking that he was at ease, knew where he was, and I was eager to be in the same place.

We stood for a while against a back wall under the vaults and watched men pray, I thinking they would object if they knew a Gentile was among them. I certainly felt self-conscious, and depended entirely on Philip to give me whatever sense possible of belonging there. His eyes were gleaming as he looked around, and he was smiling that thin smile that makes one think he is thinking of a joke but that it might just be too wicked to tell. But did I feel he was entirely at ease, knew just where he was, and saw himself as closer to understanding the Hasidim than me? Did I feel he wasn't at all self-conscious himself, but really was in a world so familiar to him it was only my being with him that gave him any sense of difference? Standing side by side, we both watched, with curiosity, a rabbi winding a phylactery about the plump bare arm of a boy. We were at the center of Jewishness, but Philip was standing apart, looking, smiling to himself.

A thin pale man with a black beard came up to Philip and me. After glancing at me, and, I thought, spotting straight off that I wasn't Jewish, he turned away so I ceased to exist, and asked Philip if he would make up the tenth man for a prayer *minyan*. Philip said, 'No, I'm just here to look.' The man insisted, with a slight whine. 'Look,' Philip told him, 'I wasn't even Bar-Mitzvaed,' and the young man turned away. When Philip and I left, the nine men, along with the boy with the black strap wound round his arm, were still waiting for a tenth to be able to pray.

Out in the square again before the Wailing Wall, outside, too, the enclosure that demarked the sacred area from the secular, at the exit to which we had thrown our yarmulkes into a box, Philip stopped and for a long while looked about, his eyes behind his glasses gleaming. He was smiling more than ever.

He asked me, 'So what do you think of it?'

I said, with a rise in my voice that went flat, 'I think it's terrific,' though I wanted to say something more. I felt I owed it to Philip to say something original about the Wailing Wall, and maybe all of

Jewishness, which he hadn't quite thought of before, but I couldn't do it. I wanted to please him too much, wanted, too eagerly, to show him my appreciation for his having asked me to come to the Holy Land with him, wanted him to believe he hadn't made a mistake inviting me.

But he said, as if what I'd said was exactly right, 'It is terrific, you're right, it is.' And he continued to stare at the square, at the people praying within the enclosures, at the Wall.

I had this feeling, which he might tell me was all wrong if I confessed it to him – that because he was showing it all to me, a non-Jew, he was not embarrassed to be where he was, and, yes, he found it all terrific.

———

Philip wanted to visit Jews who have settled on the West Bank, the people, he had said, who really interested him for being fanatics. I didn't know whom he was in touch with to make the arrangements for the visit to a settlement, but he told me he had proposed Saturday, but some of the ultra-orthodox Jews who lived there objected to our coming by car on the Sabbath. Arrangements were made for today, Sunday.

I was apprehensive about going. What did I feel about the settlements on the West Bank? Whatever my feelings, I could detach myself from them by seeing everything through the eyes of Philip, whose curiosity about the place would become my curiosity. But I was a goy, and what would the settlers feel about a goy coming to their settlement?

Last night, before going to bed, I asked Philip, 'What do you think their attitude will be towards me?'

'Hatred,' he said, and laughed.

'And what might they do to me?'

He leaned back against a wall and raised his hands to form a cross then let his head hang.

This morning at breakfast, he seemed apprehensive about my going with him, and he said, 'Look, if they ask you, say you're a Jew, so assimilated you weren't even Bar-Mitzvaed. You know nothing about where your grandparents came from except that it was somewhere in France. No one ever mentioned being Jews in your family. You didn't even know yourself until—' Then he broke off. He said, 'You can make it up. You're a writer.'

'Thanks,' I said.

Philip went to his room to telephone for a taxi. When he came back to me, he said the driver was going to charge extra because it was dangerous to drive to Ofra, the settlement we were going to. 'The Arabs in the Arab villages we have to pass through could stone the car,' Philip said, 'and us in it.' Though we joked, I felt Philip was as nervous as I. As far as I knew, he had never been in an area occupied by the military, and I certainly hadn't. We were silent waiting for the taxi to come. When it came, I thought: Well, it wouldn't be a bad death. Philip sat next to the driver, I in the back seat, and as we left Jerusalem the driver stopped at a line of people waiting at a bus stop, among them soldiers carrying rifles, and said, making a gesture to the people in the line, 'We get soldier come with us.' But instead of a soldier a young Hasid came to the car. He was pale, wore a black fedora, a white shirt buttoned up to the collar, and a black suit, and his eyeglasses were very thick. When he leaned towards the window to talk in Hebrew to the driver, his forelocks swung forward. The driver said to Philip, 'He going to Ofra too.' There was nothing to be done but offer him a lift with us, and he sat beside me, silent, in the back seat. Philip turned round to smile at me. We wanted a soldier to protect us, I thought, and we got a Hasid.

A bright, cold day, the windows of the taxi were shut. The driver drove quickly through the Arab towns, where large new houses, financed by the P.L.O., were being built with enormous antennae, like miniature Eiffel Towers, on their roofs. To occupy as much land as possible, the Arab houses were spread about at great distances from one another, and the old centers of the towns were crumbling. The new houses were made of stone, and were one with the stony landscape. I looked at Arabs from the car window, and sometimes they looked back at me. Dust rose about the car as we sped along the earth road.

The driver said, 'Ofra ahead,' and we saw, over a stone ridge, slanted red roofs with timbers like chalets in a Swiss skiing resort so far out of season the mountains had become eroded, grey rock and the valleys desert-brown. The houses looked prefabricated, and there was no meeting point between them and the landscape. Later, we were told by some of the settlers living there that the houses were not really to their personal tastes, then they shrugged.

In Ofra, Philip and I went to the office of Israel Harvel, in a long, grey, prefabricated shed. He, a Sabra, had a face that looked as if it had been gently pressed between the hands of his mother when he was a child, so he had no chin, a wide mouth, wide cheeks, and his eyes bulged; his forehead was narrow and his head so flat he had to keep his skullcap on with a bobby pin or it would have fallen off. He wore a blue shirt with a button-down collar and the sleeves rolled up to his elbows. He and Philip talked and, as attentive as I tried to be, my mind kept wandering as it always does when I try to be attentive. I was trying, mainly, to get an impression of Israel Harvel. He had a sense of humor, was totally without self-consciousness. He knew exactly what it meant to be a Jew.

He said that the settlers had been very careful in settling only on land that had been the sites of former military camps, and that they got on well with the local Arabs, who bought eggs and chickens from them.

All Philip said in reaction, again and again, was, 'A-hun, a-hun.'

As unselfconscious as Israel Harvel was, I was self-conscious, and wondered if he saw right off that I wasn't a Jew. If so, how?

A slight American woman came in, a graduate from Barnard and wearing, Philip told me later, the clothes a Barnard girl would have worn twenty years before – a black woollen skirt with black stockings and a heavy, dark cardigan. Her clothes were worn, her stockings with holes, and I imagined they were her best, put on to receive us on our visit. She was, I think, from Wisconsin, and she had a stunned look. She spoke American, but she had ceased to be American.

She said, 'Samaria and Judea are ours. It's in the Bible.'

Philip said, 'A-hun.'

She and Israel Harvel showed us around the settlement: the metalwork shop, the print shop, the school, the kindergarten. A room in a building was set aside as the museum, in which were on display grinding stones, pots and shards, coins found when digging work was done. The synagogue was being built by Arabs, the only Arabs the settlers would hire to do work for them.

Neither Israel Harvel nor the American woman asked me any questions about myself, as if they understood I was not a Jew and they would not, by asking anything personal, raise this as an issue. Even when I asked a question, they addressed their answers to Philip.

Outside in the by now warm, bright sunlight was a class of students and teacher sitting around a table. The American woman said the students were Americans learning Hebrew. Israel Harvel suggested that we sit at the table with the class, and when Philip was introduced by him, one of the students, a tall, thin young man, said, 'Wow, I never met a famous writer before.' In a high, American voice, and rising a little from his chair, this student asked Philip, 'What do you think of the settlements in the West Bank – excuse me, in Samaria and Judea?'

Philip smiled a little, the way he smiles before he is about to tell a joke, then said, 'The settlements, all of Israel – I have to tell you that everything that has to do with this country is peripheral to my real interests. I'm here because I'm curious.'

Sinking back, the student said, 'Oh.'

Israel Harvel and the American woman said nothing, but Israel Harvel did smile. The woman simply stared out into space.

We met others in the settlement who wanted to talk with Philip, all Americans from different parts of America who had ceased to be Americans. It was said that there were people in the settlement who had objected to Philip's visit and did not want to meet him. The visit had been discussed. There would be no meal.

Israel Harvel drove Philip and me back to Jerusalem. We went high above the Dead Sea, with bare, twisted, grey basalt mountains below us, and settlements on the flat tops of the mountains. Across the Dead Sea were the mountains of Jordan. From time to time, we passed a military installation on the highest spots, with Hawk missiles ('American,' Israel Harvel said) perched on stands and facing Jordan. We passed Arab villages and we passed Bedouin encampments, the black and brown tents stretched on barren ground in the lee of barren mountains. Israel Harvel said the Bedouin had battery-run television sets in their tents. Philip asked him questions about his life, his family, and he answered without, it seemed, any reservations, and he often joked.

Back at Mishkenot Shananim, Philip said, 'That trip shows up the imagination for what it is, nothing but fantasy. What we'd imagined would be dangerous to us wasn't at all.'

I wondered if he was disappointed in the trip. He said he would make arrangements for another visit to the West Bank to another settlement.

He went to his room to take notes so he wouldn't forget what had happened. I went out for a little walk, and for a while watched a camel and its rider go by, the long tassels hanging from the saddle swaying with the delicate swaying walk of the long-legged camel. In Israel, every sight becomes interpreted immediately into a question about Israel. What, I wondered, must Arab Israelis be like?

In the reception lobby of Mishkenot Shananim, I was stopped by a woman I had met earlier. She was very much of the class Philip said he found boring. With a slight frown, she asked me why we had gone to Ofra.

I said, 'I can't speak for Philip. For myself, to see it. I want to see everything.'

'What were your impressions?' she asked.

'Strong,' I said.

'But the people in the settlements are fanatics,' she said. 'They will destroy the only chance we have for peace. My son is in Lebanon now, in great danger. If those people in the settlements – who are, I know because I've met them, warm, sincere, spirited – become intransigent in their criminal acts, what will happen? You know that it is illegal for them to construct their settlements in the West Bank, so they are criminals. And how will they be removed? Will we have a civil war in Israel?'

I simply looked at her.

'Will you write about it?' she asked.

'Only for myself.'

'And Philip?'

'I honestly can't talk for Philip.'

When I saw him later on our way to dinner, I told him there was no doubt a lot of speculation going on as to why he'd become so interested in the settlements.

He said, 'I've got a girlfriend out there.'

'You know,' I said, 'the settlement people could use you, if you expressed any sympathy for them in a book, for their cause.'

'I've told them it's only out of curiosity, my wanting to see the settlements,' Philip said. 'As for the book, when I finish it, if I finish it, I'll probably never be able to come to Israel again. That would be too bad. It's a very exciting country.'

That evening, we were invited to dinner by an old couple. Other elderly people were guests. I found them all a little pompous, but they were very welcoming.

Introducing me to them, Philip said, 'This is Claire Bloom.' They had expected him to come to dinner with Claire, and hadn't told them I was coming instead.

They seemed not to be interested in our visit to the West Bank. They seemed, in fact, not to be interested in Israel so much as their lives before they came to live there. For the first time since I've arrived, the Holocaust was the subject of a conversation I was listening to, if not participating in. But I have done much more listening than talking. What most of the Sabras talked about was the Israeli economy, and among them I had never heard one of them mention the Holocaust, not even in passing. The old people at the dining table were, in their talk, in Europe during World War II. As I did, Philip listened to them without talking.

They were Dutch, Romanian, German Jews, all European. One of the men recounted the story of his being parachuted into German-occupied Yugoslavia to try to save Jews by getting them out.

What surprised me was that they started to talk about those Jews who have made livings out of the Holocaust, the professional mourners, they called them, the professional Nazi-seekers, whom they derided.

I did wonder if they took me for a Jew and thought that what they'd said should only be heard by Jews. And then I thought, I don't think so, because Jews don't have secrets.

It's the Gentiles who have secrets, I thought, not the Jews. And what is the secret of the Gentiles? What is it that they wouldn't want the Jews to know about them?

———

Today Philip went, again, to the West Bank, this time to visit another settlement. I asked if he didn't mind my not coming with him. If he was looking for reactions in me to what we saw together, I'm afraid I've disappointed him in not being original enough, not making him see what he himself doesn't see. Maybe he's already dropped the idea of having a goy as his main character. A goy in Israel finds himself the centre of his religion, and Philip's concern in his novel can't be what a Christian feels about that centre. But it is a concern of mine, and I decided, instead of going to the West Bank again, I would return, alone, to the Church of the Holy Sepulcher.

I studied the stone chalice in the Catholicon which marks the center of the world.

I went down to the chapel of Saint Helena. An Armenian priest stopped me and asked me, in shattered English, where I was from. I said, 'I'm an American.' Leaning close, he asked me if I was Protestant, and when I said, 'I'm Roman Catholic,' he grasped my hand and bumped his forehead against mine. Still grasping my hand, he took me across the floor to the side of the chapel where he switched on a light within a deep hole in the rock and told me, in disconnected words, that Saint Helena had here found the true cross. Then, still clutching my hand, he took me into a kind of storage room where he gave me a candle, a little packet of *terra sancta* with a dried flower from the Holy Land and a picture of Christ rising from the dead, and a little clear-plastic container of water from the Jordan. I gave him two thousand shekels, 'for the church', I said, and he gave me an additional handful of packets of *terra sancta*.

He was thin, with a short black beard, and his face was creased. Perhaps he was my age, though I thought of him as much older. He said, 'I get you bag,' and went into a smaller storeroom at the back of the one where we were, and I saw, through the doorway, what looked like old boxes, automobile tires, heaps of empty bottles. He was there for a long time. I waited, and I had the sudden sense that he expected me to come into this inner storeroom. I wanted to go away, but felt I had to stay. He finally came out with a plastic bag with Hebrew on it and held it open so I could put all my gifts in it, then he gave it to me and grabbed my arms and leaned forward, his eyes wide, to kiss me on the mouth. I quickly turned my face to the side, and he kissed my cheek, and I thought the least I could do was kiss his cheek in return. He kissed my other cheek, then my forehead.

While I was writing in my diary, Philip came in. He said he was both exhausted and fired up from what had been the most exciting day of his life. An extraordinary man, a very right-wing man, had taken him to a settlement, then, with a gun in the glove compartment, had driven him around the West Bank in his car. Philip said he understood the excitement journalists feel when in dangerous situations. Excited, he walked back and forth in the living room.

He said, 'You know, here I'm not thinking about myself. Fifty-one years I've spent thinking about myself. Not thinking about myself is what I've always wanted.'

'Can you imagine a novel equal to your day?'

Philip jumped up high, so his long legs bent at the knees, and he raised his arms and shouted, 'It's shit, it's shit, literature! I'm going to kick writing novels. That's all over.' Stamping the heel of a shoe, he said, 'I don't want to deal with the nice people any more. They bore me. I bore myself as a nice person, a good boy. You bore me as a good boy.'

I laughed and said, 'I don't mind your hating me for being a good boy.'

He said he would go to his room to take some notes about the past day and then rest before we went out to dinner.

I think I'm not helping Philip at all, only making him feel more helpless. We are very different, but maybe we are similar, or maybe I read myself into Philip.

Still later –

This evening we went to dinner at the house of Amos and Beth Elon. At the table, Amos Elon attacked me for saying I had been impressed by Israel Harvel at Ofra. He told me it was as if I had been impressed by Himmler. Israel Harvel was a criminal. He was the chairman of a movement that shot off the kneecaps of Arab leaders, threw bombs into busloads of innocent Arab children, wanted to dispossess Arabs of their land and homes. He said, 'You can't be impressed by him. You can't.'

I knew that in attacking me he was indirectly attacking Philip. After dinner, he and Philip went into the sitting room alone to talk. When we got back to Mishkenot, Philip said that Amos Elon had let him have it when they were alone.

———

Philip and I went to Tel Aviv. I liked Tel Aviv very much, more than Jerusalem. Philip wanted to go to the Museum of the Diaspora, a museum of information about Jews all over the world. We had to endure a lecture, with a number of other visitors, by the director, then a guide, a middle-aged woman with spectacles that magnified her eyes enormously, said she would show us around. The museums displayed fake holy books and torahs, small models of synagogues from around the world, even large fiberglass casts of some of the stones from the Wailing Wall. The guide showed us small-scale models in plaster of Jewish ceremonies throughout the world and, in a high, almost hysterical voice, praised the Jews for their virtues of family closeness, of education, of goodness, despite every attempt to destroy them. Philip leaned towards my ear and whispered, 'I can't take this, but if I just walk out it'll get into the newspapers.' The woman went on talking, and Philip interrupted her. He said, 'I know all that you're saying. It really would be better if we looked around on our own.' The woman stared at him for a moment with her enormously magnified eyes and then said, 'Oh, all right.' As we walked away, Philip said, 'I grew up with all that sentimental shit about the Jews, and I'm not going to take any more of it. I hate it. It tried so hard to make me a good boy – it made me a good boy – until I fought it, violently, and they hate me for it. I'm not a good Jew.'

We rushed to the part of the museum where visitors could sit at a computer, type in their family names or simply the name of the place their ancestors came from, and the screen lit up with the relevant information available about their general genealogies and the histories of where they were from, all in English. Philip dropped a token into a slot and typed out his name and a para-graph appeared on the screen with all the variations, ROT, ROTT, ROTH, and information about what the name meant and where it came from. The paragraph ended with the information that the ROTHS could claim as one of them the American writer Philip Milton Roth. Philip sat back and said, 'There I am.' He smiled. 'If only my mother could have known before she died that my name is here,' he said. I said, 'It would have made up for a lot.' He laughed. He punched in BLOOM. Then he punched in names in Galicia and Russia where his ancestors came from.

When he finished, I said, 'I'm going to punch in my name.'

He looked at me with a sudden expression of worry, and, quite seriously, said, 'The machine will go haywire.'

'Let me try.' I put a token into the slot and said, 'This may change my life, you know, if I find out I've got a Jewish name.' I punched out the letters and on the screen flashed a list of about fifty names approximating mine. The closest was PLOTNIK.

'It's great,' Philip said. 'Now you've got your Jewish name.' He shook my hand. 'Well, Plotnik, now you'll know what a pain in the ass it is to be a Jew. Remember, at all times, that you're a Jew, and that means you've got to be a good Jew. Remember that. Remember the virtues of family closeness, education, of goodness itself, and don't ever let anyone destroy these virtues, though they'll try. A good Jew is pious, and feels in his heart his Jewishness, and that will see him through any attempt to destroy him.' He smiled, a wicked smile. 'But the best of it,' he said, is that as a Jew you can be as anti-Semitic as you want, and the Jews may hate you for it but they'll still think of you as a Jew. You can even let the Jews know what the Gentiles have always thought about them, what the Jews have always wanted to know that is deep down in every Gentile heart, and no Jew will be able to accuse you of being an anti-Semitic Gentile, because you'll be a Jew. Now let the world know what the Gentiles really feel about the Jews.'

'This'll take some deep thought,' I said.

'Now come on, Plotnik,' Philip said, 'let's get the fuck out of here.'

He wanted to stay in Tel Aviv to see another right-wing ex-politician. I returned by bus to Jerusalem to go to the Israel Museum.

Philip, I think, isn't very interested in museums, as he isn't very interested in archaeological sites of ruined walls and excavated terracotta pipes. He likes pictures, but wouldn't, I assume, go to them for the reality it would take all his energy to try to account for.

When I saw him later, Philip said about the right-wing ex-politician he had stayed in Tel Aviv to see, 'He was too reasonable. I didn't want to see him for his reasonableness. I want the mad fanaticism of the man I saw yesterday on the West Bank.'

———

On our way to a restaurant for lunch, we stopped in a bookshop. Philip said, 'Let's see if my books are here, or if they hate me so much they won't stock them.' All the books were in Hebrew, and Philip and I, neither knowing even the alphabet, looked around in a daze. I thought of asking the salesgirl behind a counter, but then thought this might embarrass Philip. He said, 'Let's give up.' 'I'll bet they're here someplace,' I said. 'Thanks,' he said.

We had lunch with the writer Aharon Applefeld, and afterwards walked him to a bus stop from where he would get a bus back to Haifa where he lived. We walked slowly, Aharon Applefeld telling stories and laughing. He had a round, palely glowing face and made gentle gestures. His voice was also gentle. He said he couldn't write about what he had lived through when he was a boy during World War II, hiding for years in forests, living among beggars and prostitutes. He couldn't write about it because it was all too fantastic, wasn't real. He stopped and Philip and I stopped with him. He said that while he was living through the horrors, he would tell himself, over and over, that he would never, ever forget any of it, that he would remember it all for the rest of his life, day after day, if he lived to remember. He raised his arms and said, 'But, you know, I hardly ever think about it. I've forgotten it.' He laughed.

After he left, just when I was wondering about the Jews, about the Holocaust, about Aharon Applefeld, Philip said to me, 'Plotnik, you Jew, you haven't told me yet what bad things you think of your newfound people.'

London

Max, back from New York where he was for almost a month and where he stayed with Jennifer, said she is having some internal trouble because of an abortion, but she has been working very hard, and is to have a show.

I ask myself what I would have felt had the baby been mine.

When I asked Nikos this, he shrugged.

And this reminds me: someone once asked me if Nikos and I ever thought of adopting a child, and I said I had but I had never suggested this to Nikos. The friend said, 'It would be a bad idea.'

I saw Philip on his return from New York and Florida, where he saw his father. His father has a girlfriend who eats all the time. Philip said, 'I took a walk along the beach, asking myself, how could I possibly be my father's son, how can I know *anything* being his son?' His father says to his girlfriend, 'You eat too much. Why do you eat so much? Look at this girl, Phil, the way she eats. How about that.' And again to the girlfriend, 'Why do you eat so much?' The girlfriend, who is very fat, eats more.

Philip jokes about my writing about him and getting everything wrong, though I don't know if he's really joking. He keeps suggesting that I write a story about our trip to Israel – he calls me 'Plotnik' now – and that I should use him as a character, but, again, I'm not sure if he's joking or not.

I told him how I'd offended Nikos by reading out to my friends a passage from my diary about his complaining. Philip looked shocked, and said, 'But didn't you ask him first if you could do it?'

'No,' I said.

He shook his head. 'Plotnik, how long can you get away with your innocence?'

'My innocence?' I asked.

Then Philip said, 'You're not an operator.'

'Maybe I am,' I said.

Claire is in Cardiff working on a film. I stayed with Philip in their house for an hour. He told me he could parody my writing, and, as an example, he said, 'He sat on the train. The train started. His ankle was itchy. The train slowed down. He scratched his ankle. The train stopped.' Then he asked me to parody his writing. I thought for a while, then said I couldn't. He thought for a while and said he couldn't either, then he added: 'That may be a bad sign.'

Though Nikos seems to have no close Greek friends in London, he is promoting a possible exhibition of the works of Tsarouchis at the Royal Academy, and has the support of David Hockney, with whom Tsarouchis shared a model when Hockney was living in Paris and Tsarouchis was there in asylum from the dictatorship in Greece; and also the support for the exhibition from R.B. Kitaj and Howard Hodgkin.

There is a large painting by Tsarouchis called *The Forgotten Guard*, within the setting of, possibly, a coffee house; at the back are two, narrow, fluted, classical columns; at the far right is a blue window framing what looks like a small abstract painting; and in the middle, on one of the coffee tables, is a brass artillery shell used as a vase for calla lilies and lilac. Sitting at a table on the right is a guard in a loose, white, navy summer outfit, and sitting near the other coffee table on the left is a guard totally naked except for his boots. Both of these men are staring, with a combination of wonder and matter-of-factness, right at the genitals of a third guard, also naked but for his boots and a navy-issue belt and shoulder strap, his back turned to the viewer. (In fact, the three figures were painted from the same model.) All the stage-like space around the guards seems to be dark and uncontained, with a luminous cloud floating above them. (In a study, Tsarouchis depicted Aphrodite and Cupid floating in this cloud above the scene.) The title was suggested by the maker of the stretcher of the picture, who said it reminded him of military guards at El Alamein in Egypt who were so hot they wore only their accessories; Tsarouchis added the 'Forgotten' to the title because the ideas which generated the picture – among them the ancient Greek idealization of the body – would be forgotten by everyone but him, who would be the only guardian of his picture's secrets.

When I see Nikos as Greek, I see in my erotic attraction to him what I fantasize is Greek.

Oh, our love making!

I separate myself off from our love making as if someone curious to know what our love making is, and I try to satisfy the curiosity of someone else with the information: intercrural, in the ancient Greek way.

Is there *nothing* I would leave out of this diary?

We are aging together very well.

————

Keith, who was in New York, saw Jennifer, who sold a piece from her show for $50,000. Keith said, 'She's now rich and famous.' Keith and I walked up the King's Road to the Chelsea Arts Club, from where I rang Nikos, who joined us, and the three of us sat in the garden, the lawn parched yellow, and drank white wine. We talked about money.

A few minutes after we got home, Stephen rang to say how much he misses Bryan. His tone of voice made me laugh a little, but then I realized how serious Stephen was, and I became as serious as he. He is sure this is the last time he will fall in love, and is sure he has never been in love as much as he is now. He rang about five times in two hours to tell Nikos and me something about Bryan he had forgotten to tell us.

He has given us photographs of Bryan.

He said that he had shown some photographs to, of all people, John Lehmann, who commented on the acne scars of Bryan. Why Stephen would show John Lehmann photographs of Bryan has to do with a relationship between them that is theirs to figure out, if they have any inclination to figure it out.

———

In Philip Roth's study in Notting Hill, I sat on a hard wooden chair before his desk, he on the commanding side. As he turned on his desk lamp, he asked, 'Are you ready for this?'

I laughed. I had given him my novel, *The Foreigner*, to read. He said he'd only had time enough to read the first chapter. Everything I had crossed out (crossed out lightly so he could read the words underneath) he said I should put back in.

'It's interesting,' he said, 'all the information about where the narrator comes from. But otherwise, David, these pages are lifeless. I've been thinking about your writing: sensations without associations. My work is all associations.'

I knew what he meant. His work always refers to the world outside, and mine doesn't.

I said, 'I feel I am a person entirely without associations. If, say, I mention World War II, I have to create the war *inside* my book, as if no one *outside* the book has heard of it.'

Philip put his hand to the side of his mouth and whispered, 'Let me tell you – we've all heard of World War II.'

'But I can't assume that my characters have, so for them to react to World War II I have to create World War II for them, have to make alarms screech, bombs fall, buildings go up in flames, dead bodies among the rubble occur inside the book. But World War II is so vast in what you call its associations that I cross out the associations because they seem to me not to create World War II enough for my characters to react with horror, or, if it is in the character, with joy. I have to create a world that contains World War II, and because I can't, because I don't trust my own associations, I reduce all my thoughts and feelings to self-contained sensations. To get history into one of my novels I would be so overwhelmed by the contingencies of history that there would be no way I could contain them, so I suppose my novels are more or less outside of history, a-historical. And to get ideas into my writing – well, the contingencies of ideas are never ending.'

'I understand,' he said. 'I can only trust my thoughts and feelings, my ideas, in my writing when I can turn them into comedy. You've got to trust yourself more. Trust your confusion.'

I asked, 'Do you think about the shape of the novel?'

He pressed his lips together then said, firmly, 'Don't use that word again, okay?' Then he smiled. 'Stop constraining yourself so. Who're you writing for? Your professor?'

'Of course I want life in my writing, and life doesn't have shape. But there are devices that at least pin the narrative down to the page. I like repetition, using a word over and over, but always in a different context so that the word has a different connotation.'

'I don't like your repetitions. It's a boring device. Not repetition, but the opposite: variety, surprise, the unexpected.'

'I'll tell you the truth about repetitions. If I write, say, "desperate" three times – and this most often happens with abstract words – I feel that I have at least got the word down on the page, even though I still don't know what the word means. I was brought up without any real language.'

'And you think I was? I come from nowhere, too, my friend. I had to learn out of *nothing*. Even now, in conversation, I'll find the most ordinary word will suddenly put me in doubt. "Is this really what I mean – is this English?" I stop short and wonder if it's "instinct" I mean or do I mean "intuition"? We're hicks. We're real hicks. It's just because we're such hicks that we've become so sophisticated. Look at John Updike. Shillington, Pennsylvania. John's the biggest hick of all, and he's the best writer of us all.'

'I know, I know. I write with the constant fear that I'm faking the writing, and to counter the fakery I reduce the writing to the lowest vibration.'

Philip shut off his desk lamp.

As we were leaving, he said, 'I hope I haven't been too hard on you.'

I stepped towards him and he drew back a little, as if startled.

'No,' I said, 'I don't know how or why, but you reassure me.'

Later, at home, I rang him to ask what the two words are that he can't distinguish, and he said, 'You're writing that down, are you? To show what an illiterate I am? To reveal the truth about my verbal skills? Oh, David, you really are a bastard.'

How does Philip in any way fit into my London world, though he lives in London with Claire Bloom?

———

Slowly walking away from the restaurant we used to go to for lunch, Monsieur Thompson, Philip and I talked, and when he became fixed on what he was saying he stopped on the pavement and I stopped with him.

I asked him if he was frightened of dying. He stopped. His thick eyebrows curled over his gold-framed glasses through which his eyes appeared to be all black staring irises. He pressed his thin lower lip against his upper lip so they almost disappeared, and his chin became small and round. He stared at me a long time, then he said, 'Terrified.'

'So am I,' I said.

'And, terrified, I think more and more about dying and where I want to be buried,' he said. 'With my parents? I go to my parents' grave whenever I'm in Newark and cry over it. I tell myself I can't go on, but, leaving the cemetery, I go back and cry more over them. I can't leave them. If I'm not buried with my parents, where else? Where do you want to be buried?'

'I don't know,' I answered. 'But not with my parents.'

'Why?'

'I love my parents, but for the sake of my life all my life I've tried to get away from my parents, and it appalls me to think I may end up back with them as if my having come so far away from them made no difference to me.'

'I understand that about you,' he said.

I asked him, 'Can you imagine what it was like as a little boy to be inculcated, *inculcated*, with the longing for eternity? to be told, over and over, that this world is not our world, but our world is the world we will come into after death? to be made to pray with all your heart and soul for that world?'

'No,' he said.

'Then you're not a Catholic.'

'Phew,' he said, passing his hand over his forehead and shaking it, 'that's a greater relief than finding out I'm not a Jew.'

He seemed deliberately to change the subject by telling a joke, and his jokes were so funny the change was always for the better. But later, on some level wanting to draw him back into a subject he had drawn away from, I said, 'That longing I was talking about—'

Philip said, 'A-hun, a-hun.'

I knew that if he liked some of my writing he liked least in it my giving way to the very longing I was trying to convince him of now. Again, he said, 'A-hun.'

I said, 'I want to write about it, but I worry that I can't without it coming across as false.'

Philip said, 'Write about what wants to be written about, and that won't ever be false. If it's in your body to write it, it'll come across.'

'It'll occur,' I said.

'Yes,' he said, 'it'll occur.'

I, a little embarrassed by what I had said on the way, was glad that we joked at lunch. I feel most sure about Philip when we are joking, though, because I'm not entirely sure when he is joking, I never feel entirely secure.

When he said, 'Thank God I live in a totally secular world,' I thought he might be joking, then thought he wasn't, and I took what he said to mean that he was warning me, for the sake of my writing, against what I'd told him about my longing.

Maussane

I'm staying with Stephen and Natasha at Saint Jérôme, their house in the South of France.

On the ferry across the Channel, there were hundreds of schoolchildren and a group of disabled people in wheelchairs going to Boulogne for the day. The disabled people sat still in the locked wheelchairs among the running, shouting children.

Stephen, Natasha and I went to the cafeteria for lunch. The man behind the counter said to Stephen, 'Tell me what you want, sir, and I'll have it brought to your table.' Natasha ordered half a small chicken and peas, Stephen and I fish, peas, chips. At the table, I asked, 'Why were we told we would be served?' Natasha laughed. 'I suppose,' she said, 'we look important.' And because of Stephen we did look, if not important, outstanding, he large, with large red features, his hair a little long and bright white, his blue shirt hanging out of his trousers, the cuff buttons of his shirt undone, some of the buttons on the front undone, Natasha and I at either side of him.

We stayed in an hotel in the Place de l'Odéon for a night, and had dinner in the restaurant La Méditerranée across from the hotel. The waiter, showing us to a table, addressed Stephen as 'Monsieur le Ministre', and Stephen seemed bemused. We studied the menu, trying to decide, as an old man, with a thin white moustache, wearing a pale-brown summer suit and a brown and white striped shirt open at the neck, and a young, tanned, very beautiful man, wearing black trousers and a red and white checked short-sleeved shirt, were shown to the table next to ours. Natasha said, 'Oh, that's—,' and Stephen rose, smiling, to shake the old man's hand and the hand of the beautiful young man. They were the poet Louis Aragon and his friend, whom, it was said, he had fallen in love with after the death of his wife Elsa Triolet. I exchanged places with Natasha so she could sit next to Aragon, but leaned past her to say to him, in studied French, that he wouldn't remember me, I was sure, but the last time I had been to Paris with Stephen, eleven years before, we had met at dinner at the de Rothschilds. In what seemed to me even more studied French, he said that I must have been a child eleven years before. I looked across the table to his friend, who was sitting on the other side of Aragon, his elbows on the table, smoking a cigarette, and he winked at me. Stephen, Natasha, I became very excited, and ordered extravagantly, Belons, a whole *loup de mer*, profiteroles, and got drunk on three bottles of Chablis; Aragon and his friend remained calm. Stephen and Natasha talked a lot with Aragon, who said he was working like a madman, harder than he had ever worked in his life; in three years he would be eighty, and he had so much to do. The way he spoke made me think he wasn't working at all, not writing a word – and from time to time I exchanged looks with his friend, to whom I hadn't been introduced, nor had Stephen and Natasha, for Aragon was evidently keeping him apart. He had large dark eyes and bright black hair brushed back from his clear, broad forehead.

While Stephen and Aragon spoke and his friend silently ate, I, sitting next to Natasha, talked about friendship, and how important friendship is, and I felt that we were talking about our friendship, and I suddenly put an arm around her and hugged her to me, and she gave me a wide, bright smile. She, tired, left to go back to the hotel.

I sat next to Aragon. He and Stephen were still talking – or, rather, Stephen was asking him questions, such as, What did Aragon think of Spain now? Which Aragon answered in a quiet but rhetorical manner – and while they spoke the boyfriend asked me what I do, and I said, '*Je suis écrivain, un romancier,*' and I asked him what he did, but Aragon drew back from talking to Stephen and said, '*Il est acteur,*' and he was now playing in a play written by the Greek poet Yannis Ritsos. And once again in my life a connection was made that made me think that my life truly is a narrative in which everything comes together, however unexpectedly, and I exclaimed, '*Mais j'habite avec un grec qui connaît Yannis Ritsos très bien, et qui a même traduit les poèmes de Ritsos en anglais!*' Aragon and his friend looked at me. I said, '*Il s'appele Nikos Stangos,*' expecting them to react, but though they continued to look at me, it was not, I thought, with interest, but with looks of disappointment that Yannis Ritsos was not entirely within their exclusive world but was known elsewhere by someone outside their world who in fact knows the poet.

The bill came for us. It was 548 francs, about $60 for the three of us. I threw onto the table whatever money I had in my wallet, which was about 150 francs, and which I had hoped would last at least some days. Stephen said he didn't have enough to cover the bill, and went to the hotel for more. Aragon's friend left their table to talk with others in the restaurant, and I talked for ten minutes with Aragon about a singer whose recordings of 'Les Chansons d'Aragon' I had heard, years before, in Boston, Monique Morelli, and Aragon agreed, an exceptional singer, exceptional. Aragon's bill came and I saw him pay for it with a Lloyds International cheque. Stephen returned with a wad of hundred-franc notes in his hand. He gathered the money I had thrown onto the table together and stuffed it all into my jacket pocket. We all rose. Aragon bowed a little, smiled, and presented a hand, palm up, then, with a kind of swooping gesture, held it out to be shaken. His friend returned and asked me when I was leaving, and I said, '*Demain matin,*' and he said nothing.

Stephen and I walked down to Saint Germain for a coffee, but all the cafés were crowded, so we walked back to the hotel in the rain, and we talked.

MAUSSANE

117

I said, 'It was extraordinary our meeting Aragon.'

'It was as if it was arranged by God, that we should see him together after eleven years.'

'You know, I think he was bluffing and isn't doing any work.'

'No, I dare say he isn't.'

'And he wasn't a great writer. Yet why did I find him intimidating?'

'You feel that even if you know he's telling a lie it comes across as the absolute truth, don't you?'

'You feel that no matter what he does – become a Communist, reject Communism, marry, have a boyfriend – everything he does is irreproachably right because he has done it. He simply can do no wrong.'

'Yes,' Stephen said as if meditating on this.

'I feel that *everything* I do is wrong.'

Stephen laughed.

The next morning I helped Stephen to carry some books from the car – packed in a large cardboard carton which I carried and in a large laundry box which Stephen carried, its strap undone and trailing on the ground – to a bookshop not far from the hotel, where he'd been told by the writer Mary McCarthy he could sell them for a good price. They were French books he had collected or that had been given to him over the years: a very early edition of *À la recherche du temps perdu*, first editions of the poems of Valéry, plays dedicated to him with drawings by Jean Cocteau. We placed the boxes on a desk in the shop and waited for a man who asked us to wait 'two little seconds'. Stephen was impatient. I've noted that he can't bear queues or traffic jams, or being held up for any time at a petrol station or for tolls. I once mentioned this to Natasha, who said, 'Yes, it's happened in the last two or three years, since Wystan's death.' And it occurred to me that Stephen often refers to Auden in connection with something he, Stephen, disapproves of – what an awkward, vague sentence! – and I can't think of an instance of Stephen referring to Auden in connection with what he, Stephen, disapproves of! In the bookshop, Stephen paced about. He said, 'I have no idea at all

what these books may be worth.' The man came back, looked at the
dates of publication of all the books. Dust rose from them. Stephen
and I waited. There were about 200 books. The man said, 650 francs.
Stephen said, '*Très bien*.' I said to him, in English, 'But that's almost
the cost of our meal last night.' He asked, 'You don't think I should
sell them?' And I, 'No, I honestly don't. The man obviously doesn't
know who you are, so doesn't get the references to you. You should
take them back to London, where the references would be known.'
'All right,' he said, and he told the man he wouldn't sell the books,
and we carried the boxes back to the car.

We were to leave in half an hour. As I had packed, I walked
about the Luxembourg Gardens. I thought about Aragon and his
friend, and I fantasized about staying in Paris and seeing his friend,
just the two of us.

We packed ourselves into the car with a mass of boxes, bags,
suitcases, and Natasha drove us off to Provence.

At a Jacques Brel restaurant off the highway, while Natasha was
using the ladies, I said to Stephen, 'I keep thinking of Aragon and
his friend.'

'They were both very sweet, don't you think?'

'Yes,' I said, then, 'well, I don't know. I wonder about them, but
I'm sure they wonder about us, and I suspect they aren't very kind
about us, making up some story about why I am travelling with
you and Natasha.'

Stephen giggled.

'I hope we've puzzled them,' I said.

'I'm sure we have,' he said.

———

And now the clarity of Provence.

I must learn to be generous. I must. I went shopping with Stephen
the day after we arrived. There were large beautiful strawberries
at the shop, 7 francs 50 the punnet. I thought, I must buy some,
then I thought, well, I'd better save my money. Stephen bought a
punnet, and cream. In the car, he said, 'Let's say to Natasha that

you bought the strawberries and cream.' I felt a fool for not having bought them, and said, 'Oh, Stephen, you are so kind,' and he said, 'No, no, don't think about it.'

I talked to him about my jealousy. I said, 'You know, I honestly don't now feel jealous about Nikos making love with another.'

Stephen said, 'You may think that's because you don't care. That isn't true. You're not jealous because Nikos and you know one another so well that you know nothing can make you not know each other. It's the same with Bryan and me. He can do what he wants. I want him to do what he wants. He'll probably get married, have children, maybe have affairs. But we know something about each other now, and we'll know that forever. It can't be taken away. What Nikos and you know about one another is very strong. You don't have to worry about it.'

———

I've spoken with Nikos a few times. I don't like being away from him.

I said to Stephen, 'Nikos is not happy in his work.'

'Of course he wouldn't be,' Stephen said, 'having to work, even as an editor in a publishing house, in a capitalist system, which he despises, having to justify all the books he proposes financially. Of course he isn't happy. He needn't go to a psychiatrist to learn that.'

———

I've been at Saint Jérôme for about ten days, and have written some fifty pages of a novel. And, of course, I have written in here, with the idea of Nikos reading what I have written for him to know what I've been up to, and to amuse him.

I'm in my room, upstairs. The floor is wooden, so I often hear, from downstairs, Natasha shout, 'Stephen, Stephen!' as if she expects him, no matter where he is, to come quickly to her. She says to herself, 'Oh where is he?' and she shouts louder for him to come. He answers immediately, 'Yes, what is it?' and she asks, 'Where is the ———?', the blank to be filled with almost anything – secateurs for pruning the buddleia, her address book, matches for lighting

Natasha and David with the Minoan pot he made and gave to Natasha

the cooker, but most often it is the keys to the car. She and Stephen
look everywhere, and they argue about who used the car last.

I said to Stephen, 'I think it must mean something that you and
Natasha *always* misplace the car keys.'

He laughed and said, 'And there's only one set between us. But
I suspect she has a set hidden away which she won't tell me about,
just in case.'

Sometimes I hear him, in his study, in the kitchen, in the sitting
room, shout, 'Natasha!' then, after a long pause, she says, 'Yes?'

and he asks, 'Where is ——?' Once, when I was with him, he shouted, 'Where is the key to the mailbox?' and she came from upstairs down to the kitchen and they looked through a mass of keys in a drawer. 'Is this it? Is this it?' I thought: it is peculiar that they shouldn't remember a key so often used as that. The lost objects are always found, are under an old newspaper, a tea towel, a cheese wrapper, an espadrille. Stephen and Natasha lose objects because, once finished with, they put them down anywhere, as if they had completely lost any significance and they'll never need them again.

Stephen was after Natasha to write to the *New York Review of Books* to place an advertisement in it to rent Saint Jérôme during the winter. 'Yes, yes,' she would say, vaguely. Every day he would ask her if she'd done it, and she, vaguely, said she would. He said to me, 'Natasha just won't do anything unless she has thought of it first. If she asks me to buy milk and I forget she gets annoyed. If I ask her to buy milk I know she'll forget. Well, it doesn't matter.' He wrote to the *New York Review of Books*.

Stephen lit the charcoal grill outside in the evenings to grill chicken legs. He kept shouting to Natasha, up in her room, 'Is it all right to put rosemary on the chicken? Is it all right?' He made something of a mess each time: plates and forks and knives on the gravel about the grill which tilted in the gravel, bunched-up bits of paper, and when he poured cups of olive oil onto the chicken legs the flames flared up dangerously, the same with splashes of sherry, and even more so when he stuffed branches of rosemary under the grill that turned quickly into black ash. He was sweating. He almost tipped the grill over turning over the chicken legs. Natasha came down in the end to tell him if the chicken legs were done. They were very black. Natasha wore a long green smock, and was very solemn. She stuck a fork into a chicken leg and pronounced, as from a height, 'Absolutely *perfect!*'

At dinner one evening, we talked about aging and dying. I said I didn't mind getting old, and I was counting on some instantaneous mechanism in me to reconcile me to dying – as I once felt in the accident outside Paris, when the car I was in hit an oncoming lorry. Stephen said he wished that, when he became too old, he would take a pill and get it over with. Natasha said, 'You won't feel that then.' Stephen said, 'Well, I feel it now, and that's what matters.'

Natasha asked me, 'How old are you?' I said, 'I'm forty-four.' She said, 'But that's only four years older than Matthew. I think of Matthew as a child, and I think of you as belonging to our generation.' 'I've always been old,' I said. Stephen giggled. He said, 'You and Nikos can never be older than when I met you both together.'

I work in the garden with Natasha in the evening after the heat. We weed, transplant. At the end of the white path, a gravel path, cypresses on either side and white flowering plants, is my large Minoan pot, which I gave to Natasha. While we work, we talk. She said, 'I'm so easily exhausted now. I sometimes don't know what to do. Don't tell Stephen, but I've been taking sleeping pills. I try not to. I don't want to. But I often can't sleep and have to take them.' Natasha speaks, it seems, with all her jaw.

Stephen and I took a walk into the hills below the house – not hills, really, but great slabs of white stone turned up on their sides. He took some photographs. I filled my pockets with many varieties of wild flowers.

We talked about Natasha.

I said, 'She needs to rest.'

'Yes,' he said.

I said, 'You know, not long ago, I would have thought it was my entire responsibility, Natasha being so tired and having to rest, and I would have felt it obligatory to do everything I could to make her better. I felt that about all women, in fact. If they were unhappy, it was my fault somehow, or, at least, it was my fault if they remained unhappy whatever I did, because it was my duty to make them happy. I don't feel that any more. I love to help Natasha in the garden, with the cooking and washing up, and I do it out of love. I guess what I'm trying to say is that I no longer feel guilty towards

Natasha, which I once did, and now feel I can be friendly enough, loving enough, without feeling I have to be to make up for that guilt I used to feel.'

Stephen didn't answer, but appeared thoughtful.

I asked, 'You seem depressed.'

He laughed and shrugged a little and said, 'I miss Bryan.'

'Yes,' I said.

'And then I'm worried about it being all wrong.'

'Don't think that,' I said.

He said, 'I do miss Bryan. I think of him all the time.'

Every evening, the three of us play Scrabble, and Natasha always wins.

Alone with Stephen, he said, 'When I used to play with Bryan in our hotel room, he always let me win.'

———

At dinner, we drank two bottles of rosé, then played Scrabble, and I, drunk, did very well, kept using all my letters in one go, once twice in succession, and Stephen kept laughing and asking, 'What has got into David?' I won two games. Then we listened to a Brahms sextet on the radio.

———

I was woken up by Natasha, in her room, shouting in her sleep, 'Ste'en, Ste'en, Ste'en, Ste'en,' over and over again. I presumed Stephen, in his room, didn't hear.

She calls him, affectionately, Parrow.

In the morning, I woke in a state of anger against Nikos. I want to be with him. It is absurd that I am not.

After breakfast, I went with Natasha to the market in Arles. We had menthe and mineral water in the café next to the house where Van Gogh once lived, but which is now a parking lot.

Natasha said, 'I feel morally better.'

———

Nikos rang after lunch (I have not got used to 'luncheon'). Over and over and over again, I miss him. I know why I woke up angry at him: because he's not with me, as if he has left me, and not I him!

Whenever I dream about Nikos when I'm away from him, the dreams almost always have to do with his being unfaithful to me, and my reaction is rage. I never have these nightmares when I am with him.

He said over the telephone, 'Don't worry about me.'

London

Even though Nikos is away in Athens, oh the joy, the joy of being back in our home! Could I ever be more content?

I could hardly sleep the night before he returned. At the airport, I waited by the wide glass wall for arrivals, watching people come from a partition that hid customs from view. My heart was beating fast, and I was, I realized, frightened, though I couldn't say what I was frightened of. Then I saw Nikos come from behind the partition, wheeling his bag, and I ran to the doors as they slid open to meet him. All we could do was smile at each other, and all my feelings rose up into my throat too blocked for words.

With him, everything is right.

I tried to figure out what it was I felt being close to him after having been away; it was as though I was both close to him and far from him, and I saw him from a double perspective.

And this occurred to me as we made love: that though I held the person who is the centre of my life, he was in the place of someone else, someone more, if possible, in the centre. I had the curious sense that there was someone Nikos was in place of, whose absence – or, even, presence – Nikos reminded me of. I had never felt as close to Nikos as I felt then, had never loved him, as I told him, more than I loved him then, and I wonder now if this was because he made me aware of the someone beyond him who was almost accessible in Nikos, who was loving and reassuring and accepting in the presence of Nikos.

I thought I was aware of something in Nikos, in my relationship with him, that I had never been aware of before; this made me see Nikos as I had never seen him before.

Was this someone whose body is just beyond Nikos' body?

————

No, Nikos and I should never be separated, never.

As he often pleads, 'No dinner parties, not ones we give or go to, but time at home,' and, in fact, I find it a relief not to give dinner parties or to go to them, and realize they require efforts that always make me feel somewhat false in enjoying them.

And so our evenings are spent together, often listening to music after a simple supper, and to bed.

Our Saturdays are ours, sleeping in late, shopping, perhaps a meal in a pub, back home rearranging books to make room for newly acquired ones, rehanging pictures because of one we have bought – mostly by Keith, of whose works we now have a collec-tion – and then our naps together, those naps in which our love making is released into some state deeper than love making but love as deep as love can go, where Nikos becomes me and I become him, or where we both become the state of love itself, shoreless and dark and deep.

We are planning our holiday together in Italy.

————

After I told Philip about Jennifer, which I felt he did not want to hear, as if he thought I was pretending to be someone I am not, he sent me this questionnaire:

QUESTIONS FOR DAVID PLANTE

1) You speak of 'fantasy' as central to your sexual way of life. Elucidate.

2) You have slept with women and had affairs with women. A brief sexual history. What sort of women excites you?

How are they like (or unlike) the men you have desired? How is your sex life with women different from your sex life with men, if it is? Are you a different person when you are with women than with men?

3) Have you tried living as a homosexual in America? What would it be like if you transferred your life there now? What makes it easier for you in England, the society or your foreignness?

4) Would you ever like not being a homosexual? Or is it no longer an issue, if it ever was?

5) How did you 'decide' on a homosexual life? When and how did homosexual experiences become transformed into homosexual life? When and how did it first occur to you that you were homosexual? What did you do about it, think about it?

6) Who have been your homosexual mentors, the men who educated you, after whom you modelled your life? Were they lovers as well?

Il Molino

Il Molino has pictures hanging on the whitewashed walls, rugs on the floor, even white muslin curtains hanging at the windows.

Öçi came to stay. In our house, there was a matter-of-fact ease among us, so much so I felt that it was entirely natural that we, Nikos, Öçi and I, should be together, cooking together in the kitchen, sitting out after our supper under the pergola in the late evening drinking wine a farmer had brought us in a demijohn, going on walks in the countryside.

Nikos suggested we go along the abandoned road to an abandoned mill on the stream, where we would eat the bread and salami we had taken with us.

But I said, 'We always go to the abandoned mill. Let's take a way we've never been along and see where it leads us.' And I stopped and pointed to a path that leads up from the bottom of the valley into the chestnut forest. Nikos and Öçi stopped with me.

'That sounds interesting to me,' Öçi said.

'I don't know,' Nikos said, looking very doubtful.

'I should have known you wouldn't want to,' I said. 'You have no sense of adventure.'

'You think I don't have any sense of adventure, and you do. If adventure is going to get us lost, or worse, I don't want it.'

Öçi stepped back.

I said to Nikos, thinking I was joking, 'We always do what you want to do, which is always the same thing, over and over.'

But he didn't take what I said as a joke. He said, amazed by my impudence, 'We always do what *I* want to do?' and, as if his amazement increased the more he considered what I'd said, he repeated, in a higher voice, 'We always do what *I* want to do?'

'All right, all right,' I said, glancing at Öçi, who was biting his lower lip, 'we'll do what you want to do. We'll go to the abandoned mill.'

'No,' Nikos said, 'we'll do what you want to do; as you think we never do what you want to do, we'll do it now.'

I said, 'Please, let's not make an issue of it.'

Calmly, he said, 'I'm not making an issue of it. I'm simply saying we should do what you want to do. I'm ready.'

'Please.'

But he was walking towards the path off the road that led up into the chestnut forest. Öçi, still biting his lower lip, didn't move, nor did I, by him. Nikos turned round to us and asked, 'Aren't you coming?'

I said, 'Only if you don't complain on the way that we should have gone to the abandoned mill.'

'I'm not going to complain.' He smiled at Öçi and me. 'Come along for an adventure.'

As we started up the narrow path – first Nikos, who, I thought, would now take over the excursion as though he had had no choice but to take command and he would have to make the best of it, then Öçi, then me – Nikos said, 'The fact is, I am always giving in to what others want to do, and have always, all my life.'

The path became steeper and the chestnut trees closed in with great, rough trunks. Where they were thickest the path was covered with broken, thorny pods, and Nikos said – I thought: of course he would say it – that he hoped one of the sharp thorns wouldn't penetrate the sole of his canvas shoes, which he made sound all too possible. And – of course – he added that the path along the stream was smooth.

I tried to override his objections by saying, 'Look, look into the forest.'

But Nikos was not one for this kind of romantic mystery about forests – Greece, he had often told me, was not a romantic country, and was starkly without a sentimental sense of mystery – and he said, 'Never mind looking into the forest, pay attention to the path. And there may be vipers.'

Öçi, between Nikos and me, didn't speak.

I said, 'Well, then, let's go back.'

'No,' Nikos insisted, 'we're going to go wherever this path takes us.'

I said, 'You're hoping that this walk will end up a disaster and then you'll be able to say we should have taken the walk along the river.'

He said, 'If you think I'm looking for revenge for not having my way—' He didn't finish.

'All right,' I said, 'all right.'

Öçi suddenly said, 'Come along, you two.'

And Nikos, looking back at Öçi, smiled, and with that smile became as positive as he had been negative, especially when we came upon a clearing from which we could see, below us, the long, deep valley with a shining stream running down it, and, pouring over the distant mountains, white and black clouds, and Nikos said, 'Yes, look.'

I suggested turning back, but he became enthusiastic about continuing to see where the path led, as if, from the beginning, it had been his idea to follow it.

He asked Öçi, 'Do you want to go on?'

Öçi said, 'I always want to go on.'

Turning a corner in the bulldozed road, we faced a mountain-side of burned-out forest, the trees reduced to charcoal stumps with the remains of a few black branches, and as we looked over it the light darkened.

Nikos, frowning, turned to me and said, 'You see.'

A rage, like the fire that had destroyed the trees, went through me, and I shouted, 'What do I see? What?'

'You wanted to come here.'

'I did not want to come here. I didn't know this would be here.'
Öçi was standing between us, and Nikos said to me past Öçi,
'I know why you wanted to come. I know. You just wanted to
show Öçi that you have your way, that you do what you want,
that you're not bound to my way, that you don't have to do what
I want.'

'What?' I shouted.

'Don't shout,' he shouted.

I shouted more, 'I have to fight to have my way.'

'You have to fight? All I do is fight to have my way.'

'You're always right,' I said, 'and I'm always wrong.'

Nikos turned away sharply and began to walk back along the
bulldozed road. I looked at Öçi, and, saying nothing, raised my
arms out. He, too, raised his arms. We let them drop at the same
time, and we both turned to walk at a distance behind Nikos.

Rain began to fall as we reached the house, where Öçi went to
his room for, he said, a little rest, and Nikos and I stood at separate
windows and watched the rain fall.

I was embarrassed that there should be revealed to Öçi that there
was, all too obviously, a neurotic level to my relationship with
Nikos, one so crudely exposed. And that it was crudely exposed to
Öçi made it appear all the more crude to me.

The rain stopped, and Öçi, coming out of his room, asked if it
was possible to have a cup of tea, and Nikos said, yes of course, he'd
prepare the tea, and, having taken on the English habit of afternoon tea, we gathered in the sitting room where Nikos poured out
tea from a pot into mugs and handed round a plate of dry Italian
biscuits.

For supper, Öçi proposed a dish called Circassian chicken, then
we sat before the fire in the sitting room as the night became chilly
and listened to music on an old phonograph.

Öçi left the next morning, when the early mist from the stream
was still spread over the bottom of the valley. Nikos and I walked
with him to the hamlet, where a taxi that had been arranged for
him was waiting. Embracing Öçi to say goodbye to him, I could

sense in his body that he was intent on leaving us, and that, though he had come to be with two people whom he'd believed had worked out a relationship of the deepest mutuality, a relationship that, wise as it should have been, was free of contention, recrimination, accusation, he had found that ours was no different from any other neurotic relationship. I watched him embrace Nikos before he got into the car, and Nikos and I stood to wave goodbye to him as he waved out of the car window at us, smiling. Nikos and I waited until the taxi disappeared.

We bought a round pecorino cheese from the hamlet bar and walked back to our house, the mist now burned off by the sun rising over the mountains and penetrating the valley.

Nikos said, 'I hate leave-takings.'

And, as if someone very close to us had left – left to go so far it would be a very long time before we saw him again, if we ever saw him again – a sadness descended on Nikos and me as, with blunt sickles, we cut the weeds that had grown at the back of the house, where there were abandoned terraces and unpruned grapevines collapsed under rotting posts – terraces and vines we planned to bring back into working order, but which we never did. We went to the abandoned mill to sit by the stream for our lunch of tomatoes and bread and cheese.

From the beginning of our living together, Nikos has refused to discuss our relationship, particularly any 'problems' in it; and I accepted this, and still accept it, and will go on accepting it, because I know, from years of living with him, that after a day of our being together the level of 'problems' shifts itself down and the levels of mutuality shift up of themselves, not, it seems, by any intention on our part, but by our simply giving them the time to shift.

Even after our worst rows – rows that, if overheard by anyone else would make him think there was no way we could continue to stay together but would have to break up – a sudden shift occurs as long as we stay together. Nikos might tell me I am getting too much sun and to put on the straw hat he had bought me; or I, without thinking, might press my forehead to his shoulder while, in the kitchen, we decanted wine from the demijohn into bottles; or we might go out together before bed to stand among the fireflies flashing in the warm air that smelled of the stream – but these actions don't bring on the shifts so much as are indications of the shifts that occurred of themselves, suddenly, and we quietly go to bed together.

After Öçi left, Nikos and I were invited by Joe and Jos Tilson to a meal outside under their pergola.

Germaine Greer was there. She said she had been in Sicily, where, to avoid being harassed by the men, she a beautifully embodied woman, dressed all in black, as a widow would, but she got the dress wrong and was whistled at.

One day, while I was upstairs writing and unaware of Nikos, I became aware of his absence and called him. He didn't answer and I went out to find him. I walked along the road, calling. He didn't respond. Back at the house, I couldn't continue writing. Instead, I swept out the tower at the back of the house to make it our storage space for garden tools, etc., and as I worked I wondered where he had gone. I became worried. Maybe, I thought, he had been bitten by a viper. I didn't know where else to go look for him. Angry suddenly, I thought he should have told me where he was going. Then, again, I became worried, more so, and began to imagine he was in an accident, though what kind of accident in this remote valley was impossible to imagine. I even began to fantasize what I would do if he was dead. What would I do with his body? What about our flat in London? What about Il Molino? He called me from the front of the house and I ran round to him. He was carrying clippers and had been cutting thorns along the road to the bridge.

'Why didn't you look for me there?' he asked.

'I looked along the road to the fields,' I said.

He said he had been thinking. 'You don't like our house any longer,' he said; 'if that's so, we'll sell it.' He spoke as if he had been considering this for a long time, and had decided that I, not he, didn't like the house, and therefore we should sell it. His voice was sad as with a difficult resignation.

I said, 'Of course we won't sell our house.'

He said, 'I realize you are not as attached to places as I am. We've put so much into this house.'

I said, 'I suppose I think the house will never be without hundreds of things to be done to it, and then there's the road, and the land. We'll have to spend many more millions.'

'No,' he said, 'there's something else. You're bored with it all, and even dislike it.'

'But that's not true,' I said, and wondered how I could convince him it was not true.

Every day, he does something around the house as if to attach himself to it: sweeps, polishes furniture, cuts back the irises, weeds.

And I, perhaps to impress him with my attachment, have polished the floor of our bedroom, hung pictures, sickled nettles.

Nikos has left for London, and I so feel his presence in his absence.

London

A letter from Bryan arrived and I rang Stephen to tell him. He asked if we could have lunch together so he could read it. We met in an Italian restaurant in Pimlico. I handed him the letter, he tore it open, and after he finished each page he handed it to me across the table. Stephen's face became more and more dark. I read the letter and was very moved, and said to Stephen, 'He is remarkable.' Stephen was looking past me into the distance and he said, 'Yes, he is,' and I realized how deeply Stephen loves Bryan and Bryan loves Stephen. He came to the flat to write a letter to Bryan which I posted. The letter from Bryan:

On Saturday I received two letters from you and as the day was rather hectic (with preparations for my brother's engagement party here in Jacksonville), I read each of the letters through once, and then rather thoughtlessly stuck them in a bureau drawer, hoping I could read them again a bit later. Meanwhile, my mother happened upon them and, being the sort of person she is, put them aside and read them that evening. As you can imagine, she found them quite disturbing, and in fact was so upset that she couldn't even confront me about them. I eventually confronted her with their disappearance in order to bring the situation out into the open.

I don't think there is any need for me to be specific about what was said between us, but, as you might guess, she immediately cast

*you and me in the roles of the devious plotter and the innocent
victim. I told her, of course, that that wasn't so, that in fact you
were always more cautious than I, and that I was just as responsible for the development of our relationship as you were; but that
didn't satisfy her. She then asked me tearfully what the extent of
our relationship was and whether or not it had been sexual. (She
probably used a word like 'physical' or 'intimate', but the meaning
was the same.) I really didn't know how to answer her, because,
although she was begging me for the truth, I knew that if I told
her the truth in my calm, confident manner (I have this horrible
habit of keeping very collected and reasonable during situations
when I am expected to be emotional or hysterical), that it would
be incredibly painful to her. So instead, I gathered together all my
strength, affected my most sincere expression, and told her a lie. I
said that although our relationship had been a strong one, and that
indeed we did love one another, there had never been any physical
intimacy. Since your letters were fairly suggestive of what actually
occurred, the lie really fell flat, and she replied, 'I have to accept it
as the truth, but I can't really believe it.'*

*She went on to say things like that I might be ruining my life,
that I am naïve and being used, etc., etc., to which I replied things
like 'no' and 'it isn't that way at all.' She also told me that I
should demand that you return my previous letters to you and that
I should never write to you again. Of course I refused.*

*As our conversation approached its end, I began to realize that,
more than anything else, my mother was afraid that this would
somehow change my relationship with her and that she intended
to force herself into believing my lie in order to prevent that from
happening. Since that time, absolutely no mention has been made
of the letters (which she returned to me) and in fact the whole situation has seemingly been buried. However, despite the fact that it
has been shoved under the surface, it is still apparent. The atmos-
phere is one of careful civility with each of us trying his and her best
to pretend nothing ever happened, but even at its most successful
moments, I think we both realize that we are just pretending and*

if only for that reason things can't be quite the same between my mother and me.

I feel very confused about the whole situation and highly guilty as well, although perhaps not for the reason you might imagine. As I told my mother, there is absolutely nothing about my relationship with you that causes guilt, as I know what we have together is very right. What I do feel guilty about is simply that I could have hurt my mother as deeply as I did, especially in doing something that has always seemed so guiltless.

I also feel guilty in another way which I think is important for you to understand, Stephen. Although I've lied before, I feel that my lie to my mother was particularly distasteful, because with that single statement I denied both my real nature and our whole experience together. I keep telling myself that telling that lie was the right thing to do since the truth would have hurt my mother so badly, and yet I can't help but wonder if perhaps I didn't do it simply because it was the easiest way out for me. At any rate, I feel now that I have somehow betrayed you by denying our relationship so blatantly and so glibly. Can you understand how I feel?

There is another element to the situation which upsets me. Sometimes I get the strange feeling that unfortunate coincidences which caused my mother to discover the letters (i.e. my 'thoughtlessly' putting them in the bureau drawer, her 'happening' to open that drawer, etc.) were not actually coincidences at all, but rather were somehow influenced by me. Of course, I didn't plan her finding them or anything like that, but as I am not one to believe we are governed by chance, the responsibility then becomes mine.

I can remember thinking in Gainesville that it probably was just a matter of time until my family found out about us, and now I can't help but feel that perhaps that was some sort of self-fulfilling prophecy that I must have acted on as the instrument to its fulfilment. It is, I think, something like the situation you once wrote about in London Magazine where you spoke about your wallet and how you somehow knew you would lose it if you put it in your back pocket. The thought that my mother might find the letters crossed my mind, but just as you put your wallet in your pocket anyway, I left the letters in the drawer. In such instances, it's hard to believe that one didn't, somehow, even if subconsciously, desire and cause the result.

But that leads to the question of why I would have wanted her to discover them. I have considered many possible answers, but the one which seems most possible, is also the most disturbing to me. As you sensed, my mother loves me a great deal and I love her too. But lately, probably as a simple consequence of my maturing, I have found her life to be increasingly stifling, restrictive and demanding. As I think I once told you, both my parents have come to look almost solely to me to enrich their lives and provide them with a certain type of success and achievement which they themselves never had. At the same time, however, they fear that my independence will cause me to desert them and so they cling tighter and tighter to me, thus restricting the very freedom I need to grow. I have come to believe that unless I free myself of this restriction, I will never be able to realize whatever potential I have. For that reason, I have been longing to make a break of some sort from my family, to get away from them at least for a while. Perhaps this feeling is not unlike what most adolescents face upon maturing, but it must sound rather callous.

What worries me is that I might have put those letters in the drawer in the subconscious hope that my mother would find them, read them, and find that I wasn't solely her possession and that I am not what she thought I was. If this is so, then what I was doing in effect was causing her a great deal of pain just so I could escape from her life. I would like to think I wasn't capable of doing something so cruel, even subconsciously, but I'm afraid I already feel a little of the pangs of guilt whether I am guilty or not.

I know now why Auden said that one writes letters to one's self. This is the first chance I have had to really analyse my own feelings toward the situation. But this letter isn't only for me, dear Stephen; it's mostly to you. I felt that I must tell you, if no one else, the whole truth of the matter, not only because you are directly involved, but also because I do somehow feel that I have betrayed you and that perhaps by telling you I can shed some of the guilt. I only hope you don't think badly of me for it.

Before I close, I think I should make one thing especially clear. That is, dear Stephen, that there is nothing about our relationship itself which I regret in the least. While it seems tragic that anything so very right as my love for you could cause others grief, I do not feel that it is any less right because of it. I do not intend to stop writing you until the day you ask me to, and I hope that day will never come. I still very much want to see you in October or whenever possible; I still believe that we should seize and live in the present. I will write you again soon. I love you.

All my love, Bryan

———

When I was asked by someone I met at a party whose name I didn't get if I was still seeing Philip, I was surprised, wondering if there was a reason why I shouldn't, and said, 'Yes,' and was told there was recently an article by Philip in the *New York Times* about Bernard Malamud which everyone found shocking: Philip wrote that even though he knew Malamud was dying, he couldn't be dishonest and tell him he liked his latest novel. 'Everyone thinks of him as a megalomaniac.'

Yesterday morning, he rang me to tell me he had just read a story of mine in the *New Yorker* – 'A House of Women' – and he said, 'It amazes me that you wrote it, and I realize that what is always most surprising about the writing of people you know is not how like them it is, but how unlike, how improbable that it came from them. I don't know about your sex, Plotnik. There was only one word in the story that I read as a homosexual's appreciation of a woman's body, the *shone* in *her body shone*. That's idealistic. A woman's body doesn't shine. But everything else is dead right.'

He said, 'When you write about yourself, you don't allow any thinking or feeling, and, to me, your writing goes flat and dead.

When you write at a remove, you allow thinking and feeling, and the writing is alive.'

About an unpublished story I had given him a while ago, 'The Secret of the Gentiles', about which he had said nothing, he said now that he didn't like it. (He said, 'All I do is read your writing. Don't you think I should be allowed time to do my own? Well, there it is, the Jew once again submits to the demands of the goy.') He warned me against making obvious comparisons between queers and Jews, which, he said, is spurious.

Il Molino

We have decided to sell Il Molino. Nikos seems more convinced that we should sell the place than I am, though he was the one to choose the house. There are a lot of reasons for getting rid of it – inconvenience, lack of use, expense – but I feel the reason at the bottom is that our feelings towards the house and the land have changed, have become dark whereas they had once been light. We may of course have personalized Il Molino, seen the place not in itself but our fantasy of it.

We spent so many of our summer holidays trying to get the house in order, from scraping the chicken shit off the red tile floors – the house had been used as a chicken coop – to getting a pump installed in the well below the house to bring water up to the new kitchen and bathrooms when electricity came to the valley, to having a pergola for a grapevine built along the façade of the stone house so we could sit out and look over the valley and the stream running through it. We spent all of our holidays working on the house, trying ways to reduce the mould that grew up on the ground-floor walls because of dampness, trying to cut away the brambles in our woods, trying to get the plumber to come to repair the pump that was always breaking down; and then, when we felt we were in control, we would have to leave.

But this was where we planned to live our lives – eventually, when we had the house and the land in order, and when, somehow, we had the money. Nikos once planted bluebells in the woods next to the house, but a farmer's pig routed out the small bulbs with its snout and ate them.

We'll sell, but with regret, and, too, some sense of betrayal, though I can't say who or what is betrayed – our own fantasy, or, more, the people we have become close to here? Such love has gone from us into this place.

London

Öçi, visiting London, came to lunch, and brought Nikos and me, as he always did, a gift: an Ottoman tile which he'd bought in Turkey, where he'd just been.

Turkey, his Turkey, is, he said, destroyed.

From time to time, Öçi would sigh, and I didn't know if this was a sigh of contentment or a sigh of personal discontent.

He told us more about the destruction of the Turkey he had known as a boy growing up in Samsun.

I said, 'It must make you very sad.'

'I can't be sad about what no longer exists,' he answered.

And yet he continued to sigh often, and Nikos asked him, 'Are you all right?'

With a smile, he answered, 'I'm as all right as I can be all right,' which I took to be one of Öçi's ambiguous comments, into which he withdrew. I know him well enough not to try to draw him out.

But Nikos doesn't allow people to withdraw.

Nikos asked, 'But why do you sigh all the time?'

Again, Öçi smiled, and I thought he would once more say something ambiguous; and, his head lowercd, he did appear to be considering carefully an ambiguity. He looked up at Nikos and said, smiling more, 'I'm not altogether well.'

'What's wrong?' Nikos asked.

Now Öçi laughed. 'Isn't everything wrong?'

'No,' Nikos said, 'I want to know what's wrong with you that you're not well.'

I said, 'Nikos, please.'

But, as I expected, Nikos insisted, 'If Öçi is a friend we should know what's wrong with him and try to help him.'

I could only hope that Öçi did understand Nikos, and he did. He said, 'I honestly don't know, nor do the doctors in New York.'

'The doctors must have been able to tell you something,' Nikos said.

'All they said was that as I travel a lot to very strange places looking for textiles for the gallery, I might, somewhere, have picked up a strange disease. The doctors in New York suggested I come to the Hospital for Tropical Diseases here in London. That's why I'm here.'

This wasn't enough to satisfy Nikos' imperative to know. 'But what could it be?'

Öçi shrugged.

'What are the symptoms?' Nikos asked.

Again, Öçi shrugged.

To try to stop Nikos, I said to Öçi, 'It's just like you to have a rare tropical disease.'

He answered, 'I wouldn't have it if it were ordinary.'

Nikos insisted, 'I want to know what the symptoms are.'

'Come on,' I said to him.

He desisted, but he could not understand why anyone should want to be ambiguous, especially about an illness, which, in Nikos' terms, should be told to everyone and should be the concern of everyone.

He asked Öçi more about Turkey, and Öçi described the dilapidated state of the house where he had spent his youth. Nikos had never been to Istanbul to see the house where his mother and her family had lived, and Öçi said he should never go.

'Don't go,' Öçi said. 'None of us should try to see the past.'

Suddenly, about the dining table where we sat, it was as if we, all of us, were cut off from our pasts. But the sense I – and Nikos, too, as he told me later – got from Öçi was that he was cut off from more than his past.

Nikos was more attentive to Öçi than he'd ever been, in the gentle way Nikos could be attentive, not, now, by pressing for information, but by surrounding Öçi with a calm solicitude, the calm solicitude Nikos always had for anyone who was not well or simply not happy, and Öçi was not well and not happy.

This was an Öçi I had never before seen, and though Nikos knew how to talk with him, I didn't, quite. He had cut his hair short and shaved off his moustache, and his face, his nose now large and his eyebrows bushy, but his eyes, as ever, delicately surrounded by lashes, appeared pale and vulnerable. An Öçi had come forward that was unfamiliar to me.

When Nikos, now in our sitting room after coffee, suggested that Öçi and I take a walk in nearby Regent's Park while he cleaned up, I said, as if I wasn't sure about being alone with Öçi, 'Why don't you join us?'

'You two go,' Nikos said, and I realized that his saying we should go out and take a walk together was a recognition of our long relationship, the longest in my life, and a long relationship, too, in the life of Öçi, for we have now known each other for some twenty years.

Öçi said to Nikos, 'Do come.'

'You two go together,' Nikos repeated.

Regent's Park on a bright Sunday afternoon was crowded, and very few in the crowd were English. We crossed the crowded bridge over the long pond, and because of the groups gathered to look through the iron lattice railings at the swans and ducks, Öçi and I were sometimes unable to remain side by side but had to separate and follow one behind the other among people who seemed, all of them, to be speaking Arabic.

There were crowds, too, on the wide cement pavement we continued along. And the green lawn that sloped to the pond on one side of the pavement was crowded with sunbathers among whom sat circles of Islamic women covered in black veils through which they gestured with hands in black gloves.

We went along crowded pavements to the Rose Garden, where, on the green expansive grounds, we were surrounded by a circle of rough wooden posts from one to the other of which hung, in massive swags, great garlands of roses in full bloom, red, pink, yellow, dropping their loose petals. Beyond the circle were people extended in all directions, all moving among one another, as if to the far, circular horizon, and they wore white jalabiyas, black veils, red and gold saris, turbans, embroidered skullcaps, large knitted caps that sagged with the weight of dreadlocks contained in them.

Öçi smiled but didn't comment, and we walked to a bench on the other side of a lawn and sat together on it.

In our silence, he said, 'I've thought a lot about you and Nikos.' His tone was sombre.

I did not want to enter into a sombre conversation with Öçi about Nikos and me. I said, 'You can't understand why I live with him?'

'No,' Öçi said. 'I've thought that it was wrong of me to suppose your relationship with him isn't as strong and lasting as it is. The fact is, I was jealous of your relationship with Nikos, and wouldn't, in my jealousy, believe it is as strong and as long lasting as it has been. I'm not, by nature, a jealous person, but I was of Nikos' and your love for each other. I want you to pardon me.'

Raising my hands, palms towards him, I said, 'Please.'

But Öçi was looking away from me, out towards the crowd in Regent's Park.

———

Nikos gave a talk at the Hellenic Society on Cavafy. The hall was packed, Stephen and Natasha and the sisters Elizabeth Glenconner and Anne Wollheim in the front row, and many Greek men in business suits and Greek ladies in mink coats, for the Greeks are always supportive of any Greek event, though Nikos has always avoided such Greek events; the Orthodox Bishop of London was also present.

A shipowner introduced Nikos as a poet and was accurate in praising Nikos' poetry for the depthless clarity, its stark lack of imagery yet the strange illusion of its being all imagery, its bringing together Surrealism and the *sense* of a highly abstract metaphysics.

Nikos, standing at the rostrum, looked very beautiful. He read his talk in a clear, precise voice, an attack, as of course Nikos would make it, on what Greece has done to Cavafy since his death – dehumanized him by institutionalizing him, depriving him of his homosexuality, his anti-bourgeois sentiments, his true originality and subversiveness. What came across was Nikos' deeply personal association, not with mainland Greece ('that tight-lipped little peninsula' as he quoted Cavafy), but Greece of the diaspora, the Hellenic Greeks from Constantinople and Alexandria and Bulgaria and Romania and Russia. Nikos considers himself, as did Cavafy, Hellenic.

After, there was a reception. Stephen and Natasha, and Elizabeth and Anne, excited, came to me before going to Nikos, who was with the bishop, to say how good the talk was – 'very, very good'. Natasha was especially enthusiastic: 'It was so beautifully *written.*'

The man who had introduced Nikos joined us and, as if to inform us of the relevance of Nikos' life to his talk, said that Nikos' father was born in Bulgaria and his mother in Constantinople. Laughing, Stephen said, 'I never knew that Nikos is a Turco-Bulgarian,' which made the man frown. Stephen and Natasha and Elizabeth and Anne went to Nikos, left now by whatever few Greeks had gone to speak to him, the bishop not among them, and I saw our friends gather around him, he smiling brightly.

Joe and Jos Tilson were there.

An old friend of Nikos – George Katiforis, who teaches economics at the London School of Economics and whom Nikos has known since they were in Athens College together (when they were students, Nikos persuaded George to join the Communist

Party; George remained a member long after Nikos ceased to be,
which has made Nikos feel guilty about having left) – said to me at
the reception, 'Nikos is very courageous.'

Yes, he was, attacking the very people who had come to hear
him talk.

Lucca

We know Lucca from when we stayed with John Fleming and Hugh Honour in their villa in the hills outside the city. I alone am staying with them now, with the idea that Nikos and I will buy a flat in the city. The sale of Il Molino got us £30,000. We had paid £3,000, which we borrowed from a friend, for the house and land. An estate agent showed me various apartments in Lucca, and I thought one would do, in a duecento building with a brick façade and seventy-three steps up to an apartment beneath the roof, the views out over the rooftops to distant mountains, and from one the Torre delle Ore, a medieval clocktower that rings every quarter, but, as a medieval clock, not more than six times, so you have to know it's noon or midnight when the bell bongs six times. The flat was inhabited by a family, the floors covered in linoleum, the walls with wallpaper, and over the windows hung thick dirty curtains on fancy wooden rods. There is an entry hall that was used as a dining room, a kitchen, and three bedrooms. The family consists of the husband, whose job is to collect tolls at an autostrada, whom I have never met; the wife, who seems to do all the business and says she writes poetry; two plump boys; a short grandmother who wears a large wig. Without conferring with Nikos, I bought the flat for 5,000,000 lire, I reckoned about £10,000. I was invited by the wife, Ilaria, without the husband, to supper, and after played cards with her and the boys. Nikos was to

arrive in ten days. Ilaria said they could not move out in ten days. I
insisted they had to. They did in three days, though the house they
were moving to, outside the walls, didn't have windows or doors,
but Ilaria said that didn't matter. Nothing much seems to matter
to her. She works in the public library, though doing what I can't
imagine. She was impressed that I am a writer.

I had a few days to have all the furniture sent from Il Molino,
especially a large chestnut cupboard, two pieces of peasant furniture, dining table and wooden chairs with rush seats, and a simple
iron bedstead and another with a tin headboard painted with a
design in which are inserted bits of mother of pearl. Also, a number

The chestnut cupboard taken from Il Molino to Corte Pini

of abstract architectural prints by Piranesi, which we bought in London for very little. And cups and wine glasses and heavy white plates and bowls. And a rug from Greece. I bought new mattresses and towels. And I tried to clean the flat, which was greasy and impacted in all its corners and cracks with dust.

Nikos arrived, and, wearing his overcoat, went from room to room in silence, silence that I couldn't read and that made me anxious as I followed him. The place looked very derelict. He finally turned to me and I said, 'You don't like it,' and he said, 'Why do you always presume to know what I'm thinking? I love it.'

We slept together, or tried to sleep, because the bells from the tower woke us again and again.

When I got up to use the toilet and turned on the light, masses of cockroaches fled in different directions, some under the linoleum, some under the wallpaper. Though Nikos loathes cockroaches, he didn't seem to mind when I told him. And in the morning they had all hidden away.

We spent the days he was with me spraying to get rid of the cockroaches, tearing up the linoleum and tearing down the wallpaper and cleaning.

The great event was laying the rug.

Once again, we were engaged, as Nikos often said, in making our lives.

He left and I will continue to work on the flat, and, too, to have workmen in to install a new kitchen and bathroom.

London

Nikos answered the telephone and told me my brother Donald was on the line, and I hurried to speak to him, as he seldom rings. 'Hi,' Don said, 'how are you?' Without answering, I asked, 'How are you?' 'Oh, pretty well,' he said. Then he told me that Dad has passed away. He said, 'I know it's a long way to come.'

I do not want to write about my father's death.

Can I not?

After I spoke to Donald, I paced about the flat weeping. Nikos packed my suitcase. I made a few telephone calls to cancel some dates. Nikos did everything for me, yet I felt he was irritated. That night we slept badly. We got up at six o'clock in the morning to go out to an airline office for an airplane ticket. In the queue with me, Nikos kept complaining about an old man who seemed to try to break the queue to go ahead of us. I was silent. Back in the flat, I rang Natasha to tell her my father had died and to give her and Stephen my love. She did not seem to be interested, and told me that Stephen may need an operation on his knee. I said, 'Nikos will be in touch if Stephen needs help.' I hung up and Nikos shouted at me, 'Why did you mention me to Natasha? You know she doesn't like me and just mentioning my name irritates her.' I said, 'Don't shout at me.' He shouted, 'I'm not shouting, I'm telling you.' I went into my study, sat on the little bed there for guests, and I began to cry hysterically. I shouted, 'What have

I done? What? What have I done that's wrong?' He came in, sat beside me on the bed, and put his arms about me.

He came to the airport with me, by Underground. I had the curious sense of the ordinary being extraordinary when one is going far – the posters in the Underground, the passengers and their briefcases and shopping bags, the newspapers, and when the train came out from the Underground the men in orange vests working on the tracks, the houses, the playing fields.

I saw everything in the death of my father. Everything I thought and felt I thought and felt in the awareness of his death.

I said to Nikos, 'Who else but you would do what you are doing for me?' He said, 'I know you'd help me.' 'Yes,' I said, 'I would.'

Providence

Momma said, 'I slept in the bed your father died in the night after he died. I did it to lay his ghost.'

Donald said, 'It took her hours to make the bed, smooth out the sheets, arrange the pillows.'

'What did you say?' my mother asked, she now nearly deaf.

'I was telling David about your sleeping in the bed Père died in.'

'Yes,' she said, and then she looked at me with watery eyes and asked, as if this she assumed I would want to do, 'Will you sleep in it?'

She said she felt too weak to come to the parish funeral parlour where our father was being waked, and where there were few people apart from our father's seven sons.

The parish priest, whom only my brother Donald knew since when he decided to devote his life to caring for my parents and, living at home, started to go to the parish church every Sunday – the parish priest, whom I did not know, came in and knelt on the kneeler and said a rosary, and the sons stood and recited after him. Then he shook all our hands and left.

Donald said he would go home to ask our mother if she felt well enough to come.

I thought: if my father's seven sons – Robert, Donald, Raymond, Roland, René, David, Lenard – are in any way noble in looks and in bearing and in manners, it is because of our father.

Donald did come in with our mother, frail and bent over, wearing a large knitted cap. She went to the coffin in a niche surrounded by flowers, the light pale, and with difficulty she leaned over the side and kissed our father's forehead; then she looked at us, each in turn, with a look of such defeat, such acceptance of defeat, such acceptance of helpless defeat, that there was hardly any expression to the defeat except in the way she looked at us, blinking, and turned away and said to Donald that she'd better go.

Each of her sons held her and kissed her.

Oh, Momma, Momma.

In bed that night, in the bed I grew up in, I wondered why I thought my mother and father had been defeated, and why I feel I have inherited a sense of defeat from them.

Let me eulogize, as I feel the need to do –

The defeat is inherent from past generations, from generations upon generations of the French in North America, from which I come.

It is not an historical exaggeration to believe that the history of the whole of North America was determined, not in the American Revolution of 1776 which applied only to America, but in 1759, when, in what was then called La Nouvelle France and now Canada, the English general Wolfe defeated the French general Montcalm on the Plains of Abraham in Quebec, a defeat that allowed not only the English colonists of Canada to dominate there but the English colonists of America to consolidate their dominant possession of America. Unlike the immigrants of the late nineteenth century, Franco-Americans have a history in the continent of North America that goes back to 1608 – when Champlain founded Quebec. Crossing the then non-existent border between the United States and Canada by train in the late nineteenth century was for the French of Canada not so much to emigrate as to relocate within a long North American history. And the North American French had for generations worked the forests as lumberjacks across into the Dakotas and down into California without need of passports or work permits. My great-grandfather, called *le Grand Coq*, was one of these.

I like to fantasize that once our tribe was huge, was almost all of North America, and we were the great explorers, were the founders of Detroit and Des Moines and Saint Louis, and of course New Orleans, were the missionaries out to save the natives for eternity. But I was brought up in a reduced tribe, a powerless tribe in the midst of much larger and powerful tribes, and my tribe had no choice but to disband, became as irrelevant to the larger world as a decaying totem pole lying among overgrown weeds in a lot at the edge of a derelict factory town. Defeat is a strange but potent attraction, and has its own longings, its own passions.

London

Our dear Greek friend Fani-Maria Tsigakou, in London from Athens for a visit, Frank Kermode (Anita was ill), Philip (Claire was in India filming), and a mystery guest named Maryse came to supper.

When I had suggested to Nikos that we invite Maryse, whom I met just a short time ago, he said, 'She sounds like one of your neurotic women.' She is Belgian, blonde, and beautiful.

Fani-Maria arrived first, then Frank. Frank obviously liked Fani-Maria, who is dark and beautiful, very much. Then Maryse came. I should go into the oddness of inviting someone you don't know with friends you are close to. Then Philip came, carrying his folding back support, and, immediately, he turned the party into an entertaining little performance: he opened the back support on a chair and invited everyone to try it, saying, 'It may change your life. You might find it'll change your sex.' I could tell he was paying particular attention to Maryse, who, sitting in the chair with the back support, smiled at Philip.

Nikos thought Frank would like to sit across from Fani-Maria at one end of the table, and Philip across from Maryse at the other end, and he and I across from one another in the middle. I wanted to hear what Philip and Maryse were saying to one another. Maryse said to Philip, 'You're just the way I imagined you to be from your novels.' Philip leaned towards her and said,

'So are you.' They looked at one another, then Philip sat back and went silent.

Maryse looked at me and said, 'You're not at all the way I imagined you to be after I read one of your novels.'

Philip remained silent, and I, worried by his silence, asked Maryse questions about her life, which she answered with a smile and short replies – 'I worked on a ship for ten years before I came to England' – which somehow precluded one asking her why she had worked on a ship. Later, Nikos said he thought she was – is – a spy.

Philip sat up again and picked up something Frank said at the other end of the table about the Brain Drain to America (in a *Daily Telegraph* I'd read a while ago there was an article by Malcolm Bradbury decrying the loss of Bernard Williams, Christopher Ricks, and Frank, whom he called something like the best scholarly critic in England today and who has gone to Columbia University in New York, to which Frank said, 'Malcolm always gets everything wrong').

After a while, Philip began to pay attention to Maryse again, and I thought there was nothing to worry about, after all.

The next morning Philip telephoned me. He asked me what I thought about Maryse. I said she seemed to be two people, alternating: sometimes I thought she was very beautiful, other times quite ordinary; sometimes intelligent and very well read, other times not at all educated. She spoke with a precise, upper-class English accent, and seemed to have lots of money in her past. I went on for a while. Philip said, 'I agree with you.' There was a pause, then he said, 'You know what a sensitive person I am, don't you?' I thought he was being ironical, and laughed. 'You do know, don't you?' he repeated, and I realized he was serious. 'Yes, I do,' I said. 'I fell for her in a way I haven't fallen for a woman in years,' he said. 'Did you get that?'

'At the table?' I asked.

'Yes.'

'I felt that something happened. It worried me. I thought she said something to hurt you, which was why you sat back and went so silent.'

'No,' Philip said. 'I can take care of myself when people try to hurt me.'

'My instinct was: she's hurt my friend. This worried me, because I'd brought you together, so it was my fault.'

'Let me tell you, David, that that's a homosexual projection. No, she didn't hurt me. I fell for her. That's what happened. I sat back and went silent because I knew what had happened, and I thought, Christ, it really has happened. I thought of getting up from the table and leaving, but I didn't have the strength. I was trembling.'

He said she drove him home after they left together, and he asked her into the house, where he told her – No, let me get this right, or try to. (Philip said to me over the telephone, 'This is *my* story, Plotnik. If I don't use it within two years, you can have it. But until then it's *mine*.') In the car, he told her what he felt, and she responded that she felt – Wait. If I am ever going to use this, it sure as hell has to be better written. Anyway, they went into the house. She asked to use the bathroom, where she saw the photograph of Philip and Claire in a country setting ('Right out of Colette, this scene,' Philip said), and when she came downstairs she said, 'I don't think this is going to be good for either of us.' Philip took her out to her car, said, 'Well, goodbye. I won't be seeing you again, I guess.' But Maryse couldn't get the car started. Philip offered her the use of a guest room with a lock to lock herself in ('The way David used to lock his door against me when we were sharing a house in Jerusalem,' Philip said he told her). Maryse turned the key in the ignition again, and the car started.

Philip said to me, 'I had a bad night. I'm having a bad morning. I'll be over it all by 3:00 this afternoon. Give it till 3:30, and it'll be finished.'

He said that what drew him to her wasn't heat, as she didn't give off heat, but light, the light she gave off. This made me wonder about his once telling me that a woman's body does not glow, even if, in my story, her body is wet.

The writer Mary Gordon rang from New York. She said Philip's novel *The Counterlife*, which is part set in the West Bank settlement we visited, is getting great attention and praise in America.

She was feeling low, wondering if her writing has any worth. 'Does it?' she asked. 'Tell me. Does it?'

I said, 'None of our work has any worth.'

'That's true. That's so true,' she said.

———

Dinner with Claire in a Chinese restaurant. She said, 'It's amazing. Today, I haven't cared at all about anything.' She said she is suspicious of what Philip is up to in New York, but she doesn't, today, care about that either. I left her feeling up.

Paros

We are on the island of Paros.

A hippy friend in London, who comes to Greece often, advised us to come to the village of Marpissa on the island of Paros to find a house. The village is on the side of a mountain, and we are staying in a hotel on the sea below the village. We went up to the village to look about for houses that may be for sale. Nikos says I always impose my will on his, and resented my insisting that we go together to a coffee house and ask, but I kept insisting, saying I would go, and he finally, reluctantly, agreed. We were shown some abandoned houses. Looking at the courtyard and the façade over the top of a rusty gate, I said to Nikos this has to be the one. Nikos went into the port town, Parikia, to make the deal. And so we will have a house on a Greek island, paid for by what we had left from the sale of Il Molino, as was the Lucca flat.

As he is from a refugee family, Nikos can't claim to have his island in the way that many Greeks can. His mother, from Constantinople, had no interest in the Greek islands, and would never go on holiday to one, but to a suburb of Athens where middle-class people go, Kifisia. Paros is part of a Greek world that is somewhat outside of Nikos' Greek world.

The first day we went down to swim, we stopped among some bushes to take off our shorts and tee-shirts to put on our swim-suits, then, striding out on the beach, found that everyone was naked, men, women, children. The scene was a revelation in the sunlight, under the blue sky, before the blue sea. It did not take long before Nikos and I lay naked among all the brightly naked people.

The beach, Punda, has one small breezeblock shed where cold drinks and jellies and custard puddings are sold. From time to time an old man on a donkey comes along, the donkey walking delicately among the bodies, the man selling bunches of grapes which he holds out as he calls out what he must think is the English word for grapes.

Nikos does not like to walk about naked, though I like the sense, not only of permissiveness, but vulnerability in the permissiveness, of walking naked out in the world, and naked I walked along the path above the beach and looked down at the sunbathers there.

I looked down into the sea, to where it turned from blue to green, and I saw a young man swimming underwater. His arms and legs spread open then shut, open and then shut, slowly, and his long hair was pulled in with each stroke of his arms and then floated out from his head the moment he paused between strokes. He rose to the surface to expel his breath in a burst of spray and to breathe in before he dived down again, his gleaming buttocks rising above the surface. Underwater, he glided toward a flat rock on which seaweed swayed in the ebb and flow of the waves and there remained motionless for a moment as he floated face down, his arms and legs extended, before he rose up and stood on the rock. His eyelids slightly swollen from the water, he looked up at me, and then he looked away.

He gathered his hair together at the back of his head and held it, and he stood still, his chest curving out in taut curves and his abdomen curving down and then in in taut curves that converged at a fine tuft of hair and his cock and balls, and his thighs curved out and down to his knees; and there were the curves of his underarms, and the curve, just seen in the three-quarters view I had of him, of the small of his back giving way to his buttocks. He let his wet hair fall and he turned completely away and dived deep under the water.

My God, that a young man naked out in the open for the world to see should appear so sublime.

I'm not sure Nikos likes being on Paros, as he complains about everything, and hates the *panigiria* where, in a village square, loudspeakers make violent the wailing of violin and voice. But he tolerates being here for what remains of the Greece he knew: fresh goats' milk, swallows skimming the evening air, bougainvillea vines, and of course the Aegean Sea.

London

A Monday afternoon I picked up Philip from a physiotherapist in Harley Street to drive him back to Fulham. He had asked me to do this, as he was worried about getting a taxi with his knee in such a delicate state. He was very low, and made jokes in a flat voice. I said, 'You know, there is a God.' 'Why?' he asked. I said, 'There's no other way to explain your being punished by so much pain when you should feel entirely triumphant but that God is punishing you for your triumph.' He didn't laugh. 'No,' he said, 'there is no God.' Then he laughed when he said, 'Just think of how I'd be feeling if the critics had shat all over me for *The Counterlife*. I'd ask you to stop the car on this bridge' – we were going over the Serpentine in Hyde Park – 'and I'd jump over.'

We stayed in the kitchen with Claire while she prepared supper. Anita Brookner came.

At dinner, Philip said he has no more to write, and he wants to give up. Anita B. said she felt exactly the same. 'And,' she said, 'you have no idea what it's like to be alone and feel that.' Claire said she felt her acting was finished. I said, in a loud voice, 'I don't feel at all like that, and neither, really, does any one of you.'

Anita B. talked more about the loneliness of her life. I liked her, and I found her amusing, though I wondered if she thought of herself as amusing. I often think people – writers especially – are being ironical, because I assume they're too intelligent to be the parodies they appear to be, but I think I'm mistaken, as when Anita said to Claire, who was praising the freesias Anita B. had brought as a gift, 'They won't last' – pause – 'Nothing does.'

At lunch with my agent Deborah Rogers a few days ago, I asked her how she, as an agent, can take writers seriously, and she laughed a little but said nothing.

Claire went upstairs to watch a television play she'd acted in which was about a man who was dying from A.I.D.S., and which she insisted was too bad for us to watch. Philip, Anita, and I did watch it on a television set in the living room for a while. In one scene Claire, looking so isolated in her beauty, walked alone along a canal. Then the play did become bad, and Philip shut the set off.

Philip talked about the happy relationship he was having with his father in his father's late age.

I said, 'I think that when my parents die, I'll feel that there is nothing between me and eternity.'

Anita said, 'That is exactly how I feel about the death of my parents.' And she said she had once wished very much to have children.

'Did you know that you never would have any?' I asked.

'Yes,' she said thoughtfully, carefully, 'I suppose I did know.' As carefully as she spoke, she smoked a cigarette as if it were the only cigarette in the world and she was smoking it with the clear awareness of its uniqueness.

I said I thought my married brothers with children were more mature than my unmarried and childless brothers. Philip objected. He knew of people who had children who were not mature. I said, 'Look, having to deal, day after day, with egos that are fighting against your ego to be their own egos must do something to your ego we have no experience of.' Philip looked at me for a moment. 'You're right,' he said. Then he said, 'Here we are, the three of us, who will never have children.' We were silent.

It strikes me now how often, during our conversation, Philip said, 'At the risk of being sentimental,' or, 'This may sound sentimental, but,' and I realize how he's always, always holding up an iron barrier against his very deep sensitivity, which, if he dropped the barrier, would overwhelm him.

Claire came down after the play ended. Anita, as if she were thinking of using the information in a work of fiction, asked Claire about acting.

Lucca

I see John and Hugh, sometimes spend the night in the Villa Marchio, and think back at the time, on Nikos' and my first visit there, we surprised the living-in help, Gilda, when she came into the room with a breakfast tray, thinking Nikos was alone and I in another room, and found us in bed together. And I remember how, as we made love, fireflies flashed pale-green light in the room.

So much to remember, so much, and so much forgotten, so very much forgotten.

I find that when I am with John and Hugh now, for tea under the pergola by the lotus pool, I tell them more about people in London than they once told me, people I've met who are in very different worlds from their world, and I have my stories to tell about the people I have met.

They introduced me to a friend of theirs, Susanna Johnston, who with her husband Nicky has a house outside Lucca in the country. She invited me to the house, La Cavina, for a weekend, where she and Nicky and two daughters seemed to be entertaining as guests more people than there could possibly be beds for. Everyone was British except me.

I stayed on after the gang of the young left, the daughters Rosie and Sylvie remaining from the gang, but they, eager for activity, said they were going off to a disco near Viareggio, called Chez Marlene, where all the various sexes mixed. I was curious, and Susanna suggested that I go. The girls were excited, but said that to get in one had to be made up, and I said, Well, make me up, and presented my face to them to make me up with eye shadow and lash thickener and lipstick; and they proposed I wear something more in keeping with the disco and had me try on a kind of loose smock patterned with dancing girls that belonged to a Tennant young man who he had left behind. The three of us went off in the car to the disco, prefabricated, in a scruffy field, and we passed the bouncer and into the dark in which shafts of light illuminated the crowd of dancers. And the three of us danced together, I, with my makeup and my smock, one of them. There may have been various sexes present, but there were enough young men who liked young women to come up to the little group I formed with Rosie and Sylvie, our arms about one another, to take one of the girls by the arm to dance with her; but the girls always returned to me, as if I was their partner for the night and no one else would do. Then one of the girls – Rosie, I think, who was all liveliness – came back to me from having danced briefly with a boy, and, pointing to him, she said to me, 'He asked me, what are you doing here with your father?'

All this may indicate that I am hardly writing fiction, but I almost never write in my diary about writing fiction, and I am in fact working daily, for hours, on a novel, called *The Family*.

And I speak to Nikos every day. He has no interest at all in the people I have been seeing, but does not censure my interest.

———

Philip is in New York. Claire rang me. We went to see a film, then back to her house for scrambled eggs. She said, 'I'm more unhappy than I've ever been in my life.' She said this as a stark fact. I said, 'But I know Philip loves you.' 'Yes,' she said, 'and I love him.'

Tulsa

And here I am, in Tulsa, Oklahoma –
I was invited by Tom Staley, the vice president of the University of Tulsa, to a reception, given in a large ranch house behind flowering azalea bushes. Among tanned, lean people standing about tables of silver platters and dishes of food, three professors, one wearing a necklace of blue ceramic beads on a leather thong over his shirt and tie, told me that they were Native Americans. I had never before met people who told me, right away on meeting them, that they were Indian, Choctaw and Cherokee. They didn't look any more Indian than I did. Even the daughter of the hostess, who wore a diamond necklace, told him she was a sixteenth Osage, though she was blonde and freckled. Not that I knew what made an Indian, but none of these people seemed to me to be Indian.

I don't know how I'll get through the four months here at the university. I want to leave now, not because people here are unfriendly, they are wonderfully friendly, but because I want to be back in London and with Nikos.

I long for London, and I long for Nikos. Only there with him do I feel I am at home and secure in his love for me.

I tell myself, Devote yourself to your writing, for your writing's sake, and I try to do that. I stay in – except when, each Tuesday and

Thursday, I'm at the university – and I write, with great effort. But it seems to me I'm writing with a sense of total failure.

Where does my success lie? I know, I know. And I'm not there where it is.

In my first class, the students looked, not at me, but at the ceiling, a wall, or out the window at a tree in the still, outside heat. Inside, chill draughts from the air conditioning blew about the room.

When I am away from Nikos, alone, I imagine I stand inside darkness and look out, across a space, into outside brightness. There seems to me to be a gap between the darkness and the brightness, as if at some time in my life they separated and now have nothing to do with each other. I belong in the darkness. I see the brightness, but I do not belong there; and, more than ever, I feel that the brightness, even if I could get across the gap to it, wouldn't matter to me if I were there in it. But I insist: it *must* matter to me, it *must*! I must concentrate on the brightness with every effort to – to what? – to bring myself, by the force of my concentration, over into the brightness outside the darkness? No, I'll never force myself over to it. And, again, if I did do that, I know that there I would wonder why I thought being in the brightness mattered. But, from the darkness, I know it *does* matter, because out there in the brightness is the awareness of chairs, of tables, of cups and saucers and spoons, and people sitting at the tables, all out in that brightness.

I have been in that brightness with Nikos, have been for moments and for longer than moments.

I spoke to Jennifer over the telephone. She asked me, 'Have you made any discoveries about yourself in Tulsa?'

One of those coincidences in my life that make me think it is, itself, an ongoing narrative: Germaine Greer is also teaching at the University of Tulsa.

We often meet at parties we are both invited to. She said to me, 'You're so *charming* to people.' I said, 'That's because I believe in social behaviour, no matter what.' She laughed and said, 'I don't believe you when you're charming.' I said, 'You're right. I'm not really charming because I'm faking it. I can't stand most people.' She laughed again. I said, 'Here, I'm a cynic. In a cynical world, like London, I'm considered so nice. Here, where everyone is so nice, I'm a cynic. But I pretend to be nice.' She made a moue as though in doubt of everything I said.

No doubt she is right to be in doubt of everything I say.

I will leave our meeting to chance.

———

Thinking of the coincidences of my life, I went to the library to look through boxes of Jean Rhys' papers, bought by the university. Having known her, I would like to account for the coincidence of her papers being here in the University of Tulsa, Oklahoma and not in Jean's little cottage in Cheriton Fitzpaine, Devon, but I can't.

———

On my way to the airport to meet Stephen Spender, I suddenly felt very sad, I didn't know why, though perhaps there is something sad about going to meet a friend one hasn't seen in a long while at an airport foreign to both – as sad, in a way, as driving home from an airport after having left a friend off. It was dark, and Tulsa was deserted; the airport terminal, brightly lit up, was deserted. I waited in an empty lounge, by an arrival gate, for Stephen; when I saw him walking up a carpeted ramp among others, I ran to him, embraced him and kissed him, and took his luggage. We both laughed.

He is *very* big.

I was so excited to see him, I couldn't find the car in the huge parking lot and ran about as Stephen stood, his arms folded, by his luggage. I thought: not finding a car in a parking lot is something Stephen himself could easily do and has done – and yet, when someone else does what he could have done and has done, he becomes impatient. His impatience is expressed in the way he crosses his arms and the way he presses his lips together so they become thin.

I found the car, but I got lost driving back into Tulsa, though I didn't tell him. He was very lively. He told me this story: he was in a small town in Upstate New York, fog bound, so the airplane flight that was to take him to New York for a dinner at John and Rosamond Russell's to meet Jacqueline Onassis was cancelled. He decided to take a taxi. The distance to New York was 300 miles, and the taxi driver said he would drive Stephen there for $100. Stephen thought this very reasonable. After fifty miles, the taxi driver said he would like to stop for coffee; Stephen, who insisted on paying, couldn't find his wallet, and realized he had left it at the little coffee shop in the little airport in the New York fog-bound mountains. They had to go back. The taxi driver said he couldn't go back now to New York with an additional 100 miles. Another taxi driver was found who said he would take Stephen for $300. Stephen agreed. He told me it was an agonizing ride, but he was only five minutes late for dinner with Mrs Onassis.

He liked my little house. I prepared him a cold supper of ham and potato salad and opened a bottle of champagne. We sat in the living room and we talked, mostly about Bryan, who is now in Los Angeles studying zoology at the university.

He asked me to read from my diary, and he then read from his.

I gave him my bedroom, and I slept on the sofa in the living room.

———

About noon, my students Randy and Dennis came by, as I'd asked them to, thinking that Stephen would be amused by them. We all went to a fish restaurant. The boys listened attentively to Stephen, who made them laugh. I ordered catfish, which tasted like mud. Stephen said, 'The one reason why I don't like Richard Eberhart is because he loves catfish.' After lunch, the boys took us to Oral

Roberts University, which is like a world's fair, all gold windows that shine like huge mirrors. The boys led us into the Prayer Tower, in the round basement of which are different rooms, each succeeding room sealed off from the former by a door, and each representative of a period in the life of Oral Roberts, starting with the little farmhouse in which he was born, the window dark then lit up and the cry of a baby heard and then the mother, who says, 'I'm going to call you Oral.' The final room has walls of mirrors and flashing lights in which a voice booms prayers. I realized that Stephen and I were within a culture that existed nowhere else in the world. There in the final room, which the boys had arranged would be only for us to stand in, a room in which there was a constant, vibrant hum of what I took to be the hum of prayer. But I was more interested in Stephen's reaction than my own. He appeared totally absorbed. He didn't laugh, as the boys did. When we came out, he said, 'That was very interesting.' As we walked across the campus, he asked the boys, with serious interest, about the university.

The boys came back to the house for beers, there were many small sexual jokes among the boys, and Stephen laughed and I laughed, both of us, however, not sure what specifically the jokes were about.

Stephen, I realized, is always making discoveries about people. He talked about Auden, for example, as if he thinks a lot about him and makes discoveries about him he hadn't thought before. 'Wystan, while staying with us in London, never paid for anything but his gin. I had never thought of this before. I'm sure it's because . . .' Why this occurs to me now, I don't know; maybe it's because it came to me that while Stephen was with the boys he seemed to be thinking about them, to try to understand something about them that needed to be thought about.

The boys left. I wondered if Stephen was wondering about the sexual mores of the boys, who, as graduates of Oral Roberts, might have had sexual mores different from any other times in history.

And I wonder the same.

Stephen and I went to the university library so he could look
through the library of Cyril Connolly, which the university had
bought. Stephen said, 'I'm sure there are books here that once
belonged to me and Natasha. Cyril was always stealing books.'

He was interested in everything, again as if to understand something he didn't about everything there.

In the afternoon, I left him alone while I taught an undergradu-
ate class, he to write in his diary, trying, he said, to catch up on six
weeks.

In the evening, he gave a reading of poems.

I introduced him:

Though this may alarm him, I'm going to be very personal in
my introducing Stephen Spender. I'm going to try, briefly, to
say what I have learnt from him. I've known him for almost
half my life. But I think that what I have to say about him has
everything to do with him, not with me, and so if I try to
describe what he has done for me I'm also trying to describe
him in himself and what he has done for so many people in
his poems.

There have been moments when Stephen – in a restaurant, in a museum, in a taxi, walking along the street – when I
have sensed him suddenly withdraw. These moments of with-
drawal are frightening, for I wonder if he has turned from
looking outside to looking inside at what I can't see. His face
becomes blank – at most he looks puzzled. And then, if at a
restaurant, a waiter pours out a glass of wine, if in a museum
Stephen enters a room and sees a Cézanne, if in a taxi he sees
out on the pavement someone he knows standing alone on
a corner, if walking along he passes a newspaper stand piled
with newspapers with a large front picture of a child with
a belly swollen as big as its head, its arms and legs and neck
bones from starvation – and he turns, as suddenly as he had
turned inwardly, outwardly to the outside world, turns back,
I feel, with the pleasure at the sight of the wine being poured,
with wonder at the Cézanne, with love for the friend out on

the corner, and with a look of pain and near defeat at the
sight of the starving baby. It is at these moments when I see
Stephen most intimately, those moments when he turns from
whatever is inside to the outside. It's at these moments when
he is, I think, most visionary.

Wherever Stephen is, something happens to turn his
attention to the happening. Now, I don't know if it happens
because he has a way of being there when it happens or
because he is there. I've had telephone calls from him when
he has been able to report, as excited as anyone might be at
having a vision, 'They've turned over a car in the street below
my hotel window and are setting fire to it.'

I thought, before I met Stephen, that all the greatest revelations came from inside, and of course I looked for them there;
but he has shown me that the greatest revelations also come,
and perhaps more importantly, from the outside: from the
world in which we live our daily lives and often enough botch
up our daily lives as well as fulfil them.

That, to me, was revolutionary.

———

Germaine was at the reading. After, she and Stephen and I went out
to dinner. She ordered champagne. I so wanted her and Stephen to
get on. I always worry that people I introduce to each other will
not get on, and I feel responsible. They did get on. Germaine kept
Stephen laughing. When the bill came, she insisted on paying. No,
Stephen insisted, he would pay, and he searched in his pocket for
his wallet. He looked at me. He said, 'I left my wallet somewhere.' I
said I would pay, but Germaine had already paid the waiter. Outside
the restaurant, Germaine and Stephen embraced. Stephen and I
came home and searched for his wallet, but couldn't find it.

We searched again in the morning, before he was off, but it was
lost. 'Well,' he said, 'I have my ticket to Los Angeles. In a year's
time, I'll think of this as very minor.' I drove him to the airport and
gave him some money.

He has rung often from Los Angeles. He said, 'Bryan is exactly the same, and that is wonderful.'

––––––––

Tom Staley invited Melvyn Bragg and Beryl Bainbridge to come to give readings. Germaine and I went to the airport to meet them after their fifteen-hour flight from London.

They were staying in a large hotel. In the spacious lobby were hundreds of men and women wearing boots and straw Stetsons with birds' heads and feathers about the headbands, all drinking from large glasses and moving aside to allow black waiters to wheel past trolleys of enormous beef and ham joints and, in one trolley, a large abstract ice sculpture. Beryl, examining everything, said, 'What a strange place. What a strange country.'

As I drove her and Melvyn about, Beryl would stare out of the window at neon signs, at the empty night-time downtown streets, at an illuminated skyscraper against the enormous blue-black sky, and say, with an expression of astonishment, 'How could anyone describe that? *How*?'

And I would say, 'It's all too strange.'

As I saw a lot of them, we talked a lot.

Beryl talked about her life.

Melvyn said he can't talk freely about his life. He never can. He wishes he could.

We met at the hotel pool, high above the downtown Tulsa streets and parking lots; we swam, we lay in the sunlight, we sat together in the Jacuzzi.

Melvyn said he was worried about his writing. I felt he wanted to tell me, honestly, about his worries, and he tried, but he is right, he cannot confide freely. He said, 'It's the way I was brought up. I can't even express myself – my private self – in my novels. I hold back.' He said he has to invent.

During a class session to which I invited them both, Melvyn said he imagined everything in his writing; Beryl said she didn't imagine anything, and simply wrote down what had happened to her – as, in *Young Adolf*, she based Adolf Hitler entirely on her father.

One evening, Germaine took us all to a Tulsa bar. We sat at the bar and listened to the bartender recount stories about Tulsa.

She usually joined us for dinner. She talked, and the rest of us listened. After, Beryl said, 'You don't have a conversation with Germaine, do you? You get a lecture. But it's quite a lecture.'

Listening to Germaine, Melvyn often ruffled his hair and, smiling, appeared to lower his head as if to dodge under the level of the talk.

I wish I could get in the gestures, the facial expressions, the tones of voices of Germaine, Beryl, Melvyn.

Germaine sits up very straight, her shoulders drawn back, her face rather stark, her eyes focused at a distance, and her voice is high pitched, with a whine to it.

Beryl swings her head about before she speaks, as if to facially prepare herself to speak, and then announces orotundly what she has to say.

Melvyn has a nasal voice, and from time to time appears to wonder what it is he is saying.

The fact is, here in Tulsa I am with them in London.

London

Philip rang to say, 'I won a prize for *The Counterlife*, so let me take you to lunch.' We went to his club, the R.A.C.

While we were eating our sandwiches at a little table in a reception room, he talked about leaving England for America. I said I was upset that he was leaving, but thought that he'd be in London as much as ever, 'but thinking you're just visiting'. 'No,' he said, 'I won't be coming as much as ever.'

He talked about feeling a foreigner in England, feeling, culturally, very lonely. I said, 'I don't think I know what it means not to be culturally lonely.' He looked at me.

My next book, he said, should answer the question: 'What is your quarrel with America?'

After lunch, we went up to the smoking room, had tea, and, as we sat side by side in huge leather armchairs, he dictated a number of questions about my background which he said he'd like me to answer:

When did you discover that you were not a member of the great country, but of a minority? How? What incidents do you recall?

Who was the first person to make you aware of the world elsewhere?

What did you despise most about your world?

What were you most ashamed of? Why?

Which of your relatives most embodied the shame? The least?

How did you think your possibilities were limited by back-ground, and when did this occur to you?

Where did your motivation come from?

How do Francos view themselves vis-à-vis others? What is their own stereotype of themselves? Is it accurate? Partially so? Defensive? Deluded?

What was Sunday like, from morning till night?

What was your sense of history?

What alienated you from America?

How much do you think your expatriate status is a direct outcome of your tremendous cultural marginality?

Afterwards, Philip and I walked up St James's together. He said, 'You'll come to America. I'll take you to a baseball game. You'll like it. The players wear uniforms now that show off their asses.'

He got into a taxi, and I walked on feeling – lonely? Well, feeling that I had to cope with something vast which I'd hardly ever thought about and which he was leaving me alone to do. I walked through Mayfair into Marylebone and home.

Stephen looks a little older each time I see him after he's been away. I had lunch with him alone.

He said, 'I hope that one day Bryan will meet you both. You'll like him. He's pure of heart.'

After lunch we went to the National Portrait Gallery for the exhibition *Young Writers of the Thirties*: Isherwood, Auden, MacNeice, Day Lewis, and, most prominent among them, Stephen. Among the spectators, we went from case to case to lean over and study letters, manuscripts, posters, photographs. It was very odd to stand by Stephen and read a letter from him, pinned up behind glass, to Virginia Woolf. He appeared not to know what to think as he stared at the letter as if to make sense, not of the letter, but why it was there.

Then we walked through London to Marble Arch, on our way
stopping in bookshops to see what the latest are, and all the while
talking, talking, talking.

I said to myself: remember this.

As he was leaving me, Stephen asked if we could have lunch the
next day, and the next day Nikos joined us, at the Chinese restaurant Poons, and a great sense of love among us.

Stephen did appear a little dispirited, and at the end of the meal
I asked him if that was so. 'I'm worried about Natasha,' he said, 'as
always. And I think about Bryan. I'm very worried about meeting
him again. I think sometimes of holding his slender hand in my
hand and wondering, how is it possible that I should have him love
me so much, and I get worried. Maybe I shouldn't make love with
him when I see him. I don't know.'

———

Olivia Manning rang to invite me, not Nikos, to dinner, and I said
I'd be delighted to go. When I hung up Nikos said I'd sounded *too*
pleased to accept the invitation, said I'd sounded false. He calls that
my American falseness, and has to a large extent made me aware of
it so that I am more direct.

Then he said, 'She's inviting you and not me because she's evil.
I know these people. They want to trap you. You have no defenses
against them.'

I said, 'That sounds mad. She doesn't know you. She knows me
as a writer, and as she's a writer she thought we'd get on.'

'Of course she knows me, or knows about me.'

'But you always say that you don't mind if we are invited separately. Why, now, do you mind?'

'Because you don't understand. She's evil!'

I became angry. 'I don't understand.'

'No,' he said, 'you don't.'

I shouted, 'I won't listen to this hysterical overreaction to what
means nothing to me. What does it mean to you? You don't want

me to see Olivia Manning? I'll ring her and tell her I can't come.
I'll do that.'

'Stop shouting,' he said.

'I've got to shout,' I said.

I went to the telephone.

'You're not ringing her,' he said.

'I am.'

'If you ring her I'll pull the wire out of the wall.'

I laughed and said, 'You don't want me to cancel the invitation
because that will make Olivia Manning, who *should* have invited us
together, suspect it's because you're not invited, and are jealous of
me for being invited and you not.'

'I'm not jealous,' Nikos said, 'I'm not!'

'But that's what she'll think.'

He said, 'You don't understand me. You don't understand me
at all.'

'Maybe I don't,' I said.

We got into bed together.

He said, 'You don't understand that if things continue as they are
I'll have a breakdown.'

This shocked me. 'What do you mean?'

'Go to sleep.'

'I want to know what you mean. Do you mean things
between us?'

'Go to sleep.'

'No, not until you tell me.'

'Things at work,' he said.

I slept badly. I knew now that he was very very tired from
working late at night in his office, returning home just for a meal
and then to bed. I had thought he was so tired from something
other than work.

He was especially busy with the David Hockney book, *That's
the Way I See It*, which Nikos virtually (what does 'virtually'
mean?) wrote, or rewrote from typed-out tapes of David answering

questions that Nikos posed to him, Nikos on a chair in our sitting
room and David, like someone undergoing analysis, lying back on
a chaise longue.

David, Henry Geldzahler, Nikos and I went to Bradford, David's
home town, for a big publication party to be held at Cartwright
Hall.

Nikos got up at 6:00, I at 6:30, and we went out into the grey
London morning at 7:00 to catch a bus to Henry's hotel near
Gloucester Road tube station. David was standing behind the large
plate-glass doors of the hotel, reading a newspaper, and looked like
one of his paintings: a figure isolated in a simple space. He, Nikos
and I waited for Henry.

Maurice Payne, printmaker, drove us all to King's Cross, with
David sitting next to him and insisting, 'Turn here, turn there,'
which I saw made Maurice become rigid.

David had reserved a table in the restaurant car, and we sat at a
white-tablecloth-covered table waiting for a waiter to come, and
I suddenly remarked that Nikos was spirited, so spirited that to be
so spirited was everything he was in his character, so spirited that
depression, anger, hysteria could not possibly have been character-
istics. Henry said, 'David's going to try to get us all to eat kippers,
but I refuse to eat kippers.' And if it was David who talked most,
his talk was the standard of liveliness to which we all responded,
laughing. David opened the *Guardian*, as though this couldn't have
been otherwise given the level of liveliness, to a good review of the
book by Melvyn Bragg.

The waiter, wearing a white jacket with black epaulettes, came
to take our orders. For those who ordered eggs, bacon, sausage,
tomatoes and mushroom (Henry and I) he placed the knife and
fork parallel to each other, and for those who ordered kippers
(David and Nikos) he crossed the knife and fork. A long while
later he came with the orders, and by the placement of the cutlery
he knew who was having what.

David was warm, personal, bright, and I thought: you can see
David in a state of grumpy irritation and you can take that state to

be most indicative of his personality; or you can see David at his warmest, most personal and brightest, and take that as most indicative of his character. What is always indicative of his character is that he talks and talks and talks.

After breakfast, we went to a compartment. Henry took out a blindfold from a pocket and covered his eyes with it and lay on a banquette and slept, and for a while David was silent.

At Leeds, he said, 'Let's get off the train and go to the Leeds museum. We've got plenty of time. We'll take a taxi to Bradford. I'm sick of all this celebrating. I feel I'm being pushed around.'

We went to the museum. David was immediately recognized. We were shown into rooms of an exhibition that was not yet open to the public, and then were taken round the museum, where David as a boy used often to go. He wanted us to see the huge murals by Frank Brangwyn that so impressed him, he thinking: now *that* is art.

By taxi, on to Bradford. I said, 'Bradford looks like Providence, Rhode Island,' and Henry said, 'Bradford *is* Providence, Rhode Island.' We got out of the taxi at the gates of a park and walked up to the museum. The reception had started at 12:00, it was now 12:15.

David's brother Paul was waiting at the door. He said, 'Where have you been? We went to the station to meet you. The Lord Mayor's been waiting.' David shrugged his shoulders.

Henry said, 'I think I'll sit on a bench and rest for a while before going in.'

Nikos and I followed David into the foyer. Many smiling faces appeared to swell out around us, and lights flashed everywhere.

We went into the big reception hall, crowded with people, and all turned towards David as he walked in and more camera lights flashed, and more faces swelled with smiles of: look at me, look at me.

The Lord Mayor, with a golden chain about his shoulders, his wife with a smaller golden chain about her shoulders standing stiffly next to him, gave a little speech. David presented him with an etching of flowers and the Mayor said it would be auctioned off for his appeal. Henry, who had wandered in and come to stand beside me, said, peeling an orange, 'I don't think he'll win his appeal,' and Henry left.

I wondered what fantasy David is realizing for the English to make him so spectacularly popular, with bleached hair and unabashedly gay, a painter of blue swimming pools, solitary beach umbrellas casting their shadows on the sand, young Californian men in showers – images that have nothing to do with England.

David introduced me to his father, a short man, hair combed very flat, with a checkered waistcoat and a bow tie with paper polka dots of phosphorescent green and red which David said his father had cut out and stuck to the bow tie. There was a lot of dry glue around the polka dots. He was wearing a hearing aid and could hardly make out what I said, but he responded with a generalized but enthusiastic expression.

Nikos was going from person to person, talking, laughing, animated, spirited.

I ate some sticks of celery from a long buffet of food and went out to find Henry. I saw him, in the park outside, sitting on a bench turned towards a young man with long hair sitting on another bench. I hesitated. Henry turned towards me, motioned me over, and I sat beside him. I said, 'I don't want to break up anything.' 'No,' he said, 'let's talk. It's so nice to get to know you and Nikos. That's more important. And what could I do with him now?' I sat with Henry on the bench, in sunlight, while about us gardeners were digging up parterres. Henry talked about David, whom he has known for fifteen years. He said, 'David makes a strong, clear distinction between popular success, which he has, and real success, which is to paint as well as Picasso and Matisse, and that he hasn't got, and he knows it. He's just beginning.'

He said he had been given this advice by a self-made American multi-millionaire: 'Start living like a millionaire, because the style demands the money to keep it up. And the first thing in the morning, always the first thing in the morning, do what you most hate doing that day, get it done, and the rest of the day is free.'

He told me stories about New York painters and writers, and, from time to time, he'd look around to see if the boy was still there. As Henry looked at him the boy rose from the bench and walked behind us and up the steps to the museum from which Henry and I, turning round to follow him, saw he looked down at us.

I said, 'I think I'll leave you to your adventure.'

He said, 'If I'm not back at the reception in ten minutes, call the police.'

I went back to the reception. There were fewer people. David was signing copies of the book. Nikos was being interviewed. I looked at the pictures. A short while later, Henry came in with the boy, gave him a glass of sherry, and talked with him. The boy left and Henry came to me and said, 'He's coming to London, where he's never been. I'm really shaken.'

Before catching the train, we went to David's parents' house for tea. David showed us about the house, he with great amusement, and off the bedroom a storeroom with his father's belongings (boxes of elastic bands, paperclips, batteries, photographs, magazines for vegetarians, every box labeled), then out into the back garden with a clothes line across it. We had our tea in the sitting room, where there was a large television set with a large armchair before the television, where one of David's uncles sat, his back to the rest of us, as Mrs Hockney passed around cucumber sandwiches followed by an aunt who with a teapot was refilling cups. She asked Henry if he would like more, and he said, 'Yes, half a cup,' and she asked, 'The bottom half?' She asked Nikos if he would like more, and he, too, said, 'Yes, half a cup,' and again she asked, 'The bottom half?'

David's father wasn't there. His mother said, 'He'll be going from bookshop to bookshop to find out if the book is there. You never know what he is up to. In all these years, I haven't really got used to it.'

The uncle, sitting with his back to us, turned his head a little and said, 'And when he comes in and finds everyone's gone, he'll say, "Oh, they should've waited, I wanted to talk to them."'

David's mother said, 'I wish we had two television sets so I could watch David on the television tonight. Kenneth will be taking photographs of David on the television, and, what with the flashes, I won't see a thing.'

David's brother Paul, who looks as if he was once squashed and has remained squashed, said, 'Well, I've got to be getting you to the station for your train.'

In the train compartment, Henry again lifted the armrest of the banquette, took off his shoes, placed the blindfold over his eyes, lay back and fell asleep.

David and Nikos and I talked about figurative and abstract art.

I said, 'David, now be absolutely honest: once a year, doesn't a flash of anxiety pass through you that all the people who say that figurative art is dead, as those who say the novel is dead, are right?' He paused then said, 'Once a year, for half a second.'

In the evening to Kitaj's house to watch the BBC programme on David. It was odd to be in the room with David and at the same time watching him on the television.

How can I get everything in when there is so much to get in, all of it revolving about me in complicated ways that I am sure has some order in connections, but all of which connections have to be made to get everything in? I have to believe that somehow the connections will be made beyond my own ability to make them, somewhere out in the world, or out in some world, in which world everything *is* connected and what I write in here refers to that world and takes on at least some of the order of that world.

Always, always, I have the sense that order is not in me, because in me are disordered thoughts and feelings, but that order is outside me, an order of thinking and feeling in the world that does hold the world together.

And, yes, there is some order in the world of friends that I live in that holds this world together.

Kitaj and Sandra left Nikos and me off on the way to their house, Nikos on the way saying, over and over, 'It was lovely, it was really lovely, the whole day and night really really lovely.' I was reassured by his spirit.

As soon as we got into the flat, the spirit fell away from him.

He said, 'The flat is a mess.'

I said, 'Why is it you are so bright with other people, and with me you go dark?'

He said, 'I don't do that with other people, I don't. Other people don't like me. No one likes me.'

'That's totally absurd. You know it's absurd, and I'm not going to indulge you in the absurdity.'

I wasn't harsh, but firm, and I thought: if he is depressed he will show me, the person closest to me, his depression, and I am with him to help him deal with his depression.

I said, 'You're tired. Come to bed.'

He said, 'You don't like me either. I know that.'

'Come to bed,' I said.

He fell asleep immediately.

The next morning, *I* felt depressed, depressed with worry about him. It surprised me suddenly to become aware that I was not in myself depressed with worry about myself, and that I had not been depressed in a long while, not depressed as I had been when I first met Nikos. On the way to Covent Garden Opera House where Thames & Hudson were to give a publication party for the book in the Crush Bar, I wondered if Nikos was becoming what I once had been: helplessly, hopelessly, morbidly depressed.

He cured me. There was no question of that, and he cured me by loving me. No analyzing my inner world would have brought me out of that world into the outer world with him as Nikos' love for me did. Whatever the dark englobing inner reasons for my depression had been, the reasons were still there in me, but they had been diminished, superseded by an outer bright globe, and I lived in that outer bright globe with Nikos.

But I all too often was drawn back into that dark inner globe. Had I made Nikos think that he had not, after all, brought me out of it into the bright outer? Oh yes, I had given him reason to think that his love for me wasn't enough to hold me in the brightness, reason to think that I was always, fatalistically, drawn back into the dark; and, too, reason to think that if I had truly reciprocated his love by loving him I would myself be held in the brightness with him, but, evidently, I didn't love him enough.

These were shocking thoughts.

I thought: Nikos is my love and I am his love, and that's everything.

I met David in the foyer of the Opera House, and when we kissed a flash of a camera meant our kiss was photographed.

We climbed the carpeted stairs to the Crush Bar, where, in the crowd, I greeted Kasmin, Bruce Chatwin, Keith Milow, Lawrence Gowing, Germaine Greer, the artists Patrick Procktor, Howard and Julia Hodgkin, Joe and Jos Tilson, Dick and Betsy Smith, Stephen and Stevie and Scarlett Buckley, Celia and Ossie Clark, and on and on, and in the midst was Nikos, introducing people to one another with animation. He appeared very happy.

People milled around David. I heard a young Indian with a Dutch cut and many gold and rhinestone pins on his red shirt ask, 'What's it like to be famous?' and I went to David with the idea of rescuing him and grabbed his arm to pull him away and said to the Indian, 'You've got the wrong person, *he's* not famous.' David laughed.

Sylvia Guirey and I went out and up to a landing above the Crush Bar from where we looked down at the tops of heads of people below, many of them friends.

I went down to Nikos and told him I would leave with Sylvia. It was raining. We took a taxi to her house. We talked about people at the party. Then we talked about Nikos. I said, 'Nikos thinks that no one likes him.' She said, in her nasal voice, 'That's crazy. I don't know of one person who doesn't love Nikos, doesn't think he's brilliant.' 'I'm sure,' I said, 'but he doesn't think so.'

Nikos was at home when I got back. He said the reviews of the book have been terrific.

I said, 'After this evening, we will do nothing social. You're going to rest this weekend. You're in a manic state excited all day

with others and in the evening with me you crash. You have got
to rest.'

'Yes, all right,' he said.

We had a simple meal. We slept in Saturday morning and Sunday
morning, too.

Reviews of *That's the Way I See It* continue to be fantastic.

The review in the *Times Literary Supplement* praised the editing
as masterly, the book possibly a classic.

This simple-minded idea occurs to me: that Nikos now feels he
has accomplished something in the world.

He has been entirely loving.

David and Nikos in Bradford

Having received a letter from Bryan, I rang Stephen and he asked me to read it over the telephone. Then we discussed his relationship with Bryan, who has now moved to California, to U.C.L.A., to concentrate on ornithology. Stephen said he sees that Bryan will outgrow their relationship to become his own person but that is as Stephen hopes for him.

Shortly after we hung up Natasha rang. She said, 'I've been trying to ring you for hours! Who were you speaking to?'

I said, 'Nikos.'

She asked me if I would like to have lunch with her at the Royal Academy, and though I was working on my novel I thought: she must have wondered who Stephen was talking to when he was talking with me, and suspecting it was me she rang and found I was talking for as long a time as he was, and had her suspicion confirmed.

During lunch, I said, 'Do you think it's possible to be completely truthful to friends?' She studied me. I said, 'I don't think one can. One can only hope not to hurt one's friends.' 'Yes,' she said. I said, 'You're very Christian, aren't you?' She said, 'I believe in Christian morality.'

———

In the morning I went to Philip's studio with keys he had express posted to me to open it and watch over the movers packing up and moving out all his belongings – desk, chairs, books, papers, old pairs of shoes and ties and bathrobe and slippers. I helped some, but mostly stood at the window, the inside shutters pulled back, and looked out at the wide back garden in the cold late-autumn sunlight.

The movers couldn't get the large desk out of the room. They tried it one way, then another, each time catching a leg against the doorjamb. I thought I could have told them how to get it out, but left that to them. They discussed the possibilities. In the end, they unscrewed the legs. One mover had a tiny diamond stud in his earlobe.

Philip had told me to keep his typewriter.

I kept his wastepaper basket.

———————

In David's studio, Stephen and Lizzie and Nikos and me, listening to David talk. Natasha was in the South of France.

There was a pile of queer pornographic magazines on the floor beside Nikos' chair. Nikos picked up a magazine, flipped through it, and dropped it. David asked, 'Do you really want to see a good one?' Laughing, Nikos said, 'Yes.' David went up to his bedroom, came down, handed the magazine to Nikos and to me a stack of Polaroid photographs David had taken of a boy lying naked in a bath. Stephen and Lizzie sat in silence. I was embarrassed to be glancing at the photographs in front of father and daughter, and, clearly, so was Nikos, as he flipped through it rapidly, and I thought he had said yes to seeing the magazine in case David thought him disapproving of him. Stephen said, 'We've got to be going,' and father and daughter left.

Nikos and I stayed on with David to talk, of course, about figurative and abstract art, from time to time looking through pornographic magazines taken from the floor.

I asked David if he ever worried about money, and he said not even when he was poor, as he always knew there would be more.

But there was now attention of all three on the magazine David had given to Nikos: a young instructor at a military academy in a classroom of young students in West Point uniforms, the instructor at a blackboard and the class attentive to him, and many pages later the instructor and the students all have elaborate sex in the class-room, the instructor with some on his desk.

David said he wanted to give Nikos a painting, but Nikos, who does not like receiving gifts, blushed and said, 'Oh no, David,' and I said, 'I'll say yes for him.'

The next morning I rang Stephen. I said, 'I want you to know we were embarrassed by those pornographic magazines yesterday at tea with David.' Stephen said, 'I was a little annoyed, but then I kept thinking why should Nikos and David look at them? What would Christopher have felt, I wonder?'

———

Philip is very happy he decided to return to live in New York. He said he reads statements about him in the papers: Roth left England because of English anti-Semitism. He laughed.

He asked for his typewriter back.

Nikos and I had dinner with him and Claire. Ten minutes with him made me realize how much I had missed him – though, curiously, I had had the feeling, driving with Nikos to Fulham, that I didn't want to see Philip, as if he demands too much of me, more than I can give.

With a glass of wine, I wandered about the sitting room, listening to Nikos and Claire talk and laugh. Philip was upstairs. I was a little anxious. Philip came down, we embraced warmly, he stood back from me and looked at the top of my head and said, 'Oh, the baldness is extending. I offered to send you to a clinic. You wouldn't do it.' He is more bald than the last time I saw him, his nose appears larger, his eyebrows thick and wild behind the gold rims of his glasses, and the hair at the back of his neck is thick and curly, and childlike. He appears thin except for a little belly bulge.

For the three hours or so Nikos and I were there, Philip kept us, and Claire too, laughing, and, once again, I felt my admiration for his originality and wit, his charm, his intelligence, his energy.

He was talking about a writer whom everyone at the table derided: a real phony. Philip said, 'His writing is totally self-conscious.'

I said, 'You once told me never to use that word. Why should you have the privilege of using it and not I?'

He looked at me in the way a stand-up comedian will look at his straight man, expressing amazement at my stupidity. 'So you object, do you? You, the prince of self-consciousness, are so possessive of your realm you object to an outsider even repeating one of your sacred terms.'

He has bought an apartment in Manhattan, on the West Side.

I said, self-consciously, that I must go back to the States and spend some time there. He said, 'I pass groups of people in the street, all over Manhattan, every block, Blacks, Puerto Ricans, Asians, and as I pass them I hear them asking one another, "Where is Plotnik?"'

On the way home, talking about it with Nikos, I realized that I hadn't wanted to see Philip because he has returned to live in America and I have stayed in England.

Natasha, over the telephone, asking me to have tea with her and Granny, which I couldn't do, as an old friend was counting on me: 'No one cares. My mother is dying. Everyone is so bloody awful.' She was weeping. 'I'm not saying you should care, you're not family.' I said I would come in the evening. 'No,' she said, 'don't come. And I shouldn't be talking to you, it only makes matters worse. I was very upset to hear from Matthew and Maro that you had been talking about me to them. I don't want people talking about Chandler and me.' I became angry but simply listened. She said, still weeping, 'I'll hang up and pull myself together. I can't let Granny see me like this.' I felt awful. I rang the old friend with whom I was to have tea to say that I should stay at home in case Natasha rang and needed me, and she was angry at me, said I was only feeling guilty towards Natasha because of the guilt I feel towards my mother, and I should realize that. She went on to complain about the workmen in her house, and said she was too tired to go on talking. I thought: fuck her, after the hours and hours I've listened to her go on and on and on about her depression, she turns me back on myself by telling me I feel guilty about my mother!

I had to struggle to put the whole thing out of my mind.

Natasha rang to apologize.
I will not feel guilty!

———————

I found this letter from Nikos on my desk:

Αγάπη μου,
    Please don't try to suppress my complaining. As I see it, it is
necessary. It is a relatively harmless escape-valve for my neuroses,
frustrations, etc. I know it is boring and that it may seem intoler-
able. But if you could only see that it is not directed against you
and that, therefore, you don't have to defend yourself against it. Of
course it may appear that it has to do with you because you become
the focus of it, and relatively tolerant of it. You see, the neckties hung
the wrong way, the slippers in my way, the dishes left in the kitchen
sink, the dust, are only concrete excuses for my complaining. And
I feel that, well, these are such trivial things, which obviously take
on such magnitude in my mind, why couldn't I simply eliminate
them? Then I think that they become indicative of a basic excuse
for my 'big' reasons for complaining, triggered off by the trivialities.
Do you understand? This is how the trivialities assume gigantic
proportions. I hope you can see what I'm trying to say, because it
is important you should understand these mechanisms before they
do serious damage. Now, to be serious about the 'big' underlying
reasons for my complaining: I do feel I use them and I can't help it.
And this is why I started analysis. Didn't you notice that during
the two years of analysis the complaints had reduced? Each daily
analytical session usually dissipated them. Now that I haven't got
that outlet the complaints have returned, perhaps with an added
vengeance. What are they? I feel that, except for you, I have failed
to fulfil virtually all my other expectations in my life! Maybe these
expectations were unreasonable or unrealistic to begin with, maybe
they were mere fantasies. Anyway, the way I feel is this: I have
reached middle age and where am I? In a job I hate, in which I

feel trapped (but would I hate any job, as I always have, any work a surface which hides an even more basic discontentment?) and from which I have to escape or run away. My creative ambitions, i.e. my poetry, are deeply frustrated, as I find no impulse to go on, except to support you in your impulse to be creative. If your books had had no responses, as my books of poems, except for two idiotic reviews, and were bought by twenty people, wouldn't you feel as I do? So, naturally, I have to ask all sorts of questions about my poetry to which I cannot give any answers. Is it any good, is it worth it, might I be deceiving myself, will I be able to carry on never the less, etc.? Finally, I feel that my attempt, through analysis, to untangle these tangles, failed, or I failed it as, finding a convenient excuse in the analyst leaving, I abandoned it, really. And as far as I am concerned or my feelings are concerned, they constitute personal 'tragedies': in my job I am resentful, isolated and inactive, and I can't wait to get out of it and come home; in my poetry I am also resentful, isolated and always on the verge of being inactive; in my 'psyche' I am resentful, entirely isolated and totally inactive. So, the neckties, the slippers, the dishes, the dust, etc., etc., are nothing, but they are the little daily events that seem to provide temporary answers to the unreasonable question which is a constant hum behind my entire daily life: what shall I do, what shall I do? And because you are the sole exception to all this and are constant, I am hoping that you'd understand and be tolerant — as you most often are considerate — and that you'd also be willing to listen to my complaints and strong enough to allow me to use you for the role of someone who would help, which is the greatest possible help you can give to me.

I'm sorry that this has gone on at such length, but I feel desperately eager that you should be able to see clearly the true proportions of this rather than letting it turn, inside you, into increasingly defensive resentment towards me, who loves you as I have never loved anyone else in all my life.

Natasha is very vivid when she describes a person, a place, a situation, visually vivid, and she is extraordinarily articulate.

About her mother, she said she is grateful she retains a last, loving image. She described herself sitting in her mother's bedroom as her mother, very very near death, slept, and Natasha looked out of the window to the back garden where a pear tree was in bright, white blossom.

I said that seemed to be a Russian image.

'Do you think so? I suppose I am in ways Russian, from my mother.'

She talked about Stephen's homosexuality.

'You see,' she said, 'Stephen basically hates women.'

And she said this without a trace of rancour.

Leaning close to me, she said that she had, years before, given up all personal ambition, and that she feels much better since. 'You know that passage in the Bible about giving up everything to gain your soul? Well, it's true.'

Again, this was said without any bitterness, but as a statement of fact.

She talked about her relationship with Stephen.

I said, 'You've been hurt by him.'

'Oh yes,' she said, 'I have.'

We talked about relationships, which I said I accept as being basically impossible. She laughed.

'Really,' I said, 'Stephen is wicked.'

She frowned. 'Wicked? No, Stephen isn't. Stephen is an innocent, really.'

I said, 'He's wicked in a way I've always wanted to talk to you about. Whenever he sees Nikos and me, he says he has to keep our meetings a secret from you, but he also wants you to know about the meetings. It's as if he wouldn't enjoy seeing us without feeling he's hurt you.'

She laughed. 'You mean,' she said, 'like Bryan.'

I thought she would never have referred to him.

'Yes,' I said.

But I didn't want to talk to her about Bryan, and for a while during our lunch felt awkward and guilty.

She let it go.

We talked about Lizzie. She said how happy she is that Stephen and Lizzie have such a close relationship. 'He didn't want a daughter. When, before she was born, we were trying to think of a name, he wouldn't even consider a girl's name. And when she was born and he visited me in hospital, he came with a male friend, and they talked to each other across the bed and never to me as I held Lizzie. But it wasn't long before he fell in love with her as with no one else in his life, I believe, and still does love her.'

When I asked her if she would have another coffee, she surprised me a little by saying she would. I'd thought she'd accepted to come to lunch with me in the spirit with which I'd asked her: as if it were a duty.

She said, 'I don't know if I should be telling you all this.'

'Because you're worried I'll write it down?'

'When do you keep your diary?'

I told her: as soon as possible after an event, and I try simply to describe. She appeared to accept this as a matter of fact she would not oppose, but would allow.

She said, 'I used to keep a diary. I should resume it. It was all about my thoughts and feelings. If I started again, I'd try simply to describe what happens.'

For some reason, this brought tears to my eyes.

Making out the cheque to pay I suddenly couldn't remember how to spell my name, and asked Natasha, who spelled it out for me.

I walked with her to a bus stop and waited with her until she got on, hopping onto the platform and holding onto the post and turning back to smile at me, like a girl.

Nikos is in Athens.

London

Back from Athens, as Nikos unpacked – a bag of pistachios, fascomilo tea, a rug, a bottle of ouzo, a facsimile edition of Cavafy's handwritten poems, a fur hat, four pairs of straw slippers – we kept interrupting the unpacking to kiss, then we kept interrupting our talk to kiss, and then we interrupted everything to undress and get into bed and make love. We made love as if with all the sense of discovery of the first time.

In Athens, he had given his poems, many of which he had translated from English into Greek, to Yannis Ritsos, with whom he spent an evening. The next morning at 9:00 Ritsos rang him, very very enthusiastic, saying that he had been sure the poems were going to be intelligent, but that he hadn't at all been prepared to find them extraordinary. He went on and on, and Nikos, always embarrassed by compliments, kept saying, 'Thank you, thank you,' and Ritsos kept saying, 'No, I thank you!' He said he would have been proud to have written 'Pure Reason', which he thought the best – so intelligent and so passionate – and he also said, 'Now, I have very high expectations and you must not disappoint me.' The morning before he had to return to London, Nikos went to collect the poems, but Ritsos, with a bad flu, wouldn't let him into his bedroom, but passed the poems to Nikos through the door ajar, Nikos standing outside for half an hour while Ritsos repeated, over and over, how extraordinary the poems are. This thrilled me to hear.

Providence

My mother is in hospital. She said she wanted to see each of her sons, each in turn, the seven of us: Robert, Donald, Raymond, Roland, René, me, Lenard.

I waited outside the hospital room with my younger brother Lenard while, inside, my elder brother Roland was with our mother.

Weak as she might have been, our mother's dictate to all her sons was that there must never, ever be dissension among us, that we must always think the best of one another, that we must always and forever love one another.

We have abided by that dictate.

My brother Roland came out of the hospital room weeping. He said, 'Momma wants to see you next.'

She was sitting up, propped up by pillows, and she said nothing but looked at me. I sat next to the bed.

With a tone I think I had never ever heard her use, she said, 'I'm telling each one of you what I think.'

'Yes,' I said.

She said, 'I know you tried to help me, that summer at the lake house when I was feeling that no one could help me, when we sat on the glider on the porch and you listened to me talk, but you must have known you couldn't help me and so you left.'

Again, I said, 'Yes.'

She said, 'I know that you are a homosexual, living with that Greek in London.'

I lowered my head and after a silence went out and told my brother Lenard she wanted to see him now, on his own.

London

Should I force myself to write in here when I don't want to?

Nikos met me at the airport. Whenever we've been separated for any time from each other, I feel that when I see him I wonder what he has been doing in what seems to me a foreign country, because everything I had known about him appears – I can't get it, I can't get the feeling – appears no longer to have to do with him. Before seeing him, I imagine him fatter, thinner, older looking, younger looking, and all because of what he was doing while alone and in his own foreign country. No, that's not it. I'm impatient and want to get it down quickly, but I want it to be accurate. He looks, when I see him after a long separation, as if he has secrets, as if his very body has become a secret to me, and I'm both made anxious and excited by the secrets, which I know he will reveal to me at home, and which – as he goes through his agenda and tells me, 'Monday evening, dinner with John and James' – I both want to hear and not want to hear, and which when revealed as dinners with friends or plays or concerts or openings of galleries, relieve me of anxiety, but which when completely revealed as those dinners or plays or concerts or openings disappoint my excitement. We took a taxi from the airport, and in the taxi the secrets were slowly revealed – 'dinner with Anne Wollheim, a concert performance of *Pelléas et Mélisande* at the Proms' – and I felt both relieved and a little disappointed, except that I knew the big secret held in reserve hadn't been revealed – the one big secret in reserve that vibrates like some big planet at a distance from us, which we can't locate yet, which is in darkness but which is slowly drawing us to it till we see it, and which we're both frightened of.

He asked me about my mother, and I said I would tell him another time, some far-off other time, because I was back with him, and that was now.

Back home, we went into our bedroom. I undressed and got into bed and watched him undress. I looked about the bedroom, at the pictures, the books in the bookshelf, and out of the window to the trees in the park, everything familiar, and I thought: this really is my home.

I raised my arms to him as he got into bed and asked, 'Did you make love with anyone while I was away?'

He said, in a kind of self-reprimanding way, 'Yes.'

I lowered my arms. 'Who?'

He didn't say.

'Who?' I asked again.

He again spoke in a self-reprimanding way. 'With Paul.'

'What happened?'

'He telephoned one morning and I asked him over.'

'Oh,' I said.

'Do you mind?'

I said, 'I don't know,' trying to give him the impression that I did mind when, in fact, I didn't mind; the way I had dropped my arms, the way I now looked away from him, my tone of voice were, I was aware, pretence, because I wanted him to think he had hurt me, whereas I knew I didn't care, and wasn't even excited, as I'd been in the past, by jealousy. The absence of jealousy – and, emphatically, exciting jealousy – was a bewildering hollow in my feelings, and I wondered why, and was happy that I wasn't jealous. Nikos got into bed. We made love.

What do I mean by passionate love making? I mean that a trance takes us over, so that even kisses seem to be inspired, not by what we feel for each other, but what that trance we are in feels for us, and we are within the sphere of that trance, and within everything, everything, everything, every touch, becomes amazing. The most passionate moments are when we hold each other and are still, and in the stillness as if waiting for the sphere of the trance to inspire in each other what we have never yet done in making love, as if there is love making beyond love making, and the very possibility of it is unbearable and we must hold ourselves still against the unbearable.

He asked, 'Do you mind about Paul?'

I kissed him and said, 'No, I don't.'

We settled more deeply to fall asleep, and for a moment I had the vision of us, seen from above, of two beautiful young men who, after having made love in which everything was resolved, were falling asleep together.

But though I sensed him fall asleep I myself became more and more awake. I knew I wouldn't be able to fall asleep. I said, 'I can't sleep.'

Nikos woke. He said, 'Go to sleep now, please, please.'

I said, 'I can't.'

'Then you mind,' he said.

'No, I don't,' I said, because I wanted him to think I didn't care at all about Paul, but I did care, and I felt the rusty machine of jealousy get into gear.

He said, 'I didn't do it to hurt you. I don't love Paul. He may love me, but how can you object to someone loving me and my at least acknowledging that love by having tender sex with him, which was all he wanted? The sex is not important. You know that.'

'Yes, I know.'

'It's so unimportant that I wouldn't even give it the importance of making love with him, as unimportant as *that* was to me.'

'Yes, I know.'

He said, 'No one loves you more than I do.'

I held him and said, 'Yes, I know.'

'Please,' he said.

'If this was the first time with Paul,' I said, 'I would finally have accepted it, but it wasn't the first time.'

'Will you believe me that I did it for his sake, because he does love me?'

'I believe you, and I should be touched. But I can't help it – the machine has started up grinding in me and I can't stop it.'

'You can,' he said.

'I want to,' I said.

I thought: don't think of yourself, think of him.

Nikos said, 'I've told the solicitor that I want to make a will, so that, if I die, you'll get the flat for you to sell as you would like, to move wherever you would like.'

The next day, Sunday, I said, 'I'll treat this as a sickness. I've got to get over it. I will get over it, this sick neurosis.'

We had our usual Sunday morning, breakfast and the newspaper, then a walk, and lunch, and because we had not slept well we had our nap together early.

All this was two weeks ago, during which I have got over it all. I worked on *The Woods*.

———

When I got home from an evening with friends, I found Nikos asleep in his study, my novel, *The Woods*, on the floor beside the sofa. He had been reading it though I knew he was very tired. I felt I owed him everything. He woke. He said he had read a chapter and a half. He thought it the best writing I have done, but in setting and characters rather thin.

I keep thinking, 'Maybe he'll like it more the more he reads into it.'

I said, 'I want the writing to be everything, want it to be the sustaining interest in the book, more than the setting and the characters. I want the writing to be like a suspended, bright plane, with a low-level but palpable vibration.'

He said, 'It is. It's Mozartian.'

'Well, that's just what I wanted.'

He said, 'You want to do everything,' and he smiled and brushed my hair from my forehead.

New York

I am staying with Mark in the Bank.

I went to see Jennifer. She said, 'I want you to meet my new boyfriend. His name is David. I think he looks like you. He's like you in many ways, except that he lives in New York and is straight.'

(When, later, I saw Öçi briefly and told him this, he said, 'Wouldn't she have been unlucky if he lived in London and was gay?')

In her loft, we lay on her large bed. When I told her about my novel *The Family* being nominated for the National Book Awards, my reason for being in New York, she said, 'I'm so jealous.' I said, 'Well, I've been jealous of you for long enough, selling paintings at $50,000. And anyway I won't win.' This seemed to reassure her. She said, 'You were mad at me when I was in London. Why?' 'I don't know,' I said. 'But you did come to see me off. I was very moved by that.' 'I wanted to make a gesture,' I said. She said, 'I think we have a pretty intense relationship, don't you?' 'Except now I'm very tired,' I said. I yawned. She yawned. We got under the covers of the bed. I held her in my arms and while she slept I dozed. The telephone woke her with a start, so her body jolted, and my reaction was to hold her more tightly as if she had been frightened and I wanted to comfort her.

It is still true: after Nikos she is the only person with whom I feel totally free.

She said, 'You're a real drip,' and I said, laughing, 'Yes, I know.'

She had a small drinks party for me, old friends all friendly with one another; and where I met David, and I thought he was very attractive, and was jealous that Jennifer had him, as if I could have.

She asked me, 'Do you think he's like you?' 'I hope so,' I said, 'because he's very attractive.' 'He's a bit hunkier than you are,' she said. 'But I have a nicer smile,' I said. 'Yes,' she said, 'you do.' 'What does he do?' I asked. 'He's an artist, does big drawings, but I haven't seen any of them.'

David came to us. Jennifer said to him, 'David said that he does think you look alike somehow, like you told me that you and David somehow look alike.' David said, 'I think we should change the subject.'

They talked about their trip to Granada, where a revolution occurred the day they arrived.

I left after Jan and Yasuo and Michael. Jennifer and David hadn't seen each other in some days, and I thought they would want to make love.

Jennifer showed me to the elevator. She asked, 'Are you jealous?' I rested my head on her shoulder then lifted it and said, 'No, I don't think I'm jealous.' 'You like him?' she asked. 'Yes,' I said, 'I do.' She said, 'You know, I like you both so much.' I kissed her and went down the elevator to Lafayette Street; I couldn't find a taxi, so walked through SoHo to the Bank, for which I had a key, and I went to bed, as Mark was out.

In the morning, I rang Jennifer. We talked about David. She wondered if she should have a child by him. I said, 'I'm not sure that having a child can be so intentional. A baby simply happens, I think, and then you accommodate yourself to it.' 'Yeah,' she said, then, after a pause, 'Don't tell David, but when we make love I'm going to leave my diaphragm out.' I said I wouldn't tell him.

———

At lunch with David Rieff at a Jewish restaurant on the West Side. I asked him if he thinks the New Yorkers gossip more than the Londoners. 'Yes,' he said, 'but in London the gossip is about sex and in New York the gossip is about professions, for sex, no matter how complicated, can be taken for granted, and professions can't.'

Once again in New York where I have flunked out.

I wonder if I can sort out in here what has happened – or I wonder if I can account for what has happened, never mind what I think and feel.

I have slept in late, very tired. In the afternoon I'll go to the ceremony and cocktail party for the National Book Award won, in fiction, by Tim O'Brien. I should be happy that *The Family* was nominated, I should be happy for the attention the novel has got, most recently in a full-page review in the *Village Voice*. For Farrar, Straus & Giroux, *The Family* is the one novel each person has in him, and to be a writer means having many novels in one, which, apparently, I do not have.

Yesterday, invited by Bob Giroux to lunch, I was half an hour early. I sat in the lobby of the Players Club and, in one of Nikos' old suits, sweated. Bob G. came in with David Rieff. They were very friendly. We talked for a long while about travelling in Greece. Then Bob and David talked about my novel *The Woods*. I had the impression that David presumed the position of an editor. Nothing that was said was concrete: they thought it was the beginning of a book, the first paragraph of a longer book, perhaps. They said they didn't want to lose me as a writer. Bob Giroux more than implied that the publishing house would help me financially if I would agree to work on the book. I said I would take the book back and over the summer take a long, hard look at it, then decide what to do. David said I should consider my career. I said I couldn't consider my career, but only the vision I had, which I must try to realize in whatever way I could. Bob said – and this was the only definite advice he gave me – 'As a friend more than as a publisher, I'll tell you this: don't publish this book.' But I was still not sure if he was turning the book down or if he was asking me to work on it as a condition of his publishing it. They were extremely friendly.

I walked to the office with them. Bob asked me if I wanted to see Roger Straus and I said yes. Roger hugged me and said, 'We're giving you a hard time.' I said, 'I think I'm on my two feet.' I picked up the typescript. David said he had to go out to the bank, and I left with him. He said he was sorry that the business had exploded in my face, and reiterated that F.S.G. didn't want to lose me, and made me feel, vaguely, that I was still part of the publishing house.

I rang my agent Georges Borchardt to ask if I could see him. He had to give me the address three times because I kept forgetting it; when I got up to the East 50s, I had to ring him again, as, again, I had forgotten the address.

I gave him the typescript and he said, 'Good, now I'm going to send it to—' and I forgot to whom he said he would send it, and I felt as though Georges was wrenching me out of F.S.G. where I still had the impression of being a resident. I said I wanted to work more on the book. He narrowed his eyes at me from behind his desk and said, 'There's no book that can't be improved upon by being worked on; on the other hand, working on a book can destroy it. What do you want to do with it?' I said, 'I want to write another book, which I in fact have been working on, called *The Country*.' 'If it's a definite thing you have in mind, fine,' he said. I said, 'F.S.G. don't seem to have turned the book down.' 'Neither have they made an offer,' Georges said coldly; 'Bob Giroux has not yet telephoned me, though I telephoned him and left a message when I couldn't get through.' I said, 'They seem not to want to let me go. David Rieff said—' Georges cut me off with, 'David Rieff has no power whatsoever there. What did Bob say?' 'I'm not sure,' I said. 'I think he offered to help me financially.' Georges set his jaw and simply looked at me. I said, 'I feel rather awful, Georges.' He pursed his thin lips, then said, 'My plan is to send the type-script to—' and again I immediately forgot whom he intended to send it to.

In the subway, I thought that when I was back at Mark's I would ring Bob to ask him if F.S.G. would make a definite commitment or not. I did ring him and said I trusted him to keep what I was asking confidential, as this was what Georges was meant to do. He said (and I'm sure of this), 'If you are willing to work on the book, we'll make a contract.' I said I would ring Georges and tell him, and told Georges that Bob had rung me to tell me who had won the National Book Award and to propose a contract. Georges was surprised. 'Why didn't he call me?' he asked. 'I don't know,' I said. 'All right,' Georges said, 'I'll call him.'

Nikos rang me. He sounded cheerful. I told him what had happened. He said, 'I don't think you need to be depressed. I think it'll be all right. The thing is to do what Georges says.' I said, 'Georges is very angry at F.S.G.' 'He should be,' Nikos said.

That evening I went with Mark to a party given by Books & Co. for the publication of Alison Lurie's latest novel. She was, I knew, a judge for the National Book Award. As she approached me she held out her arms to me to embrace me and kiss me. She said, 'I love your book. When I proposed it, the other judges knew it and said, "Yes, sure, of course."' I said, 'I knew you must have proposed it.'

Mark and I went to dinner in a French restaurant.

In the morning, I rang Georges, who had spoken to Bob, who, however friendly, did not come up with the offer of a contract.

I am now without a publisher.

I sat at the back of the National Book Award presentation at Carnegie Hall. A strange sensation passed throughout me when I heard my name read out as a nominee, and then I felt calm, and then I felt bored. There was a reception in a huge ballroom in a huge hotel a few blocks from Carnegie Hall. The ballroom was, I think, the biggest room I have ever stepped into, packed with the greatest number of people unknown to me that I had ever been among. I took a drink offered to me on a tray and I walked around. I saw Alison, went to her, and she introduced me to Tim O'Brien, whom I congratulated.

I felt I was standing before a mansion, and from time to time a cameraman photographed me before the mansion, which I knew to be a façade, behind which the mansion had collapsed.

I heard from various people, 'Congratulations on your nomination.'

'Thanks,' I said.

Mary Lee Settle, who was another judge, said to me, 'You don't have anything to worry about now, especially with the publisher you've got.'

'Yes,' I said.

I am writing this flying over the lights of New York – green lights, orange lights, white lights, and, occasionally, a red light.

Nikos, in London, is asleep.

Oh my love, my love, my love.

Paros

We go every day, in the afternoon, to a beach we call ours, just wide enough for the two of us to lie side by side between high rocks and banks of dry grey seaweed.

———

As happens here, Nikos and I keep a calm distance from each other, though we do everything together – that is, except sleep together, but that too allows us the intimacy of a mutual distance from each other. At this calm distance, I sometimes look closely at him when he is occupied with reading, and the wonder comes to me of our being together and at the same time distinct from each other so that we are each of us the distinct self each of us is. I want him to be himself, want him to realize everything there is in him to be realized, which is a world. I don't want to impose myself on him in the world of his own thoughts and feelings, but I do, and I do by making him anxious about me. If I sigh, he, anxious, asks me if anything is wrong, and I say, no, nothing is wrong, but this doesn't satisfy him, because it is in him to believe that everything is wrong until it is proven right; and I am not sure I now have it in me to prove to him that I am, in my distinct self, in my world, all right. I rely on our mutual rituals, our reading in the mornings together, our lunch together, our walk to the beach together, our sitting together in the evening on the terrace

for our *ouzakia* and watching the moon rise over Naxos, day
after day, together and yet each of us within a world. In my love
for him, I must do everything to make sure his world remains
his, and as bright as his world should be, not darkened by mine,
and this requires my sustaining all the brightness I can, however
muted it is. I try not to sigh.

I went with Nikos to the abandoned windmills outside the village
to wait with him for the taxi to take him to the port town, and I
felt that he was going far. I should have gone with him, but then it
is probably best if I am not with him, given my thoughts and feelings. Whenever we do leave each other, it is with a sense of fatality
in the separation.

Αγάπη μου,

  *Kiorios Yannis comes every evening to knock on the door for a
visit. I hear him coming, his wooden leg thumping on the paved
street, and though I want to be alone I think it best not to be, so
open the door and he comes and sits with me in the courtyard.*

  *He asked me how old I am, and when I said thirty-five, he
nodded and said there was still time but I should be padrimenos.
I said, but I am padrimenos. Really? Yes, I said, I am married.
Where is my wife? Oh, I said, in London. In London? Yes, I
have an understanding, that I come to Marpissa to write, which is
my work, which I need to be alone to do. He frowned and said he
understood, though clearly he didn't understand, but didn't want
to let on that the ways of a xenos were too foreign for him to make
sense. He smiled and, indicating with both arms the orange tree
with its one small orange, said he hoped I would have as many
children as the orange tree would bear.*

  *I don't like to be alone here, though I am alone to write, and it
is just because I am alone to write that I feel everything is going
wrong with my writing.*

I try not to identify with my writing so much that my deepest feelings and thoughts are one with it, and the rejection by a publisher seems to me the end. Without you here, the end seems so close.

That we are happy here makes my unhappiness all the more shocking to me.

I have the breakfast I had when you were here, I write, I walk to the beach along the path that we walked every day, I follow our routine, even to ouzakia on the terrace in the evening, but behind everything is that darkness.

I shouldn't be writing this to you. I tried so to keep it all away from you.

And, no, I am not going to try to analyse in personal terms why I should be so defeated, why my failing as a writer should have an effect much greater than that failure warrants, because, as you've said, there are as many, if not more, failures than successes in the life of a writer, and, also, I have your total faith in me as a writer. No, I am not going to try to analyse what is in me as David Plante that makes me react to rejection with such a sense of defeat.

I blame the darkness that came to me when I was born, that I believe I was born into, and that I can't escape.

Nikos' letter to me:

Αγάπη μου,

Back home from the office, I found your letter, and after I changed to go out again to Stef and Roxy for supper I read the letter, and I thought I couldn't see anyone, didn't want to see anyone, because I was, and I am, so upset.

I had thought you had reached a level of confidence in yourself I could rely on, and now I find you still rely on me to bolster your confidence. I can't do it any longer, I can't.

You are much stronger than I am, you know you are, and yet you presume I'm the strong one, the one who can and will always be there to sustain you in any crisis. I have done that, and did it when, so shortly after we first met, you had a crisis started by acupuncture, and I was ready to be there to sustain you all during that crisis. I did it out of love, and I did it because we had such a short time before begun to live together, and I thought you had to get over what you called that sick time in New York you left behind to come to London, and I thought I could help you get over it. You said I did help you get over it.

Now, I can't bear knowing you have lapsed back into crisis, even if for different reasons, your feeling a failure in your writing. You won't believe me that I believe in your writing, you want approbations from agents and publishers and critics, and I'm sorry you won't believe me, but I do believe in your writing. Do you want me to enter into your sense of failure and, like you, not believe, because my believing doesn't seem to be enough to counter your sense of failure?

Forgive me, αγάπη μου, but I wonder if you are simply using this rejection of your latest novel as an excuse for indulging in what you call your darkness, and I wonder, too, if you are simply using as an excuse that past time in New York to indulge in what you call your darkness, an indulgence that may be the cause of the darkness, a self-indulgence that has been in you since you were a little boy and that you like to think is some kind of spiritual affliction. I don't know, but I do feel that when you write about your darkness you are affecting a state that has no real outer reason but whose inner reason is to have your own way, wilful as you are, and the darkness comes when you don't have your own way.

This appears so evident to me, I wonder how it can't be evident to you.

You know I admire you for being so wilful, for getting your way, but don't, please, impose your wilfulness on me, as you do, by imposing on me your darkness to relieve yourself of what you can't bear but that you want me to bear for you. You can bear it; you have to bear it; you do bear it. I can't bear it.

The fact is you are confident of yourself, so much so that any rejection of you by someone else makes you react in a way all out of proportion to how you would react if you didn't think yourself so grand, didn't think your darkness so grand.

Αγάπη μου, I know it is in you, in your very wilfulness, to stand against rejection, and to have your own way in a way that confirms the grandness of life and death and love.

I have written this to you before, over and over: I need you to bring brightness into my life.

Enough of this, which it upsets me to write about, because, as you are fully aware, I hate this kind of introspection, which leads not to any understanding but only to more introspection, and you are also fully aware of what such unstructured introspection leads to.

I did go to supper with Stef and Roxy, who send you their love, as I do, αγάπη μου, as I do, αγάπη σου

I don't write much about the critical receptions of my novels in my diary, partly because I do not want to show I care that much about the receptions that I would write about them, and partly because I am more interested in other aspects of my life. But I did write this letter to Robert Giroux, which, however, I knew I would never send:

Dear Bob,

Of course I am worried about your and Roger's reaction to my novel, The Woods. *I have a horror of trying to justify my work, partly, I think, because I'm frightened I would not be able to, but mostly because I believe all justification to be false. And yet anyone has the right to ask me, as you have, 'Well, what did you intend by—?' and I should, I guess, be able to answer. To be absolutely honest with myself, I shouldn't try to answer, because I want to write in such a way that the intention can in no way be abstracted from the writing. What I want to do is to write without any obvious intention, so if a reader were to ask, 'What is it about?' he would get no answer but the novel itself. You might ask me, 'But why write without any intention? Why not satisfy the reader's desire to know what the novel is about?' Maybe because, as I do not have an analytical mind and am incapable of them, explanations seem affectations of the mind, and any one explanation an impossible conceit. To the question, 'Is your novel about growing up, about sexual awakening?' I would answer, I don't know. 'Is it about an innocent sense of beauty lost?' I don't know. 'Is it a pastoral?' I don't know. Not one meaning ever applies; because once I have a meaning, I realize the exact opposite, or any number of variations, could just as easily apply.*

I want to write in such a way that my writing goes beyond any self-conscious meaning – and yet, having written that, I want the maximum meaning. It is always, always, always in what I do not know, in what I think cannot be stated in religion, sociology, psychology, science that I'm sure the deepest meanings are; that's where the undivided spirit is, and what I want to get into my books is the presence, however weakly got, of the undivided spirit, which survives in its own sad longing the divided and distracted mind, but which becomes whole in its awareness of what is whole outside itself. And I will succeed in doing what I want to do only when I've written a book which is, all together, a moment of awareness of that.

I tried, in my previous books, and especially in a novel called Figures in Bright Air, *to write with that awareness. I realized, however, that the very intention to force the awareness was an affectation. When I wrote* The Family, *it wasn't to break from my previous, 'experimental' work, as some critics wrote; it was to try to get closer to what I wanted my writing to do, of itself. I was, I hoped, letting the awareness occur of itself, as a revelation, with no attempt on my part to make it occur. I want the revealed sense of my writing to be an ALL, to which everything that happens refers, as objects refer to the space they are in. I am very ambitious. I want people to read me, not for what I have to say, but for the pleasure, the joy – and, oh God, if I could do this, the mystery – of awareness that most makes us loving humans. The central images of* The Woods *all have to do with space, so for a while I thought of calling the novel 'The Space'. And what should occur in the space is the awareness of space as all of space.*

How can I explain this? I will never send this to you, so I'll take a liberty that you may in fact have liked: in making love to another, the awareness of another's body is greater than what the senses perceive, because the senses can only perceive parts, but the awareness is of the whole body, and that awareness is, I believe, what makes the loving in making love. Anyone who has made love is aware of that awareness, or if attentive enough is aware of it as tenderness, as compassion, as love at love's most passionate.

I am not a mystic. I am very sceptical of the mystical, because that, too, is an explanation, and I want no explanation.

But, again you may ask, as you have asked, insisting, 'What is your novel about?' I panic. I lose my vision, I blindly invent subjects which may or may not apply. You may say, 'But there are subjects in your novel; the fact that you refer to sex, to war, to parents fills your novel with associations beyond the novel, subjects that refer to the world outside in which such subjects exist.' This is a weakness in my writing: 'subjects' lay scattered over it like bits which not only are never assembled, but for which there was never a master plan. The fact is, these bits interest me, not in terms of my justifying them, but – this is difficult – in terms of the context my writing creates, but which context expands beyond my writing, which context, again, is awareness! I believe that awareness has its own master plan, which is not mine, is somewhere outside myself as universal awareness.

In The Woods *I wanted to write a gentle but moving book, a book with a narrow oscillation but a wide reverberation; I feel I have done this. Now, if your objections to the novel are specific, I know I can deal with them, and, in my enormous respect for you, I would of course consider your suggestions to overcome the objections. If, however, your objections are general, I would not be able to come to terms with them, for they would go against the very vision of the book. In either case, I trust you to say exactly what you think.*

I've communicated with Nikos, and, through him, with
Catharine Carver, whom you of course know; they are as involved
with my writing as I am, and both, having read this letter, give it
their support.

All my very best to you and to everyone one else, including of
course Roger, at F.S.G., as ever, David

I feel this: that if I had a sexual relationship with a specific woman
I would become heterosexual, for whereas my homosexuality is
a generalized sexuality in that I am attracted to fantasy men, my
heterosexuality is particular, and I am drawn to *that* woman here,
or *that* woman there. I see that in my attraction to Jennifer, who
could not be a more specific woman.

I must say that my attraction to men is such that any one of them
young and good-looking enough would be, without my knowing
anything about them, a body to fantasize having sex with.

How Nikos fits into this is for me to wonder at, for he cannot
have promiscuous sex, but has to know as an individual someone
he makes love with, and I, in making love with him, am always
making love with the individual, Nikos Stangos.

Here I am, at my desk looking out at the rain, writing this diary
when I should be writing my novel, *The Country* –

Why is it that some event in the past, which at the time I thought
of as inconsequential, can come back to me with a great sense of
consequence? When, in what seems to me long ago because at the
time I did think it inconsequential to our relationship, I found out
that Nikos had made love with someone at the publishing house
called Paul, I passed it off as inconsequential to our own love for
each other. He didn't deny that they had made love, but he insisted
that I trust him in his love for me, and the trust seemed to me to
rise above whatever jealousy I may have had. Now, it comes back
to me as of great consequence.

Comes back to me with great consequence because of what happened just yesterday –

After our having had lunch together, I was standing with Nikos in the entrance hall of Thames & Hudson when he turned away from me to someone coming down the stairs and then he immediately turned back to me as if he hadn't recognized this young man, but I knew as immediately that he had turned away because he did know this young man and that this must be Paul. We all stood still. There was nothing for Nikos to do now but introduce this Paul to me, and as I shook hands with him, as an outer show, all of my thoughts and feeling drew back within me. Paul left, and I remained standing with Nikos, who looked at me steadily until I looked away.

I knew he would not apologize, not only because he would have thought there was nothing to apologize for, but because Nikos does not apologize, ever.

I left, and alone it came to me that Nikos and Paul are lovers, and that they are keeping this from me. When Nikos came home in the evening, I was silent. He asked me why I was silent. I tried to sustain my stark silence, but couldn't, and said I was sure that he and Paul were lovers.

Nikos became angry. He insisted not, and though he was not going to regret that he and Paul had had a tender time together, there would not be another time, and he shouted, 'I am not going to deal with this. It is your problem, not mine. Now let's have our supper.'

Let this go, let it go, let it go.

Back from America where he saw Bryan, Stephen was filled with light spirits.

He said that he went to New Orleans with Bryan, and, as seems always to happen to Stephen meeting people he knows in unlikely places, Allen Ginsberg was there. Bryan, a scientist, became irritated with Ginsberg's mysticism, and later told Stephen that he could understand that meditation could be an aid to thinking, but there were other ways of thinking – such as thinking.

They stayed, Stephen said, in a motel. He suddenly looked pensive, as if wondering if he should go on, and he did open and close his lips a number of times in, as it were, preparation of what he had to dare himself to say, which made him blush even before he said it. 'Bryan said we'd better stop making love because his left ball hurt. I said, Well, in that case you must have a cup of hot tea and an aspirin.' As he told this story his face became redder and redder, and then he laughed in short bursts so his shoulders shook.

———

Nikos is reading in typescript my novel *The Country*, about the death of my father, which he said he finds very beautiful and moving. Once, as he was reading, he turned to me, his eyes filled with tears.

———

I asked Stephen if he would read through the page proofs of my novel, *The Country*. I'm not sure he took it very seriously, but he did say, 'You couldn't be a realistic writer. You are, I think, what's called a poetic writer, but you should write against the poetry and try to be as realistic as possible. The poetry will shine through, and your writing at its best will have the quality of hallucinatory realism.'

I have dedicated the novel to Stephen and Natasha.

———

The historian Steven Runciman came to supper, as usual with eggs wrapped in newspaper, a gift to Nikos for Nikos is always asking after Steven's chickens, which Nikos feeds whenever visiting Elshieshields.

Steven said he had, a few nights before, sat next to the Queen at a dinner and made her laugh so that other people at the table turned to look. He told her about a woman he knew who swallowed her jewels.

Story after story had *us* laughing.

A lot of the stories had to do with how most of the European royals and claimants to royalty are illegitimate. For example, the Dutch Queen Juliana's real father was a peasant, because the man who married her mother (Theodore Roosevelt said of her that she was the least attractive thing he had seen on tour in Europe) simply couldn't make love with her. A peasant was brought in, blindfolded, but the child died soon after birth; a second peasant, blindfolded, was brought into the palace . . .

Steven said he is, he believes, the only expert on the subject of illegitimacy among the royal families.

He thinks Nikos and I are wasting our lives living together. 'It limits your possibilities,' he said. 'If I ever thought, for a moment, of living with one other person, a moment later I thought that I might find someone better.'

He keeps his handkerchief rolled up in the sleeve of his jacket, and pulls it out often to wipe his running nose.

He said to Nikos, 'You will inherit from me a memento to your devotion to my chickens.' Then he looked at me and looked away and I knew I would not inherit anything.

He said he would quite like to visit me in Tulsa, where he has not yet been; he has been to all the other states of the Union.

Rather drunk, he left about eleven o'clock. He wanted a little walk, he said, before returning to his club, the Athenaeum.

He gave to Nikos a limerick, which he said he composed on the way to lunch with us:

> Oh, look what a marvellous man goes
> Along there. I swoon, but then bang goes
> Any dream of romance, for as he advances
> I see it is just Mr Stangos.

Nikos said, 'You can put it in your diary.'

The next day, Stephen came to lunch with me. I told him about Steven's stories and he laughed, but then he said, 'Steven Runciman is an inveterate liar. You can't believe anything he says.'

And it seems historically very unlikely that he ever did meet the last Emperor of China, one of his most renowned anecdotes, though he came so close to the possibility of the meeting that it became, for him, an historical fact, and I think of how often he has said he likes to speculate on how history would have been different if there had been small shifts in it.

There are times when I would rather have been a scientist than a novelist; I would like to be able to investigate, neurologically, the qualities of the mind which I try to investigate, so vaguely – the mysterious power of awareness.

I pray that that mystery is everywhere in what I write.

Tulsa, Oklahoma

When one of my students, male, large but slightly plump, with black, tangled hair, looked at me, I asked him his name.

'Tony Montgomery,' he said.

His hair fell almost to below his eyes, which were narrow, and his skin, smooth in its rounded plumpness, appeared lightly coated with a reddish-brown oil. He had to be Indian.

After the hour, the student nearest the door opened it onto the outside heat, which came in like another class of large, sweating, jostling students to replace the cool, quiet students leaving.

———

The house I am renting is outside of Tulsa, on a lake.

Seen from the windows of the living room, the sky over the lake is dark red, and appears so high, so wide, so deep, that a desolation comes to me which makes me think there is no reason to be here, or there or anywhere.

I opened the refrigerator in the kitchen and in its pale light looked for my supper, cold cuts and salad, which I ate at the dining table.

The sky is now black.

The house is all inward, cold vibrations; outside is the still, great heat.

———

One of my students – a plump, middle-aged woman – came to my office to talk to me about what she couldn't talk about in class. She sat on the edge of her chair and wiped the palms of her hands with tissues as she spoke. Eleven years ago one of her sons accidentally shot and killed one of her other sons. All her effort, ever since, has been to turn that evil into good. She would like her surviving son – who is sensitive, writes poetry, but who has managed, she thinks, to overcome what he did – to write about what happened; he refuses, so she has taken it on herself to write about what happened, and she would like me to help her express 'the good that has come from suffering'.

The next morning the student, Amanda, brought me what she called an outline of what she hopes will be a novel. 'It has to be written,' she said, 'it has to be.' In the evening, I read her outline. How can I tell her I doubt she knows what a novel is? And here I face a dilemma in trying to tell her what a novel is that is the dilemma I face in writing my own novels – that is, how can I tell her that in accounting for what happened to her she must not have any overriding 'moral' about it, even to concluding that 'good can come from evil'? How can I tell her that a novel isn't a moral intention, even the elevated moral that good can come from suffering? In her life, the very belief that 'good can come from evil' has saved her. To her, a novel is a moral, perhaps the greatest confirmation of a 'moral': that, after all our suffering, life is good. And it is such a moral that I myself so want to be realized in a novel.

A telephone conversation with Nikos depressed me. I asked him to ring my accountant in London, and he, with that sudden cold way he has, said, 'Please leave me out of this. I have other priorities.' I immediately became angry and told him not to ring the accountant, that I would do it from Tulsa. 'I'll do it,' he said, 'I'll do it.' I said, 'No, I don't want you to do anything for me. You take care of your priorities.' He changed his tone of voice, which he does when he tells me I hadn't really listened properly to him or I would have understood, and he said, quietly, 'I simply told you I'm very busy.' He insisted on ringing the accountant. I got over my anger, but for the rest of the day have remained depressed – the most depressed since I left him.

I don't care about the university, don't care about my students.

———

At a faculty party, I had to concentrate to say hello, to thank for drinks and food offered to me, to understand what people were saying. Sometimes I'd look around at the groups of people in the living room, which at the back opened up, with double glass doors, onto the yard, where, too, guests stood in small groups, and wonder what I was doing there.

I saw Germaine Greer standing just by the open double doors to the back yard.

I went to her and said, 'I knew we'd meet up.'

She said, 'Let's go into the yard.'

I followed her out, past the people near the doorway, to the far back of the yard where the clothes line hung from the side of the garage to a post among bushes. Germaine raised her arms to grasp the clothes line and, leaning on it, swung back and forth a little.

She was, she said, living in a converted garage in Tulsa. When I said that I have a house on a lake, she made a moue, then said, 'You would, wouldn't you?' I said, 'You make me feel I have to apologize.' She let go of the line and laughed and said, 'A very good feeling for you to have.'

I invited her to come have supper with me.

Having known Germaine in Italy, where she had a house on the other side of the mountain from the valley in which Nikos and I had a house, having been with her when she drove all in one go from Cortona to London, having been to her flat in London and she to Nikos' and my flat for dinners, that Germaine and I would one day teach at the same time at the University of Tulsa,

Oklahoma seems to me as remote a possibility as our meeting on
a distant planet.

————

Amanda came into my office to talk about the terrible incident
eleven years ago, which she wants so badly to realize as a novel.
She told me more: how she had bought her sons the rifles, used
rifles, with the warning that they be careful; how she didn't want
them to go out hunting the day they did because Tim, the one
who was killed, wasn't well; how Vaughn, the other brother, shot
Tim. A friend was with them. They were on a slope, looking into
the woods; Tim was crouching; Vaughn, standing, was carrying his
rifle over his shoulder, his finger on the trigger; he looked away;
Tim said, 'Look,' and Vaughn, turning quickly, lost balance, so his
rifle slipped from his shoulder, and because the safety catch on the
old rifle didn't work his finger triggered the rifle and it shot Tim
in the head. The friend ran for help, and when he and help came
they found Vaughn walking round and round the corpse, plead-
ing, 'Come back, come back.' When the police rang Amanda to
tell her to come to the hospital, slowly, she knew one of her sons
had been killed. She went to Vaughn, put her arms around him as
he stared out, crying, 'His eyes, his eyes,' and she said, 'Don't talk,
Vaughn, please don't talk.' Amanda's husband blamed Tim's death
on her and tried to kill her by strangling her. They divorced, after
twenty years of marriage. Vaughn married, had a child, divorced,
became an alcoholic. Amanda struggled to make a new life and
even changed her name. She has another son, and I asked about
him. 'He's gay,' she said. 'Oh,' I said, and thought: the dysfunctional
American family. Amanda said, 'I've told Vaughn he should write
it all down. I told you, he's very sensitive and writes poetry. But he
says he can't write this. He'll leave it to me to write it down.' Then
she smiled and said, 'He told me, though, that I'd have to split the
money with him if the book becomes a bestseller.' I had felt great
grief for Amanda, and, suddenly, felt disdain. I could hardly look
at her.

Later, she came back to my office and placed an envelope on my desk then silently went out, and my revulsion is such that I can't touch the envelope.

———————

On my return from the campus to the house, I found Tony was sitting under a lamp on the sofa, drinking from a can of beer. On the table before him were five more cans of beer held together with plastic rings. Tony looked at me without smiling, but frowning a little. He pulled a can of beer from a plastic ring and held it out to me. 'I bought some more beer. You were running out.'

I took the can. 'How did you know I'd be in?'

I sat beside Tony on the sofa, popped open the can and took a long swig, some of which dribbled down my chin and neck and chest. 'Where have you been since I left you?'

'Around.'

'Did you go back to Pawhuska?'

Tony simply stuck out his lower lip.

'What's it like in Pawhuska?' I asked.

'What do you mean?'

'I mean, what's your house like?'

'It's a clapboard house with a porch.'

'You live with your parents?'

'I live with an aunt and uncle.'

'Why not with your parents?'

'I prefer living with my aunt and uncle.'

'And what do they do, your aunt and uncle?'

'What do they do?' he asked.

'Does your uncle have a job?'

Tony laughed, a slight, shrugging laugh. 'My uncle have a job?'

'And your father, doesn't he have a job?'

Tony laughed more, shrugging as he did. 'No.'

'What do you all do out there?'

'What do we do?'

———————

Germaine came to supper. She said, looking about, 'You always get the nice place to live.' I said, 'That may be because I'm nice.' I'm never sure what her reaction will be to what I say, and waited. She smiled.

I don't know why – perhaps because I was feeling so much that I was nowhere in the house and her presence brought into the house the sense of our having known each other in London and, too, her having known Nikos and me in London, there where I feel I am where I should be – I asked her to live with me.

She said she would think about it, then sighed, and said, yes, all right she would.

I gave her the master bedroom with a sundeck and a view over the lake.

I have taken the back room with two single beds and no view.

Germaine comes in from the university campus in the evening, about eight o'clock, when we have the supper that I've usually prepared. She tells me about her day.

Sometimes, if she is early, we watch the sunset over the lake, which she once described as 'looking at brutal heart surgery in a state of calm contemplation'.

———

A long talk with Nikos. At the end, Nikos said, 'Promise that our being separate from each other won't cause any uncertainty between us, please,' and I said, 'I promise.' And then that longing to be with him which seems to me to pull at my very body to transpose it to where he is.

I tried to hold back from asking if he saw Paul, but couldn't, and he said he would not discuss a fantasy that was all in my mind, not in his.

———

A very strange day. I keep thinking and thinking about it, as though something has happened that I know will change my life, but I don't know in what way.

In the morning, Nikos rang. Germaine, in her room, answered, and called me from my bed in my room, where I was still asleep. I wrapped a blanket about myself and hurried, and I stood by Germaine in her bed and she handed me the telephone receiver. Nikos told me that he had with him a copy of the *New York Times Book Review* – in which *The Family* had got a very bad review – and he read a rave review of *The Country* by the novelist Mary Gordon. He was very excited; he had an advance copy of the review, which will appear in a few days, and he wanted to be the first to tell me about it. I mentioned the review to Germaine, who did not appear interested (she expresses no interest in my writing, which I don't mind). Back in my room, I dressed and came downstairs to sit at the dining table to write. Germaine remained in her room. In the late morning, I went out to the mailbox to see if there was any post; there was a thick letter from Nikos, and two letters from my publisher, Atheneum, which contained copies of reviews. I had decided not to read any of the reviews of *The Country*; this didn't require much determination, as I told myself I didn't care what the reviews would be, though I did think it peculiar that I don't care. Back in the house, I found Germaine. I said, 'I've just received some reviews for my novel.' She said nothing. I said, 'I suppose I should read them.' She said, 'Well, I'm not going to read them for you,' and she went upstairs. I thought: I don't mind if she's not interested, I don't expect that from her. I went out onto the sundeck overlooking the lake, and opened the packet of reviews and read such sentences as: 'I don't know when I have been more moved by a novel . . . Chekhov would have been proud . . . a novel of enormous formal grace and beauty . . . one of the major novels of the year . . . I can't think of many novelists working now who could write a book as serious and perfect . . .' I threw the reviews, including Nikos' letter, down, and startling myself began to weep. In the house, the weeping gave into sobs. I didn't want Germaine to hear me, so I went out, along the back drive, and walked up and down, sobbing. I kept thinking: What am I sobbing about? What? I could only think: For your father, for your mother. I was out for about half an hour. When I came in, I found Germaine in the kitchen. Smiling, she said, 'The reviews were good, were they?' 'Yes,' I said. She said, 'I know what it feels like. And I also know what will happen now. You'll become famous, and it will be a disaster to you in all ways.' I said, 'You know about that.' Red eyed, I went back onto the sundeck to read Nikos' letter.

Αγάπη μου, αγάπη μου,

I don't know what to say about your going back or not to Tulsa next year. Of course it is very difficult for us both in many ways, and, as you know, I hate being alone without you. However, I also feel it is extremely important for you as an American writer to spend time in America every year. Not only from the point of view of experience – and there is a strong argument for that because it makes all the difference that you should be around rather than at a distance from your publisher, agent, etc. – but because it is of great importance to your writing, for you are an American writer. I feel that it is also important that you should, for a little while every year, have an outside commitment to fulfil rather than straining yourself all the time in a sort of Protestant way with trying to fulfil yourself as a writer. I think you are lucky to have that job in Tulsa, given that such jobs may get harder to come by as universities are cutting down on expenses. And there you are discovering a whole new world that should interest you. What I mean is that I think it is psychologically important to have, at least once in a while for a short time, assignments and tasks to perform which are not self-generated and self-imposed, but that get you out of yourself. Finally, and it is a last considera-tion, we may well need the money. Our financial commitment for the flat is considerable: I have to pay back on the mortgage about £580 every month out of the £850 that I earn. Then we have to pay £150 or more a month on rates and services!!! And then, running bills for telephone, gas, etc. So, that's a lot of money, and given the way things are going in publishing, I don't expect any real increase in my income. All the same, I am not saying that you should enslave yourself to a job, but that, obviously, we will have to make some compromises in the way we live so that the more important aspects of our lives together will not suffer. For instance, as things stand, it would be impossible for us to take a month off and go to Mount Athos, as we think of doing, but we do have our flat.

I am afraid the precious few moments of quiet I had here in my office have been shattered with frenzied activity. I love your letters. Please write to me often. Your letters provide a structure which otherwise is not here for me.

Here is a poem I had a moment to type. I don't know if it is any good or not.

All my love, my love.

The Necessities of the Mind

Necessities shone in the cold light
Then with words and words
In an unknown language, his.

Or he thought they shone.
He did not even think, he said.
This is what he wanted.

Decisions were unfinished
Sentences, the way he had
Of leaving things behind him.

A stranger, from another place.
This was his excuse,
The fire whose flames

Were flames of his ambition
And his desire to entrap
The unfolding mind.

And if a stranger, from another place,
Decisions would be then –
Continually, continually he wanted –

He wanted words on words,
Performances of love,
Murders of innocence,

Advice, threats and elucidations
Of the final love,
A celebration with no images.

Touch, colour, taste dissolved
In haze, a special light,
The light of endless lyricisms:

Mouth upon mouth,
Eyes on eyes,
Bodies on bodies.

If then, then the elucidation
Not of hard objects in cold light,
Not of decisions, but of proclamations,

Of a rhetoric of sighs,
Not a false rhetoric, but of appeals
To the revealing light not to reveal

A universe of images,
Glass, crystal, water,
Whose boundaries are confused.
They are body-less,
They are the truth.

———

Having read Nikos' letter, which moved me so that I couldn't sleep, I lay awake all night. Now morning, and while Germaine works in her room, I'll listen to music, read, and in the afternoon try to nap to catch up on sleep.

The weather has changed, become autumnal. The bright light is cold.

———

Germaine is in Dallas, Texas. I slept late into the morning, and deeply, then rang Nikos, waking him from a nap on what he said was a rainy English Sunday afternoon. We had a long talk, mostly about the reviews.

It occurred to me that if Nikos and I looked too closely into our relationship in itself – if we became 'internal' about it – our relationship might not last. Our relationship depends so much on the 'outside,' on its having to do with the flat, on our having enough money for the lives we live, on our being interested in each other's work, on our friends, on our being in the world together, and on the total support we give to each other. Now, there has to be a reason for our being so engaged in the 'outside', some 'inner' reason, and even to say that perhaps the reason for our being 'outward' and not 'inward' in our relationship is because we cannot face the darkness of what is 'inward' in us, and can only be 'outward', does not account for the very great support we do give each other.

I do not know what would happen to us if the outer world we live our relationship within ceased to engage us, or simply ceased – if we did not have a proper home, if we had no money, if our work failed, if we had no friends. I do not know what would happen to us if we had to rely on our inner worlds.

Nikos said that when he read the review of *The Country* in the *New York Times*, he wept.

———

After a workshop, Tony stayed behind and said, 'I'll pick you up tomorrow around noon time to go to Pawhuska.'

The next day, Saturday, at three o'clock, Tony arrived in a big car, long and in red and white, the tail fins rusted about the edges, to drive me to Pawhuska. Tony didn't say anything about being late.

'Whose car is this?' I asked.

'My uncle's.'

On the broad, interstate highway, we passed, within fifteen minutes, five mobile houses being transported slowly to the horizon. A green sign to the side of the highway stated that we had entered Osage County. The houses on the flat fields were Indian houses. The cemetery, beyond fields with cattle, was an Indian cemetery. Most of the fields were grown over with golden rod, and on them appeared, vastly separated, small clapboard houses and, from time to time, a clapboard church, and once a brick church. Some large brick houses stood back from the road among high elms, and next to these houses were smaller, prefabricated houses, or trailers. High grass and weeds grew where there might have once been lawns. Tony drove past a junk yard filled with cars parked in rows in what was like a last ceremonial parking lot for enormous, smashed-up cars. And among the houses, the churches, the derelict cars, were oil wells, their pumps rising and falling. Tony turned a corner at a yard, enclosed by a wooden fence, in which were brand-new, bright-red pumps. By the sides of the roads, at gasoline stations, outside general stores, the people I saw were Indians. They wore overalls and boots and Stetson hats. Tony stopped at a white clapboard house.

I followed Tony in through a screen door to a living room where three people were sitting in big armchairs and a sofa. They hardly moved as Tony, so off-handedly it was as if he didn't want to, introduced me to his uncle Bill and his aunt Rosa, and to his uncle Paul. Though I went to them to shake hands, they didn't get up. Their faces were smooth, flat, with flat noses, and narrow, black eyes.

Paul's hair was parted in the middle and in long, thin, loosely made braids, with elastic bands wound round the wispy ends of the braids; sparse hair grew from his chin and jaw. 'Sit down,' Paul said to me.

I took an armchair and Tony stood behind the chair so I couldn't see him.

Rosa asked me, 'Would you like some iced tea?'

I said I would, thanks.

She went out. Tony came from behind the chair I was sitting on and for a moment stood in the middle of the room before he, too, went out by a door at the side of the room. He didn't return with Rosa, who was carrying a Styrofoam cup of iced tea. She was a big-hipped woman in slacks and a blouse. Her red-brown face looked swollen, puffy about her narrow eyes. She gave me the tea, and she went out again.

'It's not as humid here as it is in Tulsa,' I said.

'Never is,' Bill said. 'It's because we don't have any lakes around here, just flat, dry land.' His face was pock-marked, his eyes red, and his short, black hair bristled.

'No woods around here, I guess,' I said.

Paul said, 'We've got the sky.'

The brothers stared out.

I looked around the room as I would have in any place that made me feel strange for being itself strange, and I fixed on details: the yellow armchairs and sofa, old, with stuffing coming out of the torn cushions; the thick, yellow-brown yarn carpet; the cedar chest in the middle of the floor with Styrofoam cups on it. On the plaster walls, rough with the marks of the trowel, were many framed black and white snapshots of Indians, some in ceremonial dress, and among the photographs were small oil paintings and watercolors of Indians that looked as though they had been done from the photographs. Above a painting of an Indian man wrapped in a blanket was a black crucifix.

There were two windows in the room, and hanging on wire hangers hooked over the tops of the window frames were costumes, bright red and yellow and purple.

I couldn't remain silent. 'What are those for?' I asked.

Without raising his head, Paul said, 'The dance.'

'If there is a dance,' Bill said.

I finished the iced tea.

Rosa came back into the living room. She sat in a corner at a desk which should have been in an office, covered with overlapping papers. She flipped through the papers, perhaps to find one.

She didn't find it, but remained at the desk, turning her office chair on its swivel towards the men.

She said, 'I think the dance should be cancelled.'

Paul and Bill didn't reply.

I asked, 'Why?'

Rosa said, 'An old woman from the Lookout Clan – they're supposed to play the drum at the dance – she was, Agnes was, found dead this morning in her motel room – and that means the dance shouldn't take place.'

His face averted, Bill said, 'People have come for the dance from all over. Some are camping out in tents.'

A fat man appeared at the screen door and Rosa got up to open it, though she could have easily told him to come in. He came in slowly. His body shook. He wore a big, short-sleeved white shirt hanging loosely out of his trousers, and he placed his hands, wrists delicately bent, on his fat chest. The corners of his mouth were so drawn down they almost touched his jaw. He hurried across the floor, as if to hide, and sat next to Bill on the sofa. With small, effeminate gestures, he patted his fat hands together, then his chest, then again his hands. Bill touched his bulging shoulder, and the fat Indian put his hands in his lap and sat still.

The fat Indian asked, 'So, is she going to be buried in the Catholic church? She was Catholic, wasn't she?'

'I guess she was for a while,' Paul answered. 'Her husband was Catholic.'

'He wasn't Catholic, was he?' Bill said. He seemed about to fall asleep. 'He was Peyote.'

'That don't matter,' Paul said. 'He could be Catholic and Peyote.'

'Are you all Catholics?' I asked.

'Yes, we are,' Rosa said.

'People are still getting ready for the dance as if it's going to take place,' the fat Indian said. He had a high voice.

'Well,' Rosa said, 'maybe they'll smoke the orchard, and it'll be all right.'

'That's what they're doing,' the fat Indian said. 'They're smoking the orchard.'

No one explained to me what smoking the orchard was.

I suddenly said, 'I'm Indian too.'

After what seemed a long time, Paul asked, 'What tribe?'

'Blackfoot,' I said.

The fat man patted his breasts, which quivered under his white shirt.

'My great-grandmother was a Blackfoot Indian,' I said.

Outside, a bell rang.

Rosa got up from her desk to go out. I watched her push a door open into a kitchen where people were gathered before a big blue and white range on which pots were steaming.

The bell rang again. It stopped, and the men got up. Bill and Paul each unhooked a costume from the window frame, and, without speaking, went out of the room and down a narrow hallway. The fat Indian, his buttocks shaking as he hurried, went out by the screen door.

I stood alone for a while, then I went out and sat on the cement stoop. Across the wide, flat land were walnut trees and oil pumps. Tony was standing under a walnut tree. When he turned, it was not to look at me, but, I imagined, at the sky.

From behind the house came a gang of people, old and young, some carrying folding chairs, others with suitcases. They went to the walnut tree where Tony was standing.

Some of the Indians placed their suitcases on a long, unpainted wooden table and opened them, and others, crouched, opened them on the ground. They took out ceremonial clothes and hung them on wire hangers from the low branches of the tree. A little boy was stood on the table and undressed to only his underpants, and as his father unpacked from an open suitcase a shirt, feathers, kerchief, beaded and woven bands, breeches, breech cloth, moccasins and handed them to his mother, she dressed the small, blond body.

Tony came to me, still sitting on the cement stoop, and he said, 'I'll take you to the dance.'

I got up and followed Tony through back yards, past broken-down cars and under clothes lines to a large shed without walls and a corrugated-iron roof, bleachers on three sides. We sat high in the bleachers, where there were few people.

All about the dirt floor, under the corrugated-iron roof, were men in ceremonial regalia on low benches. Only the feathers which stuck out of the roaches on their heads moved in a broad, slack breeze. They sat with their legs open, so their breech cloths hung loose, and their shoulders were hunched forward. At the center of the arena were men and women, in dungarees and plaid shirts and Stetsons, sitting about a big drum, and by them stood a man at a microphone who, over loudspeakers, asked for a moment of silence for Agnes, the dead woman. Then the man spoke in Osage for a few sentences. When he stopped, the drummers, with thin, long sticks, began to beat the drum, and the singers wailed. From the low benches the Indian men rose, and, lightly stamping one foot then the other so their bodies swayed from side to side, they danced round the drummers and singers. Belted about their ankles were rows of bells, which made a slow chang chang chang sound. In the horse-hair and porcupine-quill roaches on their heads their single feathers swirled. They wore bright, flowered shirts cinched in tightly with beaded belts, and kerchiefs tied loosely about their necks, and they sometimes turned to dance backwards, and sometimes jumped. A fine, grey dust rose about them.

My brother Lenard rang. He had the *New York Times* review, which he said is 'good, Dave, really good', but there was a 'so-so' review in the *Boston Globe*. He had read the novel and 'loved' it. 'It's so strange,' he said, 'to read a novel in which you know how everyone and everything looks in fact, so you can't imagine it.' Then my brother Donald got on the telephone. He, too, had read the novel and loved it, then he read the review from the *Globe*, 'lest you let the good review go to your head', which criticized the book for being sketchy. The book comes entirely from my diary.

What, I wonder, binds us seven sons together with such devotion that they would 'love' the novel I wrote about our mother and family, a novel that is dark with grief? Shouldn't I have expected my brothers to have objected, to have wanted a novel of brightness rather than darkness in portraying our mother and father? Is it, in fact, that darkness, that 'inner' family darkness in us all, that is our acceptance of one another, our understanding of one another, our love for one another? Why is it that whenever I greet one of my brothers after a separation, we embrace and a mutual sob rises up from us?

I asked how Momma is doing since the death of Dad.

'She is trying to interest herself in the outside world.'

———

Quiet, reading again Nikos' poem I am so very moved by it – moved not only by it in itself for its sensitive intelligence and beauty, but because he, my love, wrote it.

———

Amanda came to my office to discuss the writing she had presented in the workshop. She was nervous and sighed a lot. I was very British: I simply didn't refer to her proposal for the novel about one of her sons killing another.

———

A cool day. Germaine stayed home, which she rarely does. It is evening, and I have lit a fire in the sitting room, where I've been all day, writing letters, while she, up in her room, was watching a baseball game on the television, was sewing a dress, and, too, writing a monograph on Shakespeare. Someone from the faculty told me that Germaine had told him that she has found living with me very pleasant; I find living with her pleasant, too. I stay out of her way, as she stays out of my way.

I find that I want to care for her, in these small ways. I have no idea what caring for her in the larger ways would require.

Late at night, she came into my room, where I was asleep, to tell me that someone named Jack wanted to speak to me on the telephone, which was beside her bed. I was disoriented and, naked, bumped into the doorjamb on my way to her room. She said, 'Put something on, you'll get cold.' I wrapped a blanket about myself and, still disoriented, went downstairs to the sitting room to the second telephone. The time was 3:30 a.m. My old friend from college days Jack said, 'Your roommate is a fucking bitch. I'm going to come to Tulsa to tell her.' He went on and on; he was drunk. I said, 'Jack, it's 3:30 in the morning.' In Boston, it would have been 4:30. He said, 'I've just finished reading your reviews in the *New York Times*, in *Newsweek*, in *Time* magazine, and I wanted to let you know how proud of you I am. You're my old friend. I'm your old friend, aren't I?' I said, 'Jack, I'm not sure I'm not dreaming.' 'All right, all right,' he said, 'but I wanted to let you know that I love you, Dave. Still, your roommate is an asshole.' I said goodbye and hung up and went back upstairs to my bedroom. I hadn't fully woken, and as I was falling more deeply into sleep I heard the telephone ring in Germaine's room, and I knew it must be Jack. I heard Germaine say, 'Hello,' and after a minute she put the receiver down. I lay, now completely awake. I heard Germaine get up from her bed and walk about, talking to herself (she often talks to herself), then open the door to her room to stand on the landing between our rooms. I called her. She came into my room and lit the overhead light. She said nothing. I said, 'I'm very angry at him. Was he rude to you?' She said, 'He rang me to tell me my work is shit.' I sat up. 'I'm deeply angry and deeply upset,' I said; 'he had no right to insult you.' It did occur to me that I didn't know what she had said to him when he'd first rung, but I was, as if by the instinct to protect her from this drunken insult, outraged at him. She said, 'When he rang and asked to speak to you I said it was 3:30 and you were asleep. He insisted. He said, with the voice of an hysterical queen, "Will you go tell my friend Dave that his friend Jack wants to speak to him." So I came.' I said, 'I'll go speak with him.' I got out of bed and, the blanket wrapped about myself, went downstairs and dialled his number, but his telephone rang engaged, and I thought: he has taken the receiver off the hook. Upstairs, I went into Germaine's room, where she was in bed, and said, 'This has never happened to me before. I'm shocked.' She said, 'You'll see, it'll happen to you more and more. It's happened over and over to me. Like me, you'll end up with no friends.' 'Why did he do it?' I asked. 'Get back into bed,' she said. Standing by her bed, I said, 'He is a pathetic person. I've known him since I was in college, from when we were freshmen. I used to be somewhat in awe of him because he was so flamboyant about being queer. Now I find that flamboyance pathetic. Didn't he know that by insulting you he would be insulting me? I really am angry and upset.' 'Don't worry,' Germaine said; 'we neither will be able to sleep now, but we can read. And would you like a cup of hot lemon?' 'Yes, please,' I said. 'I'll bring it to you in your bed.' She brought me the hot lemon – what she, who always has the right word, calls a negus – and another pillow and a lamp from her room so I could read, and a book. 'Don't worry,' she said. 'I do worry,' I said. She went to her room, leaving the door open onto the landing between our rooms; after a couple of hours her light went out and she said, 'Good night,' and laughed. 'Good night,' I said. I couldn't read, but, propped up by the pillows, wondered what had happened between Germaine and me. The next day I felt tired, and still angry at Jack 'Don't worry,' she said; 'honestly, don't.'

What is Germaine to me that I should be so upset by her being insulted?

――――――

An example of living with Germaine being easier than living with Nikos: in the morning, I forgot to put the garbage out to be collected, my responsibility, and when, a little guiltily, I told Germaine I'd forgotten, she said, 'It doesn't matter.' Nikos would have been annoyed and said it mattered a great deal.

When I am away from him his fastidiousness amuses me; when I am with him it annoys me.

I do miss him very, very much.

———

Halloween.

I was invited by a student, Bruce, to a party. Bruce picked me up in his car, and then we picked up his friend Danny. The party was in an apartment house with a courtyard, and in the courtyard bare poplar trees on a bare patch of ground, the trees illuminated by the lights from the surrounding apartments. People were sitting on the balconies in front of their apartments, on the glass doors of which were pasted cardboard witches and skeletons and pumpkins. Danny was carrying a dress on a wire hanger and Bruce was carrying, in a brown paper bag, the wig and makeup for Danny. A fat woman on a folding chaise longue said to Bruce and Danny, 'You want apartment number 370.'

The sliding glass door to apartment number 370 was open. Inside, in the living room, was a big radio phonograph with a panel flashing coloured lights to the rhythm of rock music. On small tables among the sofa and armchairs were framed photographs of families at weddings and high-school graduations. In the kitchen three people around a round wooden table were eating chilli: they were all girls, one younger and thinner than the other two, who were fat. They were all in men's shirts and dungarees.

'Where the fuck's Tracy?' Danny asked.

'He's at Tim's,' the relatively thin girl said.

'But he's supposed to make me up.'

'He went to Tim's to get his makeup done. He said only Tim could make him up to look like a whore.'

I followed Bruce and Danny back into the living room and we sat to wait for Tracy.

Danny stood and wandered about, then went into a room at the back of the living room, from where he came out wearing panty-hose and a jockstrap visible through them. The hair on his legs was matted by the pantyhose. Glued to his narrow, concave, bare chest were two halves of a pink rubber ball.

He said, 'I've started without the fuckers,' and he went into another room.

A young man outside slid the glass door to the apartment all the way to the side and shouted, 'We're here,' and a gang of young men with naked chests came in. Their faces were bright with makeup and they were wearing big, frizzed-out wigs. Two in their midst were dressed: one in gold trousers and a black blouse, another in a short black dress patterned with little red flowers. In the apartment, they all went in different directions.

There appeared to be many rooms. Out of one came the drag queen in the short black dress patterned with little red flowers, now carrying a bull whip and snapping it and shouting, 'Come on, motherfuckers, let's get this fucking show on the road.' He/she had powerful arms and legs, his/her big feet wedged into high heels.

'I'd better go see what Danny's up to,' Bruce said, leaving me on the sofa to go into a room.

I wandered towards the back to the apartment where, in fact, there were only three bedrooms and a bathroom. The bedrooms had no furniture, but blankets spread on the floor, clothes heaped in corners, and everyone stepped on the blankets, dressing and prancing.

I watched Danny being made up by Tracy, who was in a frizzy red wig and made up to look like a terrifying whore. I leaned against a wall, where Bruce, too, was leaning, watching attentively Danny being transformed by the makeup. Circling round Danny and Tracy was the drag queen with the whip, which he kept cracking as he shouted, 'I want welts! I want black and blue marks! I want long bloody cuts!' In the midst of a heap of clothes were barbells.

I asked, 'Why are there no beds?'

Tracy said, 'That fucking roommate of ours, if he shows his face around here he'll leave with it bloody. He sold our beds to buy a dress.'

'Is it a nice dress?' I asked.

'As ugly as he is.'

Tracy did not appear to be too upset that a roommate in this apartment had sold all the beds to buy a dress.

Shyly, a very beautiful boy, naked except for a jockstrap, came into the room and leaned against the wall between Bruce and me, and faced me.

Oklahoma law requires that a man, however outwardly dressed as a woman, must wear at least one article of men's clothing: the jockstrap.

The dream of the drag queens is to go out and, as a woman, score with a policeman, then reveal the jockstrap.

Tracy shouted at the boy leaning by me against the wall, 'Hey, Brian, how's the high-school gym teacher these days?'

Brian didn't look at me, but I looked at Brian, and, on impulse, I left the room to go to the living room, where, alone, the radio-phonograph was flashing as it blasted. Outside on the balcony were two children carrying stuffed animal toys, staring in through the glass door. Passing behind them, along the balcony, two men were carrying a mattress.

I went back to the high-school boy, Brian, who was now being made up by Danny, subtly, so his face appeared to glow, tiny silver flecks sparkling on his lids and cheeks. Then Danny fitted a wig, of loose, tangled, brown hair, over Brian's head. Made up and in a wig, the boy stood and his naked body appeared so strange to me he might have been changed into someone with an altogether unknown-to-me sex.

The drag queen with the whip snapped it and shouted, 'I want long bloody whiplashes.'

Bruce went off with Danny, and Brian again leaned against the wall next to me and closed his eyes.

He opened his eyes when I said to him, his naked shoulder pressed against the wall as he turned to me, 'Don't you have someone to help you dress?'

'Not yet.'

'You're waiting.'

The boy smiled a little. 'I'm always waiting.'

'That shouldn't be. You should always be the head of the line.'

'Why?'

'Because you're very beautiful.'

The boy blushed throughout his almost naked body, a pale flush.

I asked, 'Can I help you dress?'

Bending his head to the side, the boy answered, 'If you want,' and his Adam's apple rose and fell.

'I do.'

As if uncertain about touching the boy's body, I was careful holding out the pantyhose to lift his shaved legs into, one high-stepping leg at a time; then I pulled the silvery pantyhose up over his slender hips, the padded triangle at the crotch bulging with the jockstrap beneath, the elastic band at the waist I left intentionally just below his navel. The boy held out his arms for me to slip the straps of a bra over them, the filled bra meant for a woman with a double mastectomy, and the boy turned round for me to fasten the bra at his back, the fine ridge of his backbone curving inwardly down-ward where it gave way to the reversed outward curve between his buttocks. When the boy turned back to face me, the bra appeared to me, not as a prosthetic imposed on the boy's hairless chest, but as if rising from within on delicate breasts. Now I inserted both my arms into the insides of the dress – short and silvery – to open it up and hold it high so that I would be able to lower it over the boy, who, bowing and lowering his head and wig, let it fall slackly down to his thighs, and again the boy turned for me to zip up the back. When, now, the boy faced me, the dress pulled against his thighs and stomach and breasts, the boy became fully someone of a sex too strange for me to react to with anything but wonder.

Danny, made up and wearing a slinky cocktail dress, came in, followed by Bruce. Holding out his hands so they hung loosely from his wrists, Danny said, 'My name is now KayKay. Remember that. KayKay. And I'm the sexiest, richest woman in Tulsa.'

In conversation with Germaine at supper, she said she would never weep for herself, but that she does weep for fictional characters.

We watched, on television, *La Traviata*, she on the floor, I on her bed, and she sobbed and sobbed, and I began to sob.

About a former Italian lover, Rivo, she said, 'He'll kill me.'

'He won't,' I said.

'Oh yes he will,' she said. 'And I don't mind. I don't mind if he kills me.' She shrugged. 'I don't mind at all.'

If I had said, How operatic of you, she would have said, starkly, No, not so.

Nikos' letter:

> *Αγάπη μου,*
>
> *As we talk so often on the telephone, letters have to be about something else, or do they have to be about the same thing but differently expressed? I'm no good at letters because I don't know 'what to put in and what to leave out', as I think you once said about writing. It annoys me that one should leave so much out, really. And to put everything in is overwhelming. Anyway, the telephone takes care of the news.*
>
> *And the only non-news conversation we had was about your story. I hope you don't feel badly that I think it doesn't work, because I'm convinced that you know that yourself perfectly well. Or, anyway, your own writing, your pen, knows that: the fault is there in the writing, which you must know is not up to what you can do.*
>
> *Now, αγάπη μου, I find it difficult to deal with what you wrote in your last letter to me about Paul. You say you worry about the uncertainties of my life without you here in London, and I worry more about the uncertainties of your life in Tulsa without me to reassure you. What is happening that all the past with Paul should come back to you now that we are separate*

from each other, and that that past should cause in you such anxiety because I mentioned that I see Paul from time to time? I'm angry at you because your anxiety indicates a lack of trust in me, and, what's worse, a blindness in you about the real reason for your anxiety about Paul and me. If you had not met him in the entrance of Thames & Hudson, you would not have thought more of him, I feel, beyond indulging me in my tender exchange with him. It was when you saw him that all your anxieties about him and me took you over. I had thought you'd got over that, knowing that I had gone beyond that, and that you could accept my seeing him, a colleague at the publishing house, from time to time for lunch. The facts, it seems to me, are these: you yourself were/still are taken by him, and your ego was/still is hurt because he did not show the interest in you that you thought he should have had. You felt/feel that he should have known that I'm yours, and that he should have liked you as he did me, if not liked you more than he did me. Perhaps he would have liked you if you had given him the chance, but it was you who insisted you didn't want to see him again. You know perfectly well that I am safe in relationship with you no matter what happens. The 'changes' in our relationship that you say you have had nightmares about in Tulsa are most likely to be changes you dread in your own feelings, which, though aroused by your anxieties about me and Paul, have to do with something that you are experiencing on your own. And this something you are experiencing on your own fills me with dread.

You wrote in your letter, 'I honestly feel you and I don't let one another know what we are thinking and feeling, not as we used to.' Do you realize what a preposterous reversal of the truth that is? That is precisely my complaint, my fear, because you keep telling me more and more that we can't talk about this, about that, non parliamo; you keep trying to impose a censorship and I've been protesting like mad, because you don't realize what you are imposing on me. I hate having tabu subjects with you because tabus may poison and ruin a relationship. There is nothing I would stop you

from telling me. But you have to allow me the freedom, the neces-
sity, to tell you what I want to tell you. Please try to think about
all this, my love. My love for you is perhaps the only wholesome
thing in me. Please try to leave it uncomplicated by confronting/
accepting things as they are, untainted by inner twists and defen-
sive convolutions. All my love, my love

———

I went out onto the balcony to watch the lightning flash over the
water.

———

I waited for Steven Runciman at the airport debarkation gate and
examined each passenger coming through, but he didn't appear. I
checked if it was the right flight; it was. Well, then, I thought, he
couldn't make it, and I was relieved. As with so much in my life, I
am more drawn to the idea than the fact, and I'm always willing to
give up the fact. As I was leaving the airport terminal, I saw him
standing by the luggage conveyor belt, staring into the air. I ran to
him. We shook hands. Steven never embraces. 'How did you get
past me?' I asked. He held out his arms. 'It must have been magic,'
he said.

As I drove, rain fell hard, and I lost my way on the highway.

Steven told me he had been staying in Houston, Texas with his
favourite millionaires. He likes millionaires.

I said, 'You do realize that in Tulsa, Oklahoma, you are stepping
down rather.'

'My dear boy,' he said, 'to come to you is to step up.'

I stopped at a gasoline station for directions. I'd been going east
rather than west. When I found the way to the westbound highway,
it was lunch time, and I suggested we go into Tulsa rather than the
house for lunch.

'I long to see Tulsa,' he said.

We went to a restaurant in Utica Square.

He told me stories about Anthony Blunt.

Steven said, 'Anthony, whom I knew well but never liked, was' –
and here he made a vague gesture with one hand – 'with others
sent to Germany to retrieve letters sent by the Prince of Wales,
later Edward VIII, not because they were sexually incriminating,
but because they were politically incriminating.'

I said, 'They were sympathetic to the Nazis?'

'Precisely. One must not forget that the first foreign head of
state whom he and Mrs Simpson visited after their marriage was
Hitler.'

'You see,' he said, 'Mrs Simpson was very in with the German
Embassy in London. My father, who was in the Admiralty, once
met a German at a party who told my father all that'd transpired in
Parliament that day. Mrs Simpson would get the information and
deliver it immediately into the hands of the Germans. It wasn't
because she was divorced *or* an American that she was disapproved
of – though these would have been held somewhat against her –
but because she was a Nazi sympathizer. That is the real reason why
Edward VIII abdicated.'

I said, 'I once heard Patrick Kinross say that the present royal
family should put up statues to Wally Simpson for saving the
family—'

Steven interrupted: 'For saving the family, by Edward's abdica-
tion, from Nazism, which would have destroyed them.'

I said, 'I must try to remember this accurately.'

'No doubt it will be totally inaccurate,' he said. 'You novelists
have so little respect for the hard facts.'

I laughed. I felt privileged. I think I wanted more to retain the
sense of privilege than to be accurate.

'And as for Edward's sexual tastes,' Steven said, 'Mrs Simpson
knew all about them. She'd learned about sexual tastes in Shanghai,
where she used to go to parties given by Lady ——, where, on
every floor of the house, one could witness a different form of
sexual activity. She learned quickly that what excited Edward
was voyeurism, and she catered to his taste with discretion and
imagination.'

After lunch, we went to a supermarket. Steven said, 'How I love American supermarkets.'

He is seventy-eight, he told me in the car. Every additional year, he said, he considers a gift.

We found Germaine sitting lengthwise on the sofa. I introduced them from across the room. 'Don't get up,' Steven said, 'please don't,' and he dropped his bag and, limping a little, rushed to her to shake the hand she held out to him.

I could see in her face the expression: I am not impressed. Her mouth was drawn together as were her nostrils, and her eyes were large. If she doesn't like him, I worried, what will I do?

I showed him up to his room – in fact, my room.

Yesterday, discussing with her how we would accommodate Sir Steven, as she always called him, Germaine suggested we give him her room and she would take the other single bed in my room. As she has the better room I thought she had a sense of what was most fitting for our guest. Then, today, just as I was about to leave to meet him at the airport, she said, 'I can't leave my room, I have all my things in it,' and I immediately said, 'Then I'll give him my room, and I'll sleep downstairs on the sofa.' 'You can sleep with me in my bed,' she said. 'Then I'll do that,' I said. I had just enough time to transfer into Germaine's room and bathroom my clothes and personal effects and to make up a bed in my room.

After I left Steven to unpack, I went down to Germaine. Steven stayed in his room for a few hours, resting. I helped Germaine prepare dinner – fish gumbo – which she had offered to make. She was in a lively spirit, but she is a messy cook, dropping dirty spoons onto the counter, spilling salt and rice and sauce, unwrapping butter and putting it on a plate that was used for something else then hacking at it, leaving bottles uncapped and vegetable peelings everywhere, and somehow mixing in among these pencils and sheets of writing paper, envelopes and letters, eyeglasses. She opens cupboards and drawers (leaving them open, which Nikos says all women do) looking for cooking instruments and shouting, 'What the fuck kind of kitchen is this without a mezza-luna? Fuck it, I hate this kitchen. It doesn't have anything a serious cook needs. I hate this house.' For the gumbo, she had searched in Tulsa for all the right ingredients, including *filé*. As she cooked, I put things in order. She would say, always using the Italian for my name, 'Davide, where is the salt? I put the salt here, just where I could reach for it.' 'Here, here,' I would say, and hand it to her. I asked, 'Would you prefer to be alone in the kitchen?' 'No,' she said. We were having fun together.

Steven came down for drinks. Which he and Germaine had while I laid the table. They were talking animatedly, she asking him questions about history. At dinner the questions and answers continued. Germaine, I thought, was impressed; I could tell from her attentiveness to Steven who seems to gossip about people in history as he would gossip about friends, and it is all very knowledgeable gossip. I was interested in his story about the Black Byzantine Empress.

Germaine said she had a baseball game to watch on the television. She is in love with baseball.

I had told Steven about the drag queens I'd met, and he now asked me, 'Will you introduce me to your drag-queen friends?'

In fact, Bruce, of Danny and Bruce, had invited me for that evening to a birthday party for his mother, who was visiting from Los Angeles. I said to Steven, 'We can go if you'd like. It may be dreadful.'

'I'm slightly curious,' he said.

'We'll go for exactly twenty minutes,' I said.

On her way upstairs, Germaine said, 'Thank God I'm not going.'

The party was dreadful, with skinny boys and very fat girls, and in the midst Bruce's mother in a black velvet suit with gold trim, a bouffant silver wig, silver eye makeup, and long gold earrings. She was sweating from the heat. Danny was the only one dressed in drag, and he looked pathetic.

Steven kissed Danny's hand as we left.

In the car, he said, 'We were there for more than twenty minutes, dear boy.'

'It was thirty minutes. I'm sorry.'

'Not at all. It was interesting in a way. All events are interesting, in a way. But we did stay on ten minutes too long.'

We heard Germaine, in her room, clapping and shouting as she watched the game. She came down to the sitting room to have nightcaps with us, and to ask 'Sir' Steven about the Byzantine Empire, which she said she is ignorant of.

He said, 'It is perhaps not a very interesting period.'

In her bathroom, I undressed and, naked, brushed my teeth and washed my face, then, in her bedroom, got into bed before she did. I watched her undress. She was very beautiful, raising her clothes over her shoulders and head, revealing her body naked below. Naked, she walked about the room on tiptoe, her arms extended from the elbows, her hands bent at the wrists, all of her body swaying. She got into her side of the bed and, propped up on pillows, drew the sheet and blankets to just under her breasts, which I looked at as she held up an old *Times* of London in one hand and a pen in the other to do the crossword puzzle. She read out the clues to me; I couldn't come up with any answers. She finished the puzzle quickly, shut off the light, and said goodnight.

I fell into a deep sleep.

In the morning, I got up as soon as I heard Steven moving about in his room, early. Germaine was asleep. I dressed and went downstairs to prepare breakfast, so when he came down his place was set, his orange juice squeezed, etc. He had said he didn't want a cooked breakfast.

At the table, I asked him questions about people he knew – and knows – and he responded with his vivid anecdotes. In each anecdote, there is always a simple, solid, strong dramatic event, which, after he has recounted it, makes him pause, his face long, his eyes wide, his mouth open in mock awe: someone strangled a goose, or someone pushed someone else down a flight of stairs to kill him . . . As I listened to him, I felt that his stories sustained my sense of great privilege.

Germaine came down, made a pot of tea, and went back up.

I drove Steven to Oral Roberts University. We went through the Journey of Faith in the Prayer Tower, room after room in which are kept sites from the life of Oral Roberts. We walked about the campus, the buildings shining gold. From time to time a bell rang, and the students stopped and lowered their heads and prayed, and Steven and I stopped also until the students went on. Steven said, 'It is all fantasy. Not even the Roman Church at the height of its power was capable of such fantasy. This is where I want to lecture.'

With him, I was never at a loss for conversation. I simply asked him about people and he replied with an anecdote, and all during the week he was with me he never repeated an anecdote.

Back at the house, I prepared lunch. Again, Germaine was watching a baseball game in her room, sometimes screaming. I went up to ask her if she wanted to eat with us. 'No way,' she said. I brought up a plate to her. Steven and I sat at the dining-room table; he seemed surprised that Germaine would stay in her room, as if this were not done.

I said, 'I never impose on Germaine. She knows she's welcome to join us whenever she likes, but I'm sure one of the reasons why I get on with her so well is because she knows she is completely free to do as she wishes.'

'I dare say that would be the only way,' Steven said.

He retired to his room for the afternoon. As I had no room to retire to, I lay on the sofa in the sitting room and napped.

When Germaine came down, I asked her if she was free to join us that evening. Steven and I were invited by a couple, Honey and Reg Barnes. Germaine made a face. 'I don't know what I'm doing,' she said. 'Very well,' I said. She went into the kitchen, came out, and said, 'I guess I'll come.'

I emphasized to Steven that Honey and Reg are millionaires.

They brought us to a recital – Brahms and Haydn trios – then to their house for supper, where others joined us, and a group gathered around Steven. I acted as something of a straight man by asking him questions which he, leaning towards me, listened to carefully, then he would stand back and look at the others, the audience, to answer. Germaine, talking to others at the other side of the room, didn't join the audience. Steven's stories had mostly to do with ghosts in Scotland, and everyone listened as though to a magician storyteller. He was a success, and I saw he enjoyed being a success, but I also saw he was making an effort.

The next morning at breakfast, he said, 'In society, one must give pleasure. That is the first consideration. One must also be absolutely confident of oneself, even if one isn't; one must appear to be. One must be sure that one is the most glamorous person present; even though one knows one isn't, one must be glamorous. I'm telling you, dear boy, how to get on in society.'

I said, 'I'm sure your advice will be very helpful,' and laughed.

'Of course,' he said, 'there is no society to get into. But it is wise to know just in case.'

I said, 'I also believe in one's having a duty in society. But Nikos tells me my duty makes me false.'

'Of course one is false,' Steven said. 'Of course. But one's duty often requires one to be false. To give pleasure one can't be entirely sincere. I know I am totally dull, but I make an effort to be glamorous, because I know that pleases people. No one likes being with someone dull. Do you know the story of Ben Nicolson and Lady ——? She, a monstrous old woman, said to him, in a slow and heavy voice, "You are the son of Harold Nicolson and Vita Sackville-West," which he, a gawky boy, admitted by bowing his head, and she went on, "Then why are you so *dull*?" You see, some people, as my elder brother, are born with natural charm, and others are not. I have no natural charm. I have had to learn it. It is all intentional. You will see that I sometimes slip. In a conversation with someone I will become distracted, my attention will wander, and I become, I dare say, rather blank. I must always make an effort to pay attention, to be charming.'

We went to the Gilcrease Museum, to study artefacts from the Old West and from Western Indians, about which Steven said, 'This is all so recent. One doesn't think of it as history, really, but as memory.

Still, interesting.' Then to the Boston Avenue Methodist church, designed by a woman. 'Interesting,' he said. 'All very interesting.'

Steven said to me, 'Everyone's history is world history.'

Germaine joined us for lunch. I had made cottage pie. She asked more questions about people in history, as if to connect them within history and therefore in her mind. She was particularly interested in the influence of Byzantium, especially in the person of Plethon, on the Renaissance, she a Renaissance scholar.

Steven retired to his room after coffee to write letters, he said. When he came down for tea, Germaine joined us.

She asked 'Sir' Steven about Lady Ottoline's salon, which he used to frequent. She said, 'I would like to have a salon. I would like that very much.'

'It would be difficult,' Steven said.

'Not so difficult if it were done properly,' she said. 'David and Nikos should start a salon in their new flat. They could have people come every Thursday at, say, five o'clock, for oysters and champagne and stout. It would have to be established so people would know they could, every Thursday, count on having oysters and black velvet at David and Nikos'.'

I said, 'My God, we couldn't afford it.'

'There is that,' Steven said.

'Whom would we have?' Germaine asked. 'We must be precise about whom we want and whom we do not want. Get a sheet of paper, Davide, and we'll draw up a list.'

I went for a sheet of paper and pen, but did not write on it.

She said, 'We don't want it to be all poofters.'

I said, 'Nikos and I know a *great* many people who are not!'

'Everyone must be entertaining,' Germaine said.

'Oh, that above all,' Steven said.

'Do we ourselves qualify?' I asked.

Over the following days, whenever the three of us met up, we would add to the list names of people whom we would invite to the salon.

'No actors and actresses,' Germaine said.

'No, no,' Steven said, 'they're always dreadfully dull.'

She said, 'We should have some media people. We want the salon to be known.'

'I don't think we want media people,' I said. 'It'll get known. If it's made known by the media, none of the people we want to come will.'

'I dislike publicity myself,' Steven said, 'always have.'

Germaine looked thoughtful. She said, 'Very well. But I think we shouldn't allow couples to come together.'

'You mean,' I said, 'we can't invite Stephen and Natasha *together*?'

'We can't.'

'Then I go for Natasha,' Steven said.

'Do we invite politicians as well as creative people?' Germaine asked.

'I can't see why not,' Steven said; 'they can be very entertaining.'

'What about Harold Macmillan?' Germaine wondered.

'Oh, a very good idea,' Steven said. 'Very good. He's good value, Harold.'

The list included, as far as I can remember: Rebecca West, Rosamond Lehmann (not John, whom Steven dislikes), perhaps Kathleen Raine ('Doubtful,' Steven said. 'She killed Gavin Maxwell by chopping down his tree of life, killing his otter, and destroying his letters. We want only *nice* people'), Francis Bacon ('I suppose we must,' Steven said), David Hockney ('But,' Germaine insisted, 'without his entourage. He can come only if he comes alone'), R.B. Kitaj, Joe Tilson, Frank Auerbach, Patrick Caulfield, Howard Hodgkin ('We have enough artists,' Germaine said, 'and perhaps we should invite the wives instead, because their wives are nicer'), Isaiah Berlin, Freddy Ayer, Stuart Hampshire, Richard Wollheim ('But not their wives,' Germaine said) . . . Steven said, 'But we want younger people. Who are the interesting younger people?' 'I don't think there are any,' Germaine said; 'but we must have some rich people.' 'Oh yes,' Steven said, 'it does help a salon to have some very rich people come. They can liven up an occasion.'

I can't recall the full, though unfinished, list of those who would be invited and those rejected. Steven proposed different categories: those invited every week, those every month, those once a year, and those every five years.

Here, in Tulsa, Oklahoma, we were in our fantasy in London.

Every night, before Germaine shut off the light, she did the *Times* of London crossword puzzle, calling out the words as she wrote them down, and all the while I looked at her beautiful breasts.

One morning, Steven said to me, 'I'm sorry, by taking your room, to be forcing you into a life of sin with Germaine.'

'No,' I said, 'we are like brother and sister, Germaine and I, and sinless brother and sister at that.'

He leaned towards me, his finger raised, and said, 'The sins of omission can be as grave as the sins of commission.'

When the day was sunny, Steven sat out on the sun deck. I went out to him to ask how he was and he said he was perfectly happy. He had *The Times* of London on his lap, saved, he said, from London for just such an idle moment, the newspaper open to the crossword puzzle. I asked him if he wanted a pen, and he said, 'Oh no, I do it all in my head.'

He wanted to do some shopping in Tulsa, especially for postcards. We went from shop to shop, and I saw that he badly wanted postcards of Tulsa, so much so that it would be a disappointment if he didn't find any. 'A drugstore is what we want,' he said; 'in America all drugstores have postcards.' In a drugstore, I asked a woman for postcards, but she said, 'We sure don't have any,' that 'sure' meant, I supposed, to be polite. When we found the postcards I saw Steven become excited, and I thought that one of the reasons why he had wanted to come to Tulsa was to send postcards from here to his friends.

Once, after he had told me of sailing on a pleasure craft up a river with the prince of Thailand before the war, I asked him what was the most exotic country he had been to, and he answered, with only a slight pause, 'America. It is very strange here. Very strange.'

I arranged for him to meet some professors in the History Department. They were, as Steven might have said, very dull, and I apologized after. Steven said, 'Yes, very dull. But I'm afraid that is the way most history departments will remain as long as history is not considered an art. History belongs in the English Department, belongs with literature.'

His last evening, he invited me to a meal in a restaurant in Utica Square.

He said, 'I think I'll never make love again. I don't particularly like thinking it, and preserve the vague hope that something might happen – some, as Bury might have said, historical contingency – and I will find myself in the arms of some young beauty, but I must say I doubt that it will happen. When I was in New York, a friend took me to a bar where he said gerontophiles gathered, because, of course, I could now only attract a gerontophile. Well, there were a great number of gerontos, but no philes.'

During the night, I in bed with Germaine heard Steven cough in a hard way in his room, and I wondered if he slept.

On the way to the airport, I said to Steven, 'Your life should be written.'

'No,' he said, 'my life is uneventful.'

'You can't say that.'

'Yes, I can. My life is uneventful and uninteresting, you see, because I've never been in love. I've been loved, and I've hurt those who have loved me. I, myself, have never been in love.'

He talked about his need to be reassured.

I said, 'I can't believe you need to be reassured.'

'But why not, dear boy?'

'Because of what you are.'

'That's very little.'

'No, no,' I insisted.

He said, 'You reassure me, and for that I am deeply grateful.'

We were early for the airplane. He didn't want me to wait with him. I shook his hand, and he wheeled away his suitcase, which

had casters and a little silver handle that can be folded into the case.
He didn't look back, as I knew he wouldn't.

He said he would see Nikos in London.

I have spent the entire day writing down his visit.

───────

Nikos!

He sent me this poem:

The Enchantment of Distances

Infinite, distant, pale,
Surprising distances of light, your touch.

Itineraries of your thoughts in a dark room,
The invocations of the impenetrable far.

The light hammers outside, it forges tools.
You are the interior traveller, the erotic emperor.

You comprehend through fictions, your true facts,
Your coronation is a brilliant spectacle.

Today you make another day, another day.
The labyrinth postpones receding vistas,

It multiplies the green
In ever paler screens of green.

I am envious, I want to call you back.
We go into the dark.

Miracles happen in delirious light.
Distances then diminish to a bright, insistent spot,

And then the crystal of your dream is this:
Your hand that reaches out to a glass of crystal water.

And I responded with: How beautiful, αγάπη μου, how beautiful.

And of course I read *him* into the *you* of the poem, and wonder
at him with the wonder of him as he is in himself, at a distance from
me, he the interior traveller going into the dark where miracles
happen in delirious light.

Now I have read the poem again, and I am struck by 'your
touch', and I wonder if he means *my* touch, and if *I* am with him,
the internal traveller, if I go with him into the dark, if I am with
him when the miracles happen in delirious light.

———

The sun is setting. I am not feeling well and am trying to protect
myself from incipient flu. Germaine is away giving lectures and has
been for two days. I spoke to Nikos this morning. I said, 'If you
hear that I've been sleeping with Germaine, it's true.' He laughed,
a little nervously I thought. I said, 'She's been using our sleeping
together in class as an example to her students of how William and
Dorothy slept together chastely, though I don't really understand
the comparison.' I said, 'How I long to be with you.' 'And I?' he
asked. 'I know you do,' I said.

———

A strange experience –

Though any liquor above a certain level of alcohol cannot be
bought in any restaurant in Oklahoma, even wine, the waiter serving
it arrested by a plainclothes policeman (as I've seen happen in the
fancy restaurant in Utica Square), when at a party in a club I expressed
alarm at how available guns are in Oklahoma, a woman said she
would alarm me all the more by taking me to a gun fair, if I wanted,
and I said, using the Oklahoma accent, 'shoo-are', I wanted.

She, Ruby, picked me up and parked the car outside a long, low,
corrugated building near the Arkansas River. At the door of the
building was a guard, in uniform, who asked us, as we entered, if
we had guns, because if we did, he said, we had to check them to
see if they were loaded. Ruby said, 'You didn't check the man who
went on in ahead of us who was carrying a gun.' The guard smiled.

Ruby raised her arms and said to him, 'Check us if you want, we're not carrying anything but our bodies.' She looked back at me and, with a smirk, asked, 'Isn't that right?' 'That's right,' I answered, and I felt as unprotected as if naked.

The building was windowless. Under long fluorescent lights, booths were lined up along the walls, and down the centre were tables. Men, with a few women, walked about, picking up from and putting down on the display counters of the booths and tables: pistols, rifles, machine guns. I remained behind Ruby as she walked slowly the length of the cement floor. On the cinderblock walls at the backs of some booths were displayed flags – the Nazi flag, the Confederate flag, the American flag – and hung against the flags were Nazi and Confederate and World War I and World War II weapons. One booth was filled with knives and machetes. At the end of the building a fat Indian in a Stetson was selling turquoise jewellery spread out before him on an old table. I tried to give the impression that I was looking above and beyond everything.

As we walked back through the space, Ruby met her ex-husband, Henry. They spoke as though they'd both known the other would be there. She introduced him to me, and Henry shook my hand forcefully, though, as I've noted about men here, there was something feminine about him.

He said, 'You're here to buy a gun, are you?'

I laughed and again looked above and beyond everything there.

When I heard Ruby say, 'Look at this,' I looked at her. She was holding a pistol by the barrel, which pointed at her, the handle out to him.

Henry said, 'That's an RG-4, six-shot, twenty-two-caliber pistol, a nice gun.'

Trying to laugh, I raised my hands from my sides as if the gun were loaded and being pointed at me.

'Take it,' Ruby said.

My hands still raised, I asked, 'How much does a thing like that cost?'

'Don't ask,' Ruby said. 'Just take it.'

Smiling, I said, 'Thanks, no.'

Ruby held the gun out to Henry and said, 'Buy it for me, baby, and I'll pay you back later.' Henry, with a grunt-like laugh, took the gun from her with a swagger, bought it, and gave it back to her and she put it into her purse.

I asked, in terms of a principle I knew that Ruby and Henry thought just plain self-righteous, 'Shouldn't that gun be registered?'

Henry laughed, a hard, high laugh that was meant to put me in my place.

Ruby suggested we all go to a restaurant, but Henry said he had a date. In the car, on the way with Ruby, I looked out the window at great flames, across the river, burning off gas from a well, the flames rising high against the sunset. In the parking lot, I followed Ruby into the restaurant, she carrying the gun in her purse, and I was aware of men, women, children getting out of cars and walking along with us.

Eating the meal of fried fish and beer, I was aware at another table of an old woman reaching across the table to wipe with a paper napkin the cheeks and chin of a little boy.

Her face stark, Ruby twirled her knife in her fingers like a cheer-leader twirling a little baton. She asked, 'Do you go silent in this way a lot?'

'Sometimes,' I said, 'I don't have much to say.'

'I think you're going to have to learn a few jokes in Oklahoma.'

'I'll try,' I said.

She called for the check and she paid. She also led the way out into the autumn heat and the parking lot around the floodlit mall.

'I've got to do some shopping,' she said.

'I'd like to go home,' I said.

'You just wait. I'll only take a few minutes.'

I stood outside a drugstore with a wide window through which I saw, inside, stands with greeting cards and shelves of shampoo and deodorants and hairsprays. I looked round at the people passing, and among them I saw a man with a broken nose, a woman with her mouth pulled down to one side, a teenage girl wearing one platform shoe and lurching as she walked.

———

I've had a cold for a few days. I feel low and dark. A Sunday, I sat by the fire, which Germaine kept putting logs onto, and drank hot lemon she gave me. Whenever I tried to do something for myself, she would say, 'Don't. Sit still in your armchair. For heaven's sake, don't fuss.' But I find it very difficult accepting her doing for me. I was able to do a lot of writing, the paper on a board on my lap.

One of my students told me he rises at four o'clock to write, the only time he has free. 'I need to write. I'll do anything to write. I *need* to do it.'

———

Germaine came into my room while I was in bed to see how I was. She said, 'You look awful.' I said, 'I've got a class today. I must go.' 'No,' she said, 'you don't have to. You stay here. I'm not going to let you go. Get into my bed, which has an electric blanket. Try to sleep. I'll be home early and I'll make you some soup.' I got into her warm bed and slept until the late afternoon. I lay in bed and looked out at the lake. By the time Germaine came back, I was feeling better. She made me soup. On her bed, I in it and she on it, we watched on the television the final baseball game of the World Series.

She said, 'I hope to say something about America that will make it impossible for them to give me a visa to return. It's morally wrong to be here. I'd love an excuse, any excuse, not to come back. I hate this country.'

Germaine is, she says, an anarchist.

I said I am too.

She said (the first time she has mentioned seeing any), 'The standard of your reviews is coming down. My students showed me a good review of your novel in *People* magazine. *People*! You're slipping into tasteless popularity, Plante. Be careful.'

I laughed. 'Was there a picture?'

'Oh yes, of you naked and stretched out on a rug. No, there was no picture.'

———

Still have a cold, and feel weak.

Germaine's use of imagery:

'His legs were so thin they disappeared against the sunset.' 'His legs were so thin they'd offer no resistance to any stream he stood in.'

———

Cold still won't go away. Haven't been out of the house, except to collect post from the postbox in six days. Germaine in all day.

She was very angry when she got home and found that, cleaning my room, I went into hers and cleaned hers, as we don't have a cleaning lady.

'Don't,' she said; 'just don't.'

'Very well,' I said.

I think that I irritate her more and more.

I respond so to her longing for London, for, as she said, 'the black taxis in the rain', which brought all of London back to us.

———

Feel much better, even, for no special reason, happy. It is dark and grey out, and there are white caps on the lake. There is a sailboat out, tacking, and I think: how beautiful. The trees along the lake shores have become russet and brown, and the dark sky above is enormous.

———

Germaine came in as I was about to go to bed. I stayed up. She was lively. She made mulled wine, and we both cooked a late supper, and talked happily, and after supper watched the television in her room.

She was affectionate, but she is affectionate for only short periods. She does not, I think, like people, and can tolerate them, even be affectionate towards them, for only those short periods.

I am edgy when she is in for the entire day, and stay away from her, as if to be with her, however affectionate she is for a short time, is to run the risk of her suddenly becoming irritable.

A letter from Steven. It is difficult to believe he was here, as if his having been here required, not only a strange transportation of London into Tulsa, but a strange transportation of time, for Steven is of another place and of another time which seem, in London, to be present place and time, but here in Tulsa seem of an altogether inaccessible past place and time.

He writes that on the 'aeroplane' from Tulsa to Chicago he was wedged in by a vast lady of Arab origin (born in Antioch seventy-seven years ago, she said) who asked Steven if he had heard of the space ship. The ship has been organized by Jesus to come to earth soon – in a few months' time – to pick up all true believers to take them to an eternal home in space, while the wicked who remain on earth will have the Mark of the Beast – 666 – tattooed on their fore-heads or their arms and will perish in a ghastly Armageddon. She was disappointed in Steven's reaction, though he did impress her, being as well educated as he is, by capping her biblical quotations, which, however, will not save him from being branded by the Mark.

He is 'immersed' in lunch and dinner parties, beginning with dinner with the Colonial Dames of Washington.

Perhaps what he most enjoyed of Tulsa was the uplifting visit to Oral Roberts University, of which he was able to obtain even more postcards at the Tulsa airport.

He sends love to Germaine and me.

He sent this limerick about her:

> They told me to stay clear
> Of the formidable doctor Greer;
> But with all my discerning
> I find her rather a dear.

A letter from Nikos:

> *Αγάπη μου,*
>
> *I am terrified that something may happen to my cat, Jasmine. And it worries me that you won't be tolerant of the ever-closer relationship that has developed between us. I identify with her loneliness and she with mine, I think, when you are not here. We have to count on you for support and for providing meaning. It makes me very anxious when you feel 'empty', as you said you were when we last spoke. Where will all the meaning come from then?*
>
> *Please don't feel so 'empty', αγάπη μου. All my love. Write something moving and marvellous.*
>
> *P.S. I so wish all the unpleasantness regarding Paul would wash out of your mind. I have no interest in it or in him whatsoever, let alone any relationship. This is the truth. The whole thing bores me. And I want you to tell me what to do if he phones again or writes. I don't want an issue to be created out of nothing. That's all. But I want you to be totally, totally assured that I have no interest and not a thought to spare.*

———

Amanda no longer comes to the workshop. I never see her. This is a relief.

———

A professor at the University said to me, 'What you're really inter-ested about in your writing is epistemology, isn't that true?' I said, 'Yes,' with a sense of great gratitude opening up to him from me. I said, 'I'm moved that you should have seen that. Yes, it's true.'

If it is epistemology to wonder that the mind makes connections among the disconnected to make a whole, yes, my work is essen-tially epistemological.

That the person who made this observation is French means a lot to me, partly because of Nikos' library of the current French thinkers – Barthes, Foucault, Derrida – and in part because I associate the man with these Frenchmen who would understand what epistemology is. The largest part of my appreciation of what the Frenchman said has to do with my own training in philosophy at the Jesuit Boston College, courses in logic, epistemology, ontology, all of course within the philosophical world of Scholasticism, the two goal posts of which are Aristotle and Aquinas. What remains of that training in philosophy is that there *is* objective morality, there *is* objective beauty, there *is* objective truth, all within God, who is not subjective, no, no, but the ultimate objectivity, outside of ourselves. I do not believe in God, yet I am inculcated with the belief in some outer objectivity to which our inner selves refer. If I take as an example of this belief my diary, which in the nature of a diary is meant to be subjective, I like to believe that it does, day by day, week by week, month by month, year by year, accumulate itself into an entity that is outside myself, that creates its own objectivity, and it does so by making connections, masses and masses of connections, and in the interconnections worlds apart. I like to think that my diary has nothing to do with me.

Though Germaine is invited all over to give talks on feminism, contraception, abortion, even art by women, we never talk about such subjects when we are together.

We talk, as we always talk, in a lively way, about what is most immediate – because Germaine only talks to me about what has just happened, what is most immediately relevant, as if even what happened ten minutes before is no longer relevant –

Once, at supper, she described to me her time in New York when she was at the height of her fame. She made love over and over with 'star fuckers', and she loved it. She was young and beautiful. Now she considers herself aging and haggard. She was in New York invited to a grand party, and there spoke with Alberto Moravia in Italian, and spent the entire evening with him, aware that other grand people kept passing by her, eager to speak to

her, but she disregarded them, and when, finally, she left, she left
without having spoken to anyone in the New York circles whom
she should have spoken to, much less having obtained anyone's
address or telephone number, and that was the end of it. Her New
York success was brilliant with brilliant fucking, and that was all;
and now she doesn't regret that that was all. She was never again
invited to a grand party in New York, and she didn't and doesn't
care. Germaine is a person without 'connections'. Because she is,
in herself, famous, people contact her; she does not contact people.
In the same way she says she'd easily accept dying, she says she can
easily do without her fame.

———

I am reading Stephen Spender's *World within World*, which I last read
when Nikos and I first went on holiday together, in Yugoslavia.
Nikos had taken it along with us so that I would become familiar
with Stephen's world, or worlds revolving about each other. This
was before I met Stephen, whom Nikos was in love with, and
who was then in Washington; Nikos waited for him to return to
London to tell him about me and, perhaps, to introduce him to
me, with, perhaps, the hope that we would all become friends.
I read the book out in the sunlight on a rock overlooking the
sea, and when it rained, which it did often, Nikos and I read it
together in a narrow bed. And it did open a world, open worlds,
to me. Back in London, Nikos and I and Stephen became all
together a world, he a world to us, as, I think surely, we two a
world to him.

How did that happen? If Nikos and I saw in Stephen a world
expanding outwardly, he, I imagine, saw in us a world concentrating
inwardly in our relationship. How often he would say that Nikos
and I were living the lives together that he had wanted to live.

Here, away from Nikos and Stephen and London, I almost feel
that I am thinking about a past world, though it is in fact in the
near future, and will be totally present when I am back in London
and Stephen will come to supper.

Was it because of Stephen's love for us both that Nikos and I became known as a couple? I think we are, in the world of London, known, not separately, but as Nikos and David, David and Nikos. In letters addressed to us both, Stephen has written *Dear Nikos and David Plangos*, or *Dear David and Nikos Stante*. And I cannot think of any close friends who would invite us separately.

Stephen may see in Nikos and me a world of our own inner connections, but Nikos and I see him in a world of his outer connections. He has introduced us into and opened up that world to us.

When I consider the people he has introduced us to! Now at a distance from all those people, I see Nikos and me wondering at, even being amazed by, the world Stephen opened up to us.

There are a great many anthologies in this house, and among them I have found, in *The Oxford Anthology of English Verse*, *Twentieth-Century Poets*, *Modern Poets*, poems by Stephen. At my distance from him, there comes back to me the appreciation I once had for poets whose poems I had read without having met them, an appreciation that is a form of mythologizing, and so, here, Stephen has become something of a mythological figure, someone I have to remind myself I have met and know. This is acutely the case in reading *World within World*, in which he becomes someone who belongs within the mythological world I once fantasized belonging to, and which comes back as a fantasy that it is not in London.

To get back to *World within World* –

What strikes me now is how observant Stephen is, in this book in particular, which is filled with the observations of events that expand into the history that is in them, as when he describes visiting the ruin where pieces of Hitler's desk are being sold, which pieces he bought and then, with revulsion, threw out into the rubbish.

Nikos has told me he has seen Stephen a few times for luncheon, and Stephen has struck him as ga-ga, and can't remember anything.

I feel that Stephen will not live much longer. His body is too big to support itself into old age.

I wrote to him but he hasn't replied.

He would not be pleased that Steven Runciman has stayed with me. Though they are both British, they belong to such worlds that they don't fit into each other, and Stephen knows that Steven's world is on a higher level than his own.

―――――

Because Nikos wasn't in when I rang him, I rang Stephen, who said Nikos is well, and that he and Natasha are well. He sounded pleased that I rang.

Then I got to Nikos. He was tired, but he sounded cheerful.

I feel I am doing nothing here, and am eager to *do* something.

―――――

As always, thinking about Nikos. I note a change in my longing for him. It seems to me that my longing had some guilt in it, the guilt of being away from him.

―――――

Germaine came in, about eight o'clock, looking very drawn and pale. I told her so. 'You're looking concave. That's wrong. Germaine Greer should look convex.' She stuck out her breasts. I served her supper. She never compliments me. I said, 'You're not getting enough rest.' She said, 'I use a lot of rouge.' 'No,' I said, 'that's not good enough. You must rest.' It gave me a thrill to tell her what to do. She said, 'I'm getting wrinkled, and the stress wrinkles I most resent are those here' – and she traced them down from her lower lip to her chin – 'which come from having to restrain myself from saying exactly what I think about everything.' I laughed and wanted to say, '*You* restrain yourself?' but said, 'You *should* say everything you want.' She made a face. I was pleased that she ate a lot of the supper.

While we were eating, we listened to Prokofiev's 5th Symphony on the radio. I said, 'Really, this is much greater than anything

Stravinsky composed,' and she said, 'Davide, the obviousness of that statement should make you blush in the same way you make me blush for the obviousness of my statements.'

Afterwards, we lit a fire in the fireplace, and she cracked walnuts on the hearth with a hammer and I lay on the sofa and asked her about William and Dorothy Wordsworth. I said, 'You should be writing all this down.' She said, 'There's been too much written down.' I said, 'Nonsense. I can't believe that what has been written down is as bright and perceptive as what you've just said.' At the risk of sounding patronizing, which Germaine would not tolerate, I said I would like to close her in a room and insist she write, and as I went on she crawled off on her hands and knees, across the living room, saying, 'You're just like Willy to Colette, just like Willy,' and on her hands and knees went up the stairs to her room. I shouted, 'You *need* a Willy.' She called down, 'Good night.'

I remained on the sofa, thinking of how light in spirit and clear in mind she can be, brilliant ideas coming to her, it seems, one after the other.

She once talked to me devisively about feminist writers, about whom I know very little, and about whom she said, 'None of them can express the joy, the passionate joy, a woman can have in contemplating a man's body. They grudgingly give into making love with them. They're so mean, so lacking in imagination. It's as though a male body couldn't possibly bring joy to them, but only grey suffering. They don't know what it is to love and long for a man.'

She had also said, 'I want, most nights, to sleep alone in my own bed. I can't bear sleeping every night with a man. I'd rather sleep on the floor. The best way to live with me is to leave me most of the time alone.'

———

Some of Germaine's students, who happen to be also mine, complain to me about her: they can never do anything right, she insults them, she makes them feel small and stupid (Germaine might say, 'They are!'), but they all admire her and have learned a great deal of hard knowledge from her.

I was with a few of them in a classroom after a class, and because they did admire her I felt I could say, 'Germaine's greatest power over people is to make them self-conscious. She will question me about the socks, the shoes, the trousers, the shirt I'm wearing, and when I say they're what I've always worn she says, well, they look odd. She is probably unaware that she has that power, but she has it. I've made a pretty good effort not to allow her to make me self-conscious. I've been very deliberate about it. It has been an effort.'

Germaine came into the room and, in an impromptu meeting among the students, she and I talked about writing, about writing turned to the inside world and writing turned to the outside worlds. She said, 'All most current women writers are interested in is their dim, damp inner worlds.'

I was reminded of her once saying she doesn't try to understand herself – a futile, and, what's more, an utterly boring operation.

Suddenly surprising me, Germaine said to the students, 'Davide has the strictest boundaries to his world of anyone I know,' and she raised her hand in a salute and said, 'and I respect the boundaries. I never try to cross them.'

The students and I laughed.

The students think of Germaine and me as a couple in our own world, a couple outside their world, and because we are in our own world we, they assume, understand each other in our mutuality, as if we were both foreigners speaking our own language and in that language we can say whatever we want about each other. In fact, we often speak Italian to each other. The students all know we live together.

———

In the evening, at a supper of tinned soup, lively talk with Germaine, and I thought: I'll miss this.

About Nikos and me, she said, 'I think of you both as two beautiful men who met and ran off together to live outside the homosexual world. It's as if you were never in it. Do you think you'll be together forever?'

'I think so,' I said.

'I think so, too. I'm a true romantic. I always want someone new. I mythologize the unknown man. I've mythologized the football coach, I know; if I do make love with him I'll wonder why the fuck I wanted to. I'll want someone else, someone new. I quite like making love with old friends as long as it doesn't go on too long. But what I really like is the man after the current one, whom I haven't met. And I know this all has to do with my father. It's not very interesting because I understand it all. I don't think I'm interesting. There it is. Now, why the fuck doesn't the coach ring me? He said he would. He started it. Well, he'll be sorry if he doesn't ring. I'll have my revenge.' She wailed, 'I don't want him. I really don't want him. Why do I think of him so much? He's married. I don't like getting involved with a married man. What the fuck am I doing pining over a married man I know I don't want?'

———

I wish I could put everything, everything, everything into this diary: letters, my students' stories, books, conversations, and, too, apples, oranges, bottles, glasses, tables and chairs, doors, windows, houses, trees, clouds and sky.

———

I said to a mutual friend of Germaine and mine, 'Just when I'm about to leave, I feel Germaine won't have anything to do with me, has rejected me.'

'I know, I know,' she said. 'She'll reject and reject. And yet – if it's a "yet" – she told me the other day that what she most fears in her life is rejection.' She added, 'She likes your book.'

'Does she? She only told me that she dislikes novels. She hates the form.'

'Well, she likes at least the first part.'

I said, 'I can't imagine Germaine a little girl.'

'Oh, I can, and there are times, now, when she becomes a little girl.'

Germaine is going to Guatemala for Christmas, alone.

She is the most isolated person I know. Her accommodation to her isolation is ruthless; and it is an isolation she herself causes.

———

My brother Donald rang me to tell me our mother has died.

I sat on the sofa in the sitting room and wondered where I was, where I have been since I left home those years ago, as if everything that has happened to me since I, in my late teens, did leave to go to college, has been irrelevant to my life at home in the parish of Notre Dame de Lourdes, as if that parish were a palisaded fortress of French-speaking colonists holding themselves out against the Yankees of Providence, Rhode Island, the United States of America, in which we had no part, and which palisaded world has made me feel I have no part in the world.

She died alone, during the night, in a hospital.

Germaine came downstairs and stood before me.

I said, 'My mother has died.'

She said, 'Now there is nothing between you and eternity.'

As it is only a week until the end of the semester, I can leave.

I rang Nikos to tell him about my mother, and he said, 'Oh, your mother,' and I knew he was weeping.

He is very upset that he will not be able to welcome me when I return to London as he has to go to Athens.

———

I gave up my car, and on my last day in my office I asked Germaine if she wouldn't mind driving me back to the lake, whenever she herself would go; I asked her reluctantly, as, always, I do not want to impose on her. She said, '*Va bene. Non ti prioc.*' Then two students came into my office and when I told them I didn't have a car offered to drive me to the lake. I rang Germaine to tell her and she said, 'Oh,' as if I was wasting my time with two students, and she sighed.

At the lake house, the students, Randy and Dennis, sat with me in the living room, drinking whiskey. The door banged open and Germaine came in carrying a large paper bag. We all stood. She said, 'Don't get up. I've got to go out to the car again.' Randy and I went out with her to the car to help her, but she refused the help and carried the bag herself back into the house. She said nothing to me, and nothing to Randy and Dennis, as though they were beneath her acknowledging them. She said, 'In typical fashion, David [not Davide] has not lit the fire, and there is nothing prepared to eat.' A fury passed through me. She said to Randy and Dennis, 'He does nothing.' She looked at me. 'I don't mind. Don't think I mind, I don't expect it.' I was furious and embarrassed to be called down before the students, and I almost said, 'Fuck you, I've done more domestically for you than you have for me, much more.' I asked her if she would like a drink, thinking: This is the last night, and never again will there be another. 'I've got to make myself some soup,' she said, and went into the kitchen. The students, as if it were their duty, followed her in. I stayed out, and went in only to say I was going upstairs to pack. She was chopping vegetables while the boys asked her questions, which she answered cursorily, often sighing.

Randy said he would come upstairs with me while I packed, and in my room I told him how angry I was with the way Germaine was treating him and Dennis, never mind me. I said, 'She brings her boyfriend, the coach, here, to fuck, and I don't mind. I treat him well, and after she leaves to get back to the campus I offer him coffee.' Then I said, 'Never mind.'

When we went downstairs, I found Germaine joking with Dennis. She offered us all some of her soup. She told us, laughing, about her affair with '*el coacho*' (about which she has written an article in *Cosmopolitan* magazine), and was very funny. She put her arms around me and kissed me and said, 'You look very tired. You must go to bed.' 'Yes,' I said, 'I must.' The students left.

I have been writing this on the airplane to New York.

Though ill, up all night with diarrhoea, Germaine drove me to the airport.

Providence

As my brothers and I entered the funeral home, my brother Robert, the eldest, turned away from the casket and went quickly to the opposite end of the room, unable to face our mother dead, and I went to him. 'So many things,' he said. 'So many things.'

My brother Donald: retired Marine Corps major, standing at the casket, he saluted our mother sharply then walked out of the funeral home before anyone else, without looking at anyone else, as if he was alone.

My brother Raymond said, 'Her sufferings are over, she's at peace with Dad.' He explained how he received the news of her death: just as he was coming home from evening Mass the telephone rang, and it was the doctor from the hospital who told him that he was sorry to inform him that his mother had expired, but Raymond said nothing until the doctor asked him if he was there, and Raymond said, Yes, I'm here, and would the doctor repeat what he had just said? which the doctor did, Your mother expired this evening, and Raymond asked, Doctor, at what time did she expire? and the doctor said, At seven twenty-four, which was just the time the priest at Mass was elevating the Host and Raymond was praying, Please, God, come and take my mother. Her sufferings have been so great. Come and take her.

My brother Roland: weeping beyond consolation. His family didn't touch him, but stood near him as he wept.

My brother René: he did not come, he could not bear to see our mother dead and, dead, alone.

I?

My brother Lenard: he stood apart, he wept.

We did not want to have anything to do with this death. We were mostly silent.

There were few people at the wake.

After he said a decade of the rosary at the side of the casket, the pastor of our parish shook the hands of all brothers, all sons, and he said, 'You are her seven crowns.'

The undertaker asked us if we wanted her wedding ring removed before the casket was closed; we all said, no, let her be buried with it.

What did she die of? No one knew. Her heart gave out. The doctor who had informed Raymond had asked if the family wanted an autopsy, and Raymond had answered, No, no. She suffered too much in life. Don't let her suffer in death.

The funeral Mass in the parish church, that brick church among tenement houses, with the stained-glass windows donated by the wealthy parishioners, their French names inscribed at the bottoms, and the painting above the altar of the miraculous appearance of Notre Dame de Lourdes to the girl Bernadette Soubirous.

The priest sprayed the coffin with holy water from an aspergillum so the water dripped off the edges.

He said, 'We commend the soul of Albina Marie Odile to you, Lord –'

I thought: She has gone with Dad into the North American forest.

After we left my mother's casket in the cemetery, I said to my brother Robert, 'Do you mind if I don't join you all for coffee? I don't think I can face it.' He held me close to him.

I asked Donald if he would take me to the country house, where he was living. He did, and left me alone there. Snow began to fall.

I walked about the living room, and from a dusty table picked up a book about the Russian repulsion of the Germans in World War II and opened it to a double-page photograph of a young woman lying in the snow; one breast was exposed and the other had been cut off, so I saw the edges of her ribs; she had been hanged, so her neck was arched back, her chin raised, as if she'd been dragged through the snow after she'd been hanged; her face looked alive still, her eyes closed against what was happening to her still alive. Inserted in the bottom left-hand corner of this large photograph was a small photograph, perhaps a school photograph, of the same young woman, smiling a little, looking out, her wavy hair drawn back. Her name was Zoya Kosmodemyanskaya, a Communist partisan who, at eighteen, set fire to a German stable to divert attention from a partisan operation. She was captured and tortured and hanged in November 1941, in the village of Petrishchevo, near Moscow.

On a shelf I found my books, and took down *The Country*, and opened it and read:

My mother and father were born, as I was, among the ghosts of a small community of people of strange blood. They were people who saw that they were born in darkness and would die in darkness, and who accepted that. They spoke in their old French, in whispers, in the churchyard, among the gravestones, in the snow, and with them, silent, were squaws with papooses on their backs, and the forest began beyond the last row of gravestones. They were strange to me, and yet they were not strange.

When I thought about God and our religion in French, God and our religion were familiar. I prayed to my Canuck God.

Seigneur, Seigneur, ayez pitié de nous.

Philip once told me that my parish is my Israel.

I wish I had not written the book as fiction, for it does come, word for word, from my diary.

On Airplane to London

Before the airplane took off, I noted, at the far end of the row of seats I'm in, Allen Ginsberg stand up and take out from the overhead locker a canvas bag from which, still standing, he took out and put back papers and magazines as if he couldn't decide which ones he wanted to read. As there were not yet passengers between us, I leaned forward, when he sat, and introduced myself. I said we'd met years ago through Stephen Spender. 'Oh yes,' he said, 'I met you in New Orleans.' He thinks I'm Bryan. 'No,' I said, 'I'm another friend of Stephen.' Ginsberg smiled. Then the passengers came to take the seats between us.

I realized I have little interest in Allen Ginsberg.

London

Some extracts from letters that Jack Kerouac wrote:

. . . that horrible homelessness all French-Canadians abroad in America have . . .

All my knowledge rests in my 'French-Canadianness' and nowhere else.

English . . . is not my own language. I refashion it to fit French images.

Isn't it true that French-Canadians tend to hide their real sources. They can do it because they look Anglo-Saxon, when the Jews, the Italians, the others cannot . . . the other 'minority' races.

The French-Canadian story I've yet to attempt.

By French-Canadian he meant Québécois-French-Canadian-American.

———

A lovely evening with Nikos. When he returned from work, cold, he got into a hot bath, and while he soaked in suds I sat on the toilet and we talked. It didn't matter what we talked about, the tone was everything, and the tone was familiar. I left him to go down to the living room, where I had prepared some hors d'oeuvres for him – mussels and bits of lobster and spring onions and thin slices of toast – and drinks, and we talked more. For our supper we had a grey mullet baked with dill and lemon, and talked more.

Nikos said, 'How lucky we are to have what we have.' Then he said, 'Spit three times, because we may lose it all.'

'We won't lose it,' I said.

———

I spent an afternoon with Natasha's mother, Granny, now staying at Loudoun Road while Stephen is away. She sat by the window and looked out and appeared very gaunt. Her lower teeth are missing on the right side, and her upper teeth on the left side. She had a kerchief tied about her hair. She turned to me when I sat next to her and smiled. She is deaf. To communicate with her, I wrote out questions in a notebook and she answered by speaking. I asked her if she would like to do a drawing if I held the board, but she said that she was too weak. 'I keep getting weaker. I wonder if I'll ever recover.' I asked her if she would like me to do a drawing for her, which she might advise me on. She said yes, and asked me to draw the flowers I had brought for her and which Natasha had put into a jug. The drawing, I think, went well, and she'd say, when I showed it to her for her advice, 'That's quite good. But you should make the jug bigger.' I'd make the jug bigger and then draw in more flowers to fill the jug. The more I progressed, the more critical she became. 'You haven't got the jug big enough.'

The telephone rang, and, as Natasha had left the house, I went out and answered. When I got back to Granny, I sat to continue the drawing, thinking to myself, this is a better drawing than any Granny could do, but, looking where the jug of flowers had been I saw that Granny had moved it and I couldn't continue drawing.

Natasha came in. I asked her if she had heard from Stephen. She said, 'He's back in Gainesville, Florida. He keeps going there.' She smiled and asked, 'He doesn't have an *amant* there, does he?' I shrugged my shoulders. She said, 'He says he works well there. He's working very hard.'

———

Stephen is back from America. He told us this:

Natasha went to the airport to collect him. She said to him, 'You must ring Nikos. He has a lot of business to discuss with you.' Stephen said, 'I'm so tired, I don't want to talk to anyone today.' 'But you should ring him,' Natasha said. Stephen rang Nikos, and then went into the sitting room and found Natasha in tears. She said, 'The first thing you always do when you get home is ring Nikos.'

I said, 'While you were away, Natasha came to dinner a couple of times. She was lively and affectionate.'

'I know,' Stephen said, 'it's only when I'm away that she really likes you both. Maybe I should stay away for good.'

I laughed. 'Or maybe Nikos and I should stop seeing you for the sake of Natasha and you.'

Stephen said, 'Bryan is a healer. In his attentiveness and loving, he's a healer. He has the love of people which those who deeply love animals have.'

He seems to have put aside the play he is working on. 'Maybe,' he said, 'I'll rework it later.'

He is trying to rework a play he wrote many years ago, *Trial of a Judge*, and has shown it to many people in the theatre world, all of whom send back praise but excuse themselves with the old excuse: theatre is in a bad way, the cost of putting on a production prohibitive, and on and on, which he, I think, attempts to believe is the case.

I don't tell him that I hear from my agents the same about publishing, and I always suspect that it is an excuse.

Then he asked me if I would help with editing and rewriting some old short stories. I said, 'Stephen, I'd feel very presumptuous doing that.' 'No,' he said, 'I need help with my writing now.'

He, Nikos and I met for lunch.

The food was delicious, the waiter was beautiful. We talked about Anthony Blunt being exposed as a former spy for the Soviet Union, and as we all know Anthony the talk seemed to be gossip about a friend.

Stephen said, 'I'm thinking of calling *The Times* and saying, 'I'm the hundred and first man.' He laughed.

He loves people. He is tremendously on the side of life, and he moved me more and more to love people, and to love life, too.

———

Before he left for the South of France with Natasha, Stephen gave me to read a diary he kept while he was in America. He is most moving when he writes about old age and dying, and about his love for Bryan.

He wrote this:

> People to me mean, more and more, a span of at least 50 years, at one end of which are the children, and at the other end the old. Between these are the young who have ceased to be children – Matthew, Maro, Lizzie, David and Nikos for example. Beyond the perimeter of the old are the dead with whom one feels increasing intimacy.

———

Mario Dubsky came to tea. He looked gaunt. He said he had had a revolting accident in a cubicle of a men's toilet, an attack of diarrhoea. I didn't know how to react when he told me he has the virus, which I had known from Öçi. Nor did I know why he had come to visit me. I listened to him talk mainly about his painting, which seems to be in the school of Auerbach and Kossoff for the heavy use of the paint, and I wondered if there was something Jewish, European Jewish, in the heavy use of such paint.

Then, as if this was the point of his visit, he told me that Öçi is H.I.V. positive. (As David Hockney has said, that word 'positive' has now become a terrible negative.) I asked Mario how bad Öçi's condition is, and he said Öçi is having treatment for the sarcoma – I didn't know what that meant, and when Mario explained that it is a form of cancer that appears on the skin in black patches, I had a vision of Öçi's face – but the cancer may be untreatable.

In a kind of dark thrall, I asked what causes the virus to infect.

Mario seemed not to be talking about himself but about the illness as separate from anyone, a homunculus that exists in itself and that sends out rays that infect people – that infect, as the favourite people of the homunculus, homosexuals.

It's possible that homosexuals are especially vulnerable to the virus because of a homosexual lifestyle of clubbing all night and drugs and anonymous sex in the baths, all of which weakens the immune system.

I thought: Well, Nikos and I are safe on that account.

And where did the virus start from?

It's thought, from monkeys in Africa.

Monkeys in Africa? And how did it spread from monkeys in Africa into the homosexual world?

Some people think that the predominantly gay airplane stewards, travelling from city to city all over the world, spread the virus through sex.

From monkeys in Africa to airplane stewards?

Mario did laugh. He said research has begun, but it's not known how long it will take before a preventive vaccine, never mind a cure, will be found.

I said, surely science is equipped to find a vaccine quickly.

As long as the virus seems contained within the gay world, there isn't much incentive for research.

Yes, I see, I said, and I saw the gay world made round, a world which Nikos and I belong to because of a virus that distinguishes us within that round world.

Mario said it has been suggested that people with A.I.D.S. should have a mark on their foreheads to let others know to stay away.

That can't happen.

Mario shrugged.

With evident irony, Mario told me that his parents, Jewish refugees from Vienna, had refused to have him circumcised when he was an infant, wanting him to be assimilated into Anglican England; but as he matured his foreskin gave him such pain when he had an erection he had himself circumcised in a hospital, not for any Jewish identity, but to make sex pleasurable.

He looked very tired, and when he said he had to go I felt that he wanted to stay, and I should have told him to stay, but I wanted him to go. Afterwards, I thought that by letting him go I betrayed the round homosexual world, inclusive of Nikos and me, a world I should be committed to, at least enough to have asked Mario, one of us and ill because one of us, to stay and spend the night.

I carefully washed in very hot water and suds the cup he had drunk from.

He had not said *what* sexual activity caused the virus to infect. Could kissing?

Every morning, I examine my face in the mirror for any sign of a black patch of cancer.

———

Natasha has gone to the South of France to pick olives. Stephen invited Nikos and me to dinner at Loudoun Road. He also invited Keith Walker, who asked if he could come with a new friend, a lorry driver named Richard. Stephen asked, 'Now what should I prepare for a lorry driver? What about a roast? Lorry drivers always like roasts. And what'll I have for pudding? Lorry drivers always want pudding.' He was very amused. I said I'd prepare the pudding.

Everyone thought the lorry driver marvellous.

Nikos and I stayed on and Stephen talked of Bryan.

He seems not to care if Natasha finds out or not.

———

Before Nikos shut the light off on his side of the bed, which has become part of the ritual of our falling asleep together, he asked me, 'Are my poems any good?'

'They are more than good,' I said. 'The fact that you won't send off your poems to the Greek publisher seems very strange to me. It's as if you were purposely blocking the publication.'

'Maybe they're not good enough.'

'They are beautiful.'

'I don't know.'

'You must know.'

'Well, I don't.'

'I'm telling you.'

He shut off the light and said, 'Let's go to sleep.'

Lucca

I am in Italy, in Lucca, in our flat here, waiting for Nikos to join me for the winter holidays. He rang me to tell me that Öçi has died. His brother Tony, whom I had lost touch with, had rung to let me know, and, in my absence, told Nikos.

Nikos said, in a tone of deep commiseration, 'He was your first love.'

It was night; I went out to walk around the town walls. The full moon was encircled by very fine rings of green and red. I was alone on the walls.

The feelings his death rouses in me, like the feelings one can only have for one's first love, are like no other feelings I've ever had for anyone else. My feelings are so unlike any I'd ever had, I think they could not have been roused by Öçi's death, but by something else that happened to him. How could I, out in the light of a moon surrounded by red and green misty circles, account for those feelings, and, much less, grasp what that something was that happened to Öçi? Everything around me was incomprehensible – the bench by the side of the path around the top of the walls – and I was presented, as never before, by this incomprehension. I said, 'How strange.' I kept repeating, 'How strange,' and the more I did the more tears rose up and rolled down my face.

Nothing gave more uniqueness, and in their uniqueness more strangeness, to the things of the world than death did, and Öçi's death – if it was death – made all my world one of uniqueness and strangeness. There was no wholeness in this world, and there couldn't be, not even in the world in which Nikos and I lived our lives together, and would live them together until our own deaths. Öçi had shown me that longing for wholeness was a vain longing, however much I had so longed; and if wholeness was impossible, purity in wholeness was impossible.

But there was another purity, and this was the purity of the clearest apprehension – the apprehension, without longing, of every single thing in all its most detailed particularity, every spoon, apple, glass of water. I sat on a bench and in the reddish-greenish moonlight stared at a shoe, an old shoe, left on the path, and it penetrated no deeper than my merely staring at it, yet on that level of something that I could not name, but I was struck with the force of wonder, wonder totally free of any longing for the world to be in any way other than the way it was, but great wonder.

I placed my hands on my wet face and looked from the shoe to the tree trunk near me, to the highest branch of the tree, to the moon, and once again I said out loud, 'How strange, how strange.'

Öçi, the most embodied person I had ever known, his very body sensitive to the great pleasures of the world, the greatest of these being sex, was dead, and over the afternoon and evening and nightfall his death became to me a vast darkness against which the objects of the pleasures of the world shone; against which a fragment of Coptic embroidery, a faience Egyptian scarab, the marble head of a small Cycladic figure, a glass of ouzo and slices of cucumber, a pomegranate, a silk scarf, a sandal, a glove, an eye, a breast and nipple, an erect cock, a naked foot shone out with the most vivid particularity in that vast darkness behind them that went out and out and out, as deep as the deepest space. It wasn't, I thought, these objects in the mind – a spoon, a key, a coin – that gave the darkness meaning. No, it was the dark in the mind that gave meaning to the objects in the mind. Öçi was always, always, entirely particular, in himself and in what gave him pleasure – the way he might, as we talked, pick up from somewhere a feather and pass it back and forth across his face – but, by a strange mental and moral and spiritual apprehension, it is his death that gives to me the overwhelming sense that death gives meaning to the meaningless details of life. And death is all *out there*, out in the dark, the grand and sublime dark.

Of course we say about the dead that they are with God.

Öçi was my first love, and he revealed, and he does still reveal, so very much to me.

And when I consider Nikos and me, everything about our lives together makes me think, 'How strange.'

London

We were very eager to see Stephen, just back from three and a half months teaching in America, months that he said he thought would never end. Nikos said, 'Now you won't go back.' Stephen said, 'Well, maybe.' He looked very well.

Natasha had spent some time with him in Atlanta, Georgia. There he often said he would like to go to California, and Natasha said she would like to go with him. She knew he wanted to go to see Bryan. Finally, Stephen said they should go together. His and Bryan's sexual love had ended when Bryan wrote to him to end it. In California, he saw Bryan for lunch before introducing him to Natasha and asked him, 'Do you know anything about animal perception?' Bryan said he was doing research in hearing in birds. His principal research is in how small Arctic birds generate heat at low temperatures. Stephen asked, 'Could you talk about the hearing in birds for an hour and a half?' Natasha proposed a picnic, and she, Stephen, Bryan and Bryan's new friend went out into the desert for the picnic. 'Natasha and Bryan got on very, very well.' But Natasha never mentioned Bryan afterwards, except once, to say that Stephen should invite Bryan to stay with them in Saint Jérôme. 'I think that's a bad idea,' Stephen said to her.

She is now at Saint Jérôme with what Stephen calls a lame duck, of whom she cares for many.

Nikos said, 'Surely, Natasha knew about your homosexuality before you married.'

Stephen said, 'In fact, I wrote her a letter before we married telling her I would, all my life, be attracted to boys.'

When he and Natasha were in Atlanta, she helped him edit his diary.

After he left, Nikos and I felt spirited because he had been spirited.

———

Nikos woke me to say that Jasmine is in a very bad way. I got up. She couldn't stand. With a heavy voice, Nikos said we would have to take her to the vet. I said, 'You don't think it would be better to let her simply, quietly die here with us?' 'No,' he said. While we got ready, Mustafa, her son, licked her all over. Jasmine was very still when Nikos lifted her from her pillow, but as he put her into her wicker basket she clawed the edge. Nikos closed the lid and held the basket on his lap as I drove up to Lavender Hill to the vet. I kept thinking: life is all we have. Nikos got out before me and I parked the car and went into the vet's surgery and sat in the waiting room. Nikos came out of the back room carrying the basket, tears running down below his glasses, followed by the vet in a white smock. I said I would pay, and Nikos, hardly able to speak, said, no, he wanted to, and he made out a cheque. Weeping, he said to the vet, 'Goodbye,' and the vet said, 'Goodbye.'

He put the basket with Jasmine's body in it into the boot and we went to our dear friends Richard and Sally Morphet's house in Stockwell. Richard's enthusiasm for the world of art would itself, I think, have made him the curator of paintings at the Tate. And though Sally, at the Foreign Office, is in another world from Richard's, both worlds come together in talk at their dining room table, that includes the politics of non-aligned countries, about which Sally is so informed, and Richard's knowledge of Bloomsbury artists. They had promised Nikos that when Jasmine died she could be buried in their garden; he had, that morning, called them, and Richard had said that their cleaning lady would be waiting for us. We went through the house into the garden, all spring green, with flowering lilac and clematis along the fences, and at the back of the garden found the spade that Richard had left for us.

As we dug, in turns, a black cat appeared, the Morphets' cat, called Agenda, who began to play about the deepening hole; she'd circle the hole, then dart away, once after a bumblebee which she caught in her paws then released, then she would return to look down the hole. Then she jumped onto the basket and sniffed along the edges.

We dug down about three feet, to clay. Nikos took Jasmine, wrapped in a towel from the basket, and, tears dropping from his face, placed the corpse in the bottom of the hole. We covered the corpse. Nikos broke some blossoms from a lilac bush and placed them on the grave.

Nikos is in Athens, invited to give a lecture.

Jennifer was in London for a while with her latest lover, Mathieu Carrière, a German actor. I saw them both at Max's, he away. When I went to pee she came with me into the toilet and while I was peeing she asked, 'What do you think of him?' 'I hardly have any impression of him,' I said, 'but I like him.' After I finished peeing, she pulled down her knickers, sat on the toilet seat, and peed. She said, 'I really like him. I hope it works out.' She wiped herself with toilet paper.

She left with him to go to Berlin, and returned to London alone. She was again staying at Max's, who told me she was there; she didn't ring me and I didn't ring her. Then I did. I went round to Max while he was at work, and Jennifer and I had lunch together, inconsequential, and I left her feeling that nothing had happened, and then wondered if I had wanted something to happen.

Sylvia invited her and me. At the table, both of us drunk, I told Jennifer that I thought she wasn't interested in me any longer, and

I wasn't going to be interested in her unless the interest was recip-
rocal. As if we were alone, we talked, louder and louder, and the
others said nothing. I said she expected me to be interested in her
work when she was not at all interested in mine. She said some
things I've forgotten. Of course we laughed at lot.

She didn't ring me. I rang her. We had lunch in an Indian
vegetarian restaurant. All the dishes were exotic; we left it to
the waiter to choose for us. I recall the food more than I recall
our conversation, which had mostly to do with Mathieu, still in
Berlin.

She was just about to move into Howard Hodgkin's flat in
Coptic Street while Howard was in New York, staying in her loft.
She was frightened, she said, of spending the night alone. Mathieu
would arrive the next day. I said, 'I'll spend the night with you.'
'That would be terrific,' she said. When over the telephone I told
Nikos, I sensed that out of an encompassing acceptance of Jennifer
in both our lives, he said, 'Sleep with her, I don't care.' I said, 'I
won't sleep with her.' She and I went to an Italian restaurant, where
she ate little, and I felt she was restless. We went to a movie, then
to Coptic Street.

She was lying on the floor, a glass of wine, an ashtray, a crum-
pled pack of cigarettes, torn bits of paper around her. Her dress
had looked like a bright, clean, stiff sheet of blue tissue paper; now
the dress was wrinkled, torn where a button had been pulled off,
sodden with water and spotted with wine stains. Looking down at
herself, she said, 'God, I'm a slob.'

The telephone rang and she went into another room to answer.
I heard her say, 'I'll be all right. David is staying the night with me.'
Then a pause, and she said something else I didn't understand. I
knew she was speaking to Mathieu, and I hoped he was anxious
about my staying the night with her.

I got up before she did, and left.

Mathieu came, and I didn't see Jennifer.

Then Mathieu left again to go to Berlin, and Jennifer rang me.
She asked me if I would go to the Royal Ballet with her.

I worked hard at my desk. In the evening I went to Jennifer in Coptic Street. She talked about Mathieu as she went into and came out of her bedroom, and finally came out wearing a beautiful dress that looked like a large pink sheet of tissue paper. We went to the ballet.

The dancer dancing the part of Giselle was a friend of Mathieu. Jennifer said she was in love with him. She had left tickets off at the box office, but Jennifer couldn't remember her name. She said, 'It's Eva Klopaklopaklopa or something.'

After the ballet, she came home with me for supper. She took off her shoes and lay on the floor.

Jennifer told me that when she had been in New York and ill, and had rung me to ask me if she was going to die, and I protested no, no, perhaps thinking she was exaggerating, she in fact *was* in great danger of dying.

She said she was trying to have a baby with Mathieu, but she doubted, now, if she could because of her past illness.

She asked, 'Do you still want a baby?'

'Yes,' I said.

She said, 'You could have had one years ago with me.'

Suddenly, I felt something give way in me, a sadness.

She said, 'I don't think you really wanted one.'

I said, 'I can never tell, in myself, if my desires are literary or not. I don't know if I want a baby because of the *idea* "baby" or because of the *fact*. I don't know.'

'I know that about you,' she said.

She asked if she could spend the night.

I made up the bed for her in my study. She borrowed a tee-shirt as pyjamas.

In my bed, asleep, I had many dreams about paper dresses.

In the morning, I got up when I heard her up. She was dressed in her pink dress, now very wrinkled. I rang for a taxi, and she left. From the window, I saw her, in her wrinkled dress, get into the taxi. The morning light was bright.

San Francisco

I am here with Nikos, he at a College Arts Association conference, I simply to be with him.

While he was at the conference, someone took me to the Castro district of the city, a queer ghetto, if a ghetto can be of its own making by the inhabitants. Walking along the street we passed many very beautiful young men, and also many not so beautiful young men, and some very much older men, and all, it seemed to me, belonging to a world. I am aware of belonging to a world, of world and world within worlds, but I felt I did not belong in this world.

Not only because, in a gay bookshop, none of my books were available, but because the gay world seems not to consider me to belong, not in any way that matters to the gay world.

Whatever world Nikos and I do belong to in London, never do we think of it in terms of sexes, so it is a world that perhaps identifies itself more in terms of a shared interest in – in what? – in a culture of literature and art and music and philosophy.

The men of the Castro also live lives of literature and art and music and philosophy, and they have another bonding identity, A.I.D.S.; and, oddly, instead of condemnation by the outside world, that plague within the inner world seems to be inspiring sympathy in the outside world, sympathy for mostly young men who are dying because of making love. The plague is opening up that inner world to the outer.

Perhaps there is something strangely romantic in the young dying because they make love with one another, the romance of fated love, and especially fated among people who were considered to be fated in their sexuality for being outsiders.

And this brings me to our meeting Bryan.

Stephen so wanted Nikos and me to meet him, and himself rang Bryan in Los Angeles to tell him that we would be in San Francisco and to ask him, please, to drive all that distance for us all to meet. We rang him, and arranged to meet.

He appeared, a thin young man who on sight did appear to be an outsider, if only because of the sense he gave of being more absent than present, more spirit than body.

His hair was long and fine, his slightly pock-marked face pale. He wore a loose, faded shirt, as if indifferent to what he wore. He did appear to be exactly as I would have imagined a young man would appear whose great love was to be alone in the Arctic, for long periods, studying Arctic birds, in touch with a base camp only intermittently. He appeared to me, in himself, at a distance from the world.

He talked about the recent vast oil spill in the Arctic, and he said, with a look in his eyes as of seeing from a distance the oil on the ice, 'Even if all the pollution were stopped now, it is too late.' He said this as with a vision much wider in his knowledge of the world than any vision Nikos and I have.

He could only stay a short time, as he had to return to Los Angeles.

We said how much Stephen had wanted us to meet him, and he smiled a faint smile, hardly raising the corners of his lips.

He said, 'Stephen,' again as if at a far distance from Stephen, then said, 'I would never want to hurt him,' and his tone suggested his accepting Stephen's love for him more for Stephen's sake than his own, he, at his distance, able to live without love.

Stephen is, I saw, the more loving love, and Bryan wants Stephen to know he appreciates that love, which – again at his distance – Bryan doesn't himself now quite feel in return.

Perhaps there was even in his tone the implication that Stephen was being somewhat foolish in his romantic love for Bryan, a romantic love he, however, would not disabuse Stephen of. He suddenly appeared older and wiser and more experienced in love and in the world than Stephen.

He said he is working in a support group for H.I.V.-positive gay men.

London

Nikos got into bed with me.

I said, 'I wish your life were happy. I worry about you.'

'Don't worry about me,' he said.

'Well, I do. I worry about you, and I'll worry about you while I'm in Lucca. I honestly don't want you to be alone. Perhaps I should put off going to Italy.'

'You go.'

'But I don't want you to be alone.'

We were lying close together, he holding an arm over me.

He said, 'You go. If you stay there may be problems.'

A strange sensation passed through me. 'What problems?'

'Problems, just problems. I want to be alone. No, I don't really. But I do, I want to be alone.'

The sensation passing through me was so strong, so unfamiliar, that I wondered about it. 'If you want to be,' I said. 'I understand.'

'Let's go to sleep,' he said.

I said, 'But I must tell you before I leave: that I do love you, that I do love you and will do everything for you. There's no question of that in my mind and there shouldn't be in yours.'

'I know that,' he said, and kissed me.

France

Now on a train, in the Gare de Lyon, Paris, on my way to Italy and Cortona and then Lucca, alone in the compartment.

In Paris, I stayed three days with Jennifer and Mathieu, who were married in New York. Jennifer may be pregnant – having spent two weeks or so in a clinic in Germany where pregnancies are induced by injections of hormones, etc., and artificial insemination with Mathieu's sperm. She used a lot of technical terms to explain it all. But she thinks she isn't pregnant.

She looked fat, her face rough and red.

The first evening, I went out to dinner with them to a friend's apartment, a French couple with two daughters. We talked about Italy. Mathieu said he wasn't very keen on the country because he had never had an Italian boyfriend. There was a slightly shocked pause, and he looked surprised at what he had said. He didn't correct himself, and we all went on talking. On the way back to their apartment, he and Jennifer had a fight about money and about time, or the lack of time, Mathieu will be able to spend with her in the next four months because of his acting.

She said, 'I hate Paris. I hate it. I'm only here because of you, and if you're going to be away, I'm not staying. I'm going back to New York.'

They shouted at each other, and Mathieu called her 'a fucking bitch', but I never felt that their fight would go so far that it would break up their marriage. They seemed deeply married.

The next morning they both apologized for fighting before me.

I said, 'Do you think I don't understand?'

Jennifer asked me questions about my relationship with Nikos – how long have we been separated from each other, how do we feel when we come back together?

The flat was filled with workmen everywhere, banging, sawing, grinding. I slept on a sofa in the midst of it all, and woke up to the noise with work started around me at 8:30 each morning. Among the workers were three American artists whom Jennifer and Mathieu had hired to paint the apartment, finding it cheaper to pay for their fares plus work, and also that the work would be better done than by Frenchmen. The three were homosexuals.

One evening, Mathieu out working, they, Jennifer and I sat before the fireplace, in the midst of building rubble, and ate roast pork and potatoes and salad (prepared by an Italian who comes in every day and who told me she had never worked in such disorder – but, she said, even if there were cupboards to put dishes away, and hooks for clothes, there would still be disorder), and the five of us talked about sex.

Jennifer's brother Jeff has taken more steps towards a sex change: he has had his beard removed by electrolysis and is taking elocution lessons to speak and laugh as a woman does. He now dresses all the time in women's clothes, even at his job, which he has no intention of changing. He is an electrician.

We talked about homosexuality and heterosexuality.

She said she thought that homosexuals did not mature because they did not take responsibility in the world.

I said she was being naïve.

'Well,' she said, 'they've opted out of so much.'

'Like what?'

'Relationships with women.'

I looked at her. 'But I have relationships with women.'

She said nothing.

'And I feel great responsibilities towards the world in my work and in my relationship with Nikos.'

'But you're an exception.'

'I don't think I am.'

'You don't belong to a homosexual subculture like almost all homosexuals do.'

The three artists were silent.

'No,' I said, 'I don't. Nikos and I don't. But I belong to the subculture of writers, as you do to artists.'

I didn't know what the point of our talk was.

I asked her about David, her former lover. She said, 'When he told me he felt he had gay tendencies, I told him to go out to the bars and find out if he really did. Well, he really did. I don't see much of him any more. He said something really devastating about me, which got back to me – devastating because I know it's true: Jennifer is a legend in her own mind.'

I accused Jennifer of being anti-homosexual.

She denied it, with reservations.

I said I'd begun to think that everyone had his or her own particular sex.

She agreed with that.

One afternoon we went out for a walk about the quarter, looking in shop windows. We went into a shop where she tried on different dresses and asked me what I thought of them, then bought the two I liked best. 'Don't tell Mathieu I bought them,' she said. 'He'll be even angrier with me than he already is.'

While we lounged about the messy apartment, often on the floor with pillows, surrounded by rumpled newspapers, coffee cups, bottles and ashtrays, books, bits of wood and plaster and empty tins of paint, as if wallowing in it all, we talked. From time to time she would say, 'This place really is a dump, but it *will* be pretty – won't it?'

Mathieu was in and out, and when in he never seemed to sit in one place for long, except at his typewriter, in the middle of the living room, to continue writing a script, to be called *Champagne Breakfast*. But when he was attentive to me, however briefly, it was with a lively interest.

I came into the living room once and found Jennifer in his arms, and I said, 'Now that's lovely.'

Why did I feel, with her, somewhat dispirited?

She said to me, 'I think you and I are now on the same level of success.'

'No,' I said. 'You make much more money than I do.'

I am alone in the compartment.

Train shaking.

Lucca

Doris Saatchi came to Lucca, where she had never been, to stay with me in the Villa Marchio while John Fleming and Hugh Honour are away and I am caretaking. She is interested in looking for a house in the Lucchesia.

In Lucca, we stopped to look inside a church that had just been restored, its interior reduced to the stone nave with stark columns on either side and the stone apse, the only colour a fresco within the curve at the top of the apse. White light beamed through the high windows along one side of the nave. I said nothing.

Doris said, 'The fact is, colour doesn't move me. Neither does visual narrative. But space and light do.'

In a bar near the old opera house the estate agent Nigel Sudius–Hill was waiting for us. An appointment had been made before Doris's arrival for him to take her to see an abandoned monastery high in the hills outside Lucca. Nigel, English, works as an agent for Sotheby's in London.

An hour outside Lucca into spring-fresh countryside, higher and higher up, round hairpin curves, into chestnut woods, I thought we'd left the industry of Lucca far behind, but, round a sharp curve, a dam appeared, and round another, higher curve, something like a small electrical power station. Doris had said she wanted a view, and the view was of the entire plain, with Lucca and the industrial suburbs, and, beyond, mountains, dark green, high-peaked mountains folding smoothly into one another, and beyond the mountains the gleaming sea.

Nigel opened the door into the monastery courtyard, over-grown with weeds, and Doris said, 'This is interesting.' To one side of the courtyard was the large chapel, deconsecrated; all that remained in the high, stone interior was the altar, broken. Doris said this would be the place to hang pictures. We went through the courtyard again into the monastery, which had had structural work done to it by people who had run out of money, and Doris walked about the small, cell-like rooms knocking on walls to find out if they could be removed or not, as she wanted open spaces. She was thinking, and when she thought, I realized, she became silent and seemed to withdraw to the point at which she seemed not to be attentive to anything Nigel or I said, not even to be attentive to the monastery. Suddenly, she said, 'Okay.'

On the way back to the car she picked a bouquet of wild flowers.

I knew she was not going to buy the monastery.

Doris sat in the front with Nigel who drove us to the Villa Marchio. I was in the back, and as they talked I realized they had met before. I heard him say, 'You did know that Charles and his new wife were looking around Lucca for a place. I showed them some. But they didn't buy.' Doris, smiling a little, said, 'I did hear.'

At the villa, they sat under the loggia, and I went for drinks with them. Doris wanted only a glass of fizzy mineral water. They made plans to see a large villa, outside a village, and after a whiskey Nigel left.

Doris said to me, 'While you were getting the drinks, Nigel told me I'm the most intimidating woman he's ever met.'

'How?'

'Because I never seemed to be paying attention to anything he said, and he was embarrassed about saying anything.'

'But you were paying close attention,' I said.

Doris wore a blouse of white cotton, and in the evening natural silk, but both appeared identical in style. She kept the cuffs unbut-toned and turned back once, the top buttons undone.

We went to a restaurant in the hills outside Lucca. With glasses of prosecco, Doris said the villa of John and Hugh, as beautiful as it is in what it represents of art history, has decided her against getting a house around Lucca. She said, 'It's too civilized for me.'

As always, she spoke with long pauses, thinking, and during the pauses she often delicately brushed away strands of hair from her face with her finger tips, or pulled gently at an eyelash. It occurred to me that there was, after all these years, still a Southern softness in her international voice.

I thought, here I am alone with Doris, as I almost never am in London, so I asked her what made her collect art.

It doesn't matter, she said, what you collect, it could be seashells, but the impulse is to have every single example of seashell that exists. When she met Charles, more or less hired him for the advertising agency Ogilvy, he was collecting Superman comic books. She interested him in collection art.

I said, 'The fact is, you initiated the Saatchi Collection.'

I remember when I first met Doris. Jennifer was staying with her and Charles in their house in Saint John's Wood, where Jennifer was designing, on many different tiles attached to walls and fireplace, their dining room, and Jennifer invited me to come to see what she had done. Charles hardly spoke to me, but at a distance played backgammon with his brother Maurice, and Doris led Jennifer and me to Jennifer's room, where we lay on the bed together and joked, as we always seemed to do when we were together.

Doris and Charles lived in a late 19th century former chapel which Doris had chosen because it was an exaggeration of everything that comprised English architecture, from brick walls in herringbone pattern to fretwork eaves. John Betjeman loved it, and, perhaps due to him, the house was listed. The inside was closer to what Doris was already tending towards – white-walled, generously proportioned spaces – but it was the outside I remember. And I also remember that she and Charles had acquired the ground floor of the house adjoining theirs and opened a doorway into it, and there, in the otherwise bare rooms, they installed pieces of their growing art collection. I especially recall a large John Chamberlain sculpture, car fenders crushed together, in the centre of a stark white room.

It was for their art collection that, just when they were starting to have trouble in their marriage, they created their museum in London. Doris found the site, a disused paint factory and depository, just a block or so away from their house in Boundary Road: a vast, simple structure, its 'dog-tooth' glazed roof supported by exposed metal trusses. She took Charles to see it, and he, too, thought it was perfect except for the walls, which weren't high enough to show the enormous pictures they had acquired. The architect Max Gordon, their close friend, advised them – the solution wasn't to raise the roof, but to lower the floor. Doris was completely involved with Max Gordon in the design of the space. The museum came to be known by its address, Boundary Road, and opened in March of 1985 with works by Donald Judd, Brice Marden, Cy Twombly, and Andy Warhol.

The show lasted eight months, and was replaced, in December of 1985, by a show of the works of Carl Andre, John Chamberlain, Dan Flavin, Sol Levitt, Robert Ryman, Frank Stella. This lasted until July 1986, and in September a new show of Anselm Kiefer and Richard Serra opened. The Saatchi Museum had established itself as perhaps the most important private museum of contemporary art in the world.

Neither Doris nor Charles ever appeared at the openings, but you were always aware of them. It was as if they became abstracted presences, became the space of the Saatchi Museum, in which the spectacular works they bought were made public. From the street, you went through a narrow metal door, painted gun metal grey, which was opened by someone inside with a click when you pressed the buzzer, and you entered a courtyard that had been a loading and unloading area for lorries with a petrol pump and that looked transformed only because it was so empty, so *clean*. There was a sense of power in the emptiness of an industrial building taken over by two people for their personal use, and it was

especially the emptiness that made the space such an expression
of personal power. And the sense you had of power had to do
with what Doris and Charles were able to do. At the same time
you were drawn to go in, you resented, a little, their museum.
Museums, you felt, should be municipal and belong to the people,
and this was entirely private and you were there only because
you were allowed to be by the Saatchis. They had the power to
make it something of a privilege for you to see their collection,
but only in their absence. A guard in a uniform opened the door
with its narrow glass panel inset, and you went into the space, long
and wide, on three levels, the walls white and the concrete floor
battleship grey, and show after show amazed. Any initial resentment gave way to this amazement at what the Saatchis did, and
you realized that your idea that all museums should be municipal
was itself a received idea, simply because no municipal museum
would have been capable of putting on such shows. The Saatchis
were determining a new way of appreciating art. If there were
precedents, I didn't know of them.

Nikos, who was in principle against such a show of privilege,
was impressed. Nikos has always liked Doris, and she him.

You didn't know who was responsible for what in the shows,
which artists were in because of compromises between Doris and
Charles, and which transcended their deepening differences. The
last show Doris had anything to do with was 'New York Now',
Parts 1 and 2, the first part shown from September 1987 to January
1988 and the second part from February to April 1988. Doris had
ceased to have anything to do with the museum but still thought
of the collection as representative of a generation, and she did add
to the collection works by Ashley Bickerton, Robert Gober, Peter
Halley, Jeff Koons, Tim Rollins & K.O.S. After the last show closed,
the works disappeared – some presumably into great warehouses,
some apparently into auction houses and dealers' back rooms – and
never appeared again in the museum.

I asked Doris if she and Charles considered the accusation that
they were harming artists by buy and dumping when buying, and

she said, simply, that they had bought out of enthusiasm. They hadn't known much about contemporary art, but learned as they went along, and if their buying had any influence in the sales of the work, she supposed, yes, that they influenced the sales value of the artists' works. After their divorce, Charles began to sell off more and more of the collection, starting with the Warhols and Twomblys and Minimal works that they had acquired early and that been their joint favourites.

I said that she had a rightful place in art history, because the Saatchi Collection in Boundary Road is an important part of art history, and none of it would have happened without her. Surely he must know that the history of the collection and the museum would be known, and her essential role would be revealed.

She was tired, and I thought, seeing the shadows appear about her pale blue eyes and her sharply angular face behind her light, straight hair become even paler than it was normally, how Russian she looked.

Back at the villa, and we each went to our room for the night. In the morning, I found the double doors of her room were a little open, and I saw, through the crack, Doris, in a white silken dressing gown, standing at a window, wide open, and, in total stillness, looking out at the garden and the view of hills beyond the garden wall. I had one of those odd moments of wondering who she was, who I was, and what we were doing in this villa.

Cortona

I'm in Cortona alone to close an old account in the bank.
Walking along the high street, I saw, in the distance coming
towards me, Germaine, carrying plastic bags of shopping. She
was with a man. As we advanced towards each other, we smiled,
and near her I said, 'What am I supposed to do? The last time we
communicated, you said you were not disposed towards me.' 'I'm
not,' she said. I leaned forward and put my hands on her shoulders and kissed her cheeks. She laughed. 'Where are you having
lunch?' she asked. 'Wherever you are,' I said. She introduced me
to the man, who, his voice high with the improbability, said,
'Oh, I know who you are.' I said, 'You mean, the writer who
wrote a book about difficult women?' He seemed to step back.
About my age, rather effeminate, he was an Australian staying
with Germaine.

Outside a bar in the street, she encountered two people with
whom she was to have lunch, and when she introduced me to
them, a man and a woman, they appeared amazed, and I thought:
Germaine so condemned me to them that they could only have
been shocked that I was with her.

I know about Germaine's condemnations, the least of which is
to reduce someone to a slimy toad.

I became excited being with Germaine, and talked too much.
Germaine went down an alley, and when I said, 'This isn't right,'

she said, 'Stop fussing, you're always fussing.' She knew that we could go into the restaurant by the back way.

The five of us stood around a big square table, the others not sure where to sit, but I said, 'I want to sit next to Germaine.' She laughed, that affectionate laugh she has, which is really a giggle.

As much as I had talked excitedly on the way to the restaurant, I said very little during lunch, but looked at Germaine as she talked. She was beautiful, her hair pinned up in loose loops. Her hands were dirty and scratched from working in her garden.

She said that no reviewer had understood her book, had 'got it all wrong', especially in America. I expected her to rage against them, but she appeared indifferent, and said nothing more about *Sex and Destiny*, as if she was shrugging off both the book and the reception of the book. Sitting next to her, I as if involuntarily often touched Germaine, on her arm, wrist, shoulder. She reciprocated while talking by touching my arm, wrist, shoulder, in a kind of distracted way.

In fact, I felt distant from her.

From time to time, she attacked the Australian, who when he spoke roused Germaine to say, 'If you want to join the conversation, you've got to do better than *that*,' and he said less and less.

And then, I can't recall how, there burst from Germaine a stream of vituperation against the writer Ann Cornelisen, who wrote a novel about four women staging a train robbery, one of the characters based on Germaine. 'Her portrait of me is grotesque. That she should have used the stories I told her is monstrous, and that she should have got them all wrong is more than monstrous.' Ann has a house outside of Cortona. We used to see it when we were at Il Molino.

I reached out for one of Germaine's hands and raised it to my lips as if to kiss it but bit into it, hard, then dropped it. Astonished, Germaine looked at me.

I asked her, 'Will you come stay with me in Lucca?'

'No,' she answered. 'I hate Lucca. It's dark and damp.'

I laughed and thought: *Lucca* is damp.

She said she was cold, and I rubbed her back.

I said to her, 'You should know by now never to be friendly with writers.'

She made a moue at me.

Somehow or other, she and I started to talk about anger. I said, 'Very few people have ever seen me angry.' I again grasped Germaine's hand and looked hard right into her eyes and said, 'You would be amazed by my anger,' and again I dropped her hand. She drew in her chin and simply stared at me.

She said to the Australian, 'Come on. We've got to go. We've got to dig up the carrot patch.'

I called for the bill. Germaine took out her money, many 50,000-lire notes folded together with coins in a clear plastic refrigerator bag.

I said, 'I want to pay.'

Everyone else insisted on sharing, Germaine too.

Germaine and I walked together along the high street, the balding Australian some way ahead.

She asked me where I was staying, as she knew that Il Molino had been sold, and I said in a hotel; I had the momentary sense that she was about to tell me to come stay with her.

'I supposed you're going to have a nap now,' she said.

Again, I had the sense that had I said, no, I don't want a nap, I want to do something, she would have asked me to her house.

'Yes,' I said.

We walked in silence for a while.

'I know you don't like me,' I said.

'Not much.'

I put an arm around her so we stopped walking.

I said, with a coyness belied, I hoped, by something deeper, 'Well, I like you.'

She giggled and said, 'Stop it.'

I withdrew my arm and said, 'I'm not going to say any more.'

We walked on.

She said, 'You know that I don't believe in censorship.'

'I do know.'

'Publish and be damned.'

I laughed. 'One is.'

She laughed too.

She said, 'Do you think we'll go on seeing each other in these haphazard ways?'

'Oh, that would be nice,' I said.

London

Had lunch with Philip in an Iranian restaurant in Notting Hill. Instead of joining us, Nikos went to a demonstration in Trafalgar Square against the killing of whales, seals, against all forms of maltreatment of animals for scientific research, against the cruel breeding of animals for food, against blood hunting as a sport. He came home with many badges. I can't recall how many charities he belongs to for animal welfare, animals helpless against humans.

We met for dinner at Sue Flanagan's. She is divorced from Barry, and is doing everything – from icy cold baths to herbal medicine – to combat cancer, and her face beamed with her smile.

Friends of hers said they have bought Germaine Greer's flat in London. She has moved to a short bicycle ride from Cambridge. The friends of Sue said that Germaine has become active in Ethiopia, where she goes often, and where, trying to help the children dying of starvation because of the famine, she holds in her arms babies who die there, she taking the risk of being kidnapped and held for ransom. And what can I say but that Germaine is a woman who would die for a selfless cause, with no concern about her own death?

New York

Philip invited me for a meal in his new apartment. Claire is in California. Philip ordered a Chinese meal by phone. We had a bottle of wine. As he hadn't had wine in weeks, he got very drunk and kept saying, in a high voice, 'Ou-ee, ou-ee, am I drunk.'

He gave me a copy of the typescript of his latest book, called *Deception*, which I read when I got home, about 9:30. I rang him the next day and said I was very worried about Claire's reaction. He said she hadn't read it, but he was going to give it to her over the weekend to read, and he'd tell her the main woman in the book was in reality someone he knew over ten years ago, just before he and Claire began to live together – 'She can't mind about an affair that happened over ten years ago, can she?' I said I didn't know how she could believe this, given the immediacy of the affair in the book. He said, 'I'll tell her it's mostly invented.' I said, 'Even if it is invented, won't Claire be humiliated by everyone's assuming it's the truth?' He said, 'She knows what it is to live with a writer.'

Over the telephone a couple of days later, I asked Philip if Claire has read *Deception* yet. 'No,' he said.

———

As I'm in New York I went to see the ceramicist Andrew Lord in his studio. I recalled the time, in London, when we went one day to see a collection of Chinese porcelain. We were alone in a

room, looking at delicate vases in an illuminated glass case, and I
had such a sudden sense of Andrew's body next to me I turned and
put my arms around him. He laughed, a light, shy laugh, and his
body seemed, abruptly, to elude me and I dropped my arms. We
continued to study the porcelain.

He wears jeans and tee shirts, and his hair is crew cut.

As powerfully present as he is, Andrew is elusive because his
centre is somewhere outside himself, and he is himself drawn to it.
That centre is his work in clay. His obsession keeps him isolated for
most of his life in his studio, where he is remaking the mortal body
in large, powerfully present pots.

The studio is a long, narrow, high space on the Bowery, the only
decoration a row of geraniums along the sill of the wide, grimy
windows. The domestic appliances in the stark space – a refrigerator,
a stove, a washer and drier, an electric kettle, all dusty and smeared
with clay – suggest that he actually lives there, but they seem never
to be used and to have nothing to do with domesticity.

Andrew, in the midst of plastic bins filled with clay and water,
cardboard boxes, raw, bisquitted pots on the floor, appears entirely
isolated from any life outside, transferring into his work the impressions of all the most vital experiences of the body – the body
sleeping, making love, ill, dying.

He has devised different ways of working the clay to give it its
sensual, both delicate and brutal, presence. One way is to remove
all the marks of his fingers from the surfaces so they are smooth,
and the pots finished in this way have what he calls 'round shapes'.
Another way is 'modelling', in which the imprints of his fingers
pressing the coils of clay into one another are left. (Andrew never
throws the pots, and uses only hand-turned wheels. His equipment
is basic: apart from two wobbly wheels, he has a pugging machine he
keeps covered with a damp rag, and a simple electric kiln.) He has
four variations on 'marking' when the clay is still wet and pliable –
touching and holding, impressing with his palm and fist, pressing
out the clay with his fingers with as much pressure as the clay will
stand, and squeezing. The gold dribbles that appear on the pots are

not meant as mere decoration, but according to an old Japanese use, to cover cracks. Some pots were cast in copper or tin.

(I mention it as an aside, giving no more importance to it than Andrew does, that his work is called pottery only in the sense that pottery is for him material that transcends pottery and becomes sculpture.)

He has made a series of large pots called Biting, Smelling, Hearing, Swallowing, and Breathing.

He asked a dentist to make a plaster cast of his own teeth, and with these Andrew experimented with impressing teeth marks into the clay, but the result wasn't satisfactory, and Andrew himself bit into the clay, over and over, all round the pot, raising what look like welts. Then, for Smelling, he pressed his nose into the clay, for Watching pressed a closed eye. For Hearing, he would press an ear, for Swallowing press his throat, and for Breathing press his bare chest. The effect is both of lumpy crudeness and sensitive fragility, and baroque.

I saw, dominant on a waist-high wheel, a gray clay sleeping head on its side, a great funnel rising out of its temple. Andrew said he had made a dozen or so of these heads, until he felt this one was right. The earlier sleeping heads were resting on metal shelves, and among them were skulls that formed the bases of pitchers with thick, looping handles. The sleeping head and the skull were part of a new series, to be called Sleep, Touching, Phallus, Blood, Death. Touching would consist of hands reaching out to one another across the open space from the rim of a pot, the tips of the fingers in contact. Phallus would be a two-headed snake, the heads erect glans. Blood would be a round, flat dish on three finely curved legs, glazed red. They would be cast in bronze, some, because of the thickness, without being first fired in the kiln.

And so, the body in the body of his work.

The sense of mortality, and, more, of grief, I felt from these works made me go silent. Andrew went to the sleeping head on the wheel and turned it round to look at it, then he abruptly told me, as if he all at once decided that so personal a revelation had to be made about his work, that what had impelled him to do this most recent work was the memory of his finding himself in bed with someone who suddenly began to bleed from his anus, unstoppably, until the sheets were soaked in blood.

The young man was Ritt Warsworth, one of the first people Andrew knew who died because of A.I.D.S, when people died very quickly after they were diagnosed.

London

Philip rang last night from Connecticut. He said he and Claire married a week ago. After their wedding, they went home, got into bed, and read. He said, laughing, 'I believe now in fidelity. Fidelity is terrific.' Philip laughed quietly and said, 'I've become filled with the milk of human kindness, so much so that I'm becoming Christian. I'm not only asking people to forgive me, I'm forgiving people who have offended me. If ever I've offended you, Plotnik, I ask for forgiveness.'

As ironical as he was being, I felt, beneath the irony, a composed stillness. I was impressed by how composed he was, but there was something in the composure that worried me.

We talked about our writing in the world, and he used a strange simile: he said that for readers the wires that used to give an electrical charge to the chair of literature are cut, and the charge gone.

———

Stephen and Natasha, Anne and Elizabeth to dinner. Stephen and Natasha, as if father and mother to the rest of us, sat at each end of the table. There was talk about a Belgian ex-Dominican (Dominic de Groon?) whom Nikos and I have met from time to time at drinks parties, and whom everyone else at the table knew. I asked how he had become a friend of everyone.

Natasha said, 'Oh, I introduced him round. You see, Stephen and I were in Geneva, Stephen at the literary conference and I along with him, and one day a young man joined us to go up in the lift, a good-looking young man, and as we went up I saw him and Stephen making eyes at each other.'

I suddenly felt awkward, and noted that the others at the table felt the same, Stephen blinking a lot, Nikos silent, and Anne and Elizabeth saying, 'Oh, really?'

Natasha said, 'At luncheon in the hotel restaurant, the young man came to our table and asked Stephen, "Have I seen you somewhere before?" and I realized it was time for me to powder my nose while they talked about the sexual activities of monks, because I found out later that he was a Dominican monk, and a very sweet person.'

Stephen kept blinking, the rest of us kept fixed smiles until Natasha stopped, and the talk changed quickly.

I would have thought Natasha would have been the person quickly to change the talk.

———

Nikos answered the telephone when Jennifer rang. They had a long talk about what is going to happen to us all in old age, a great worry to Jennifer. Then I spoke with her. She sounded drunk. Mathieu wasn't back yet, but she was expecting him that night.

She asked, 'What do you think about him?'

'I like him,' I said. 'I think he's intelligent and sensitive and self-aware.'

'What do you think of us together?'

'You seem very good together.'

'Relationships always seem better from the outside than they are on the inside.'

'Yes.'

'I want to know if you're upset about our being together.'

'Do I have a right to be?'

'I'm not asking you if you have the right or not to be, I'm asking if you are upset.'

'Yes, I am.'

'But?'

'I'm happy that you're together.'

She said, 'You've always made me think that if it wasn't for Nikos you'd be with me.'

'I'd like to think that's true.'

'I'd like to, too,' she said. Then she said, 'I can see why you're with Nikos. You and I are undetermined. We need systems to determine us. He's very systematic.'

'Yes, he is.'

'I like that about him. I see why you like that about him. If I met him at a party I would be attracted to him.'

———

I found on Nikos' desk his address book. I opened it to see if Paul's name was in it, and I found the name and the address crossed out, and I felt that I had imposed on Nikos a will that he tells me is stronger than his will, and I wanted to go to him and insist that he see Paul if he wants to, but I won't.

I sensed Nikos was depressed and when I asked him why he brought up Paul, who, he said, he's seen to tell him why he wouldn't see him again.

'What did you say?'

'I said that I'm incapable of having sex with someone unless it means something to me, and having sex with him doesn't mean what it has to mean for me. Sex is a very special act for me. You can have sex with someone and that is the end of it, but I can't, I can't, even if I try. Paul was asking too much of me.'

'And that depressed you?'

'Yes. I was rejecting him, and I didn't want to, and that depressed me.'

When we were in bed together, he said, 'I'm nothing, really, for anyone to want to make love with.'

'How can you say that?' I asked. 'You know how important you are to me in every way, and an essential way is to make love with you.'

'You don't need me.'

'I do need you.'

'You're strong in yourself, stronger than I am.'

'I'm only as strong as the person I'm closest to. I've been made strong by your love for me.'

'Maybe somewhat.'

'Essentially. I know I could never have done what I've done without you.'

'But,' Nikos said, 'you've done it. You have your success, you have your money. You're on your own now.'

'Oh, I see. Really, you're only drawn to those young men who, you think, need help, and not yet on their own.'

'Yes, I am. You're not one of them.'

'Well, I honestly don't think my success, whatever that is, and my making money, however little that is, and certainly not my being more social than you are, can make me independent from you. Yes, I feel that it will make me feel less guilty about taking so much from you, and that means I'll be closer to you.'

'Will you?'

'Yes.'

'You've put up with a lot from me, more than anyone else would, or has.'

'You've put up with a lot more from me.'

'I'm always in need of reassurance,' he said. 'You reassure me when you're here, but when you're away I'm very uncertain of myself, and I think no one likes me, everyone finds me tedious, a heavy Middle European.'

'That's not true, and you know it's not true. You are loved.'

'I know that I am, but I feel that I can't be loved.'

'I want to reassure you.'

'You do, but I need your physical presence to be really reassured. I need it, though I have no reason to demand it from you, because you are on your own. But I do need it.'

———————

At Bianchi's restaurant, Stephen talked about Wystan Auden. He said Wystan once said something which he, Stephen, took very seriously, as he thought it was meant to be taken, and Wystan put his hands to his head and said, 'Don't tell me you too take me seriously?'

Then Stephen told this story: He was having luncheon with Evelyn Waugh at Lady So-and-so's and the luncheon was a great success. Stephen and Evelyn Waugh talked on and on until Evelyn Waugh said, 'I was meant to have my watch repaired before leaving for Dutch Guiana tomorrow, but I see it's now too late,' and Stephen said, 'Well, give it to me, I'll take it round to Garrard's myself and have it repaired,' so Evelyn Waugh gave him his jewelled gold watch. It was too late to bring it round that day, however; Stephen took the watch home with him and put it in a drawer of his desk. That evening, Francis Bacon came to dinner with two of his friends, young thieves, and while one young thief helped Natasha in the kitchen the other prowled around the house. The next morning, about six o'clock, Stephen woke thinking, 'The watch!' and he immediately went downstairs to look in the drawer, and found it was gone. He rang, not Francis, but Frank Norman, who said he'd get the watch back. Stephen told Lady So-and-so what happened and she wrote to Evelyn Waugh, and Evelyn Waugh wrote a severe letter to Stephen that put an end to their friendship. A while later, one of the young thieves came to Stephen with the watch and said, 'Somebody played a dirty trick on me. I don't know how I got this watch, but here it is.' All the jewels had been taken from it.

Stephen was on an excited high about telling stories, which made him laugh when he told one, so that he would seem to withdraw from the general conversation to think of a story, and then, having thought of one he found amusing, he would lean forward and interrupt the general conversation with the story, which would have no connection with the previous one.

He would start a story by opening and closing his lips in preparation.

'I just had a terrific idea. I thought I'd write to *The Times*: "Sir, When Richard Crossman and I were at Oxford as undergraduates we had a sexual relationship. I am the Norman Scott of Richard Crossman's life. For £50,000 I will reveal my name."' Stephen's laughter was greater than his ability to express it, so it shook his body. I asked, 'Did you go to bed with him?' 'Yes,' he said, 'we went to bed together out of hatred for each other.'

And then: 'I was once very much in love with Lucian Freud. I remember telling T.S. Eliot how much I was in love with Lucian. Eliot said, "There's nothing I understand more."'

———

Nikos thinks Stephen is very depressed. I rang him to ask if so, and he said, 'Yes, I am,' as if surprised that I might have thought he wasn't. He feels he has so little time left to finish the work he wants to do, which he never seems able to get to. I said, 'I hope you're not worried that Bryan hasn't written to you in a long while.' 'I do think a lot about him, you know,' Stephen said. 'But I don't allow myself to expect anything from Bryan. Wystan said that an older man who loves a younger must never expect anything from him. Bryan will change. He has to change. He's only twenty-one. But I'll always love him, and I know he will always love me for what we have had together.'

———

Nikos rang from his office to say that, at lunch time, he had gone to visit Mario in hospital, but Mario was asleep. The nurse caring for him was as if protected from any virus that might be flying around the room. Nikos said that Mario, almost naked in the bed, looked very beautiful.

———

I rang Kitaj. He sounded strange, and said he would ring me back. He did, hours later, and sounded stranger. I said, 'You sound in a terrible state, Kitaj.' He said, 'I am.' I didn't know what to say, because I felt I couldn't ask him what was wrong. I asked, 'Is there anything I can do?' and I felt that thrill of alarm when you know something terrible has happened. In a low, hoarse voice, the voice of a man broken, he said, 'No, there's nothing anyone can do.' We hung up and I felt very upset. Kitaj is a very private person – he never talks about his former wife, Elsie, who killed herself – and I thought I couldn't ring him back to ask how he was because I was so very concerned.

———

Kitaj and Sandra have married. Nikos and I were invited to their wedding in an old synagogue in the City. As we were approaching the archway in a modern office block that opened into a court-yard beyond, I saw Stephen rushing through the archway to join Natasha, who was ahead of him, all of us a little late. At the door-way to the synagogue, within the courtyard, Nikos and I embraced Stephen and Natasha, as if the occasion, a wedding, inspired embraces. Natasha wore a green frock and a green hat with a dark green feather on the brim. We went in.

Kitaj was wearing a black suit and a bright red shirt with a black tie. He embraced us closely and kissed us, and I felt in his strong male embrace more than affection, but a sense, too, of – of what? – of compassion, the compassion of someone who has suffered and whose embraces are expressions of that compassion, the compassion of recognizing in others such suffering. He was wearing a black skullcap. David H. was beside Kitaj, also wearing a skullcap, blue with white piping, and kissed us. We were given white paper skullcaps, and the men were separated from the women to sit at opposite sides of the synagogue.

I sat next to Stephen. Behind us were John and James, wearing the hats they arrived with, as if not to have to wear the skullcaps.

The best men were David H., Kitaj's son Lem from his previous marriage, and Lucian Freud. They and Kitaj and the rabbis, in top hats and morning suits and clerical neckbands and white and black striped shawls, all waited under a canopy for Sandra to appear from a side door at the back of the synagogue, on the arm of Frank Auerbach, followed by Kitaj's adopted daughter Dominie, who is Indian and wore a white sari, her midriff bare, carrying a bouquet of violets. Sandra was smiling. She wore a kind of golden hat, around it a white lace veil, and red velvet and gold jacket and a black blouse.

(She said later that she had tried to look as much as possible like Rembrandt's Jewish Bride.)

The congregation stood during the short ceremony under the canopy. Talking to Kitaj and Sandra, the chief rabbi told them that they must use the talent they have to praise God. Kitaj repeated some words in Hebrew, and when the rabbi asked him to repeat some words in English, Kitaj seemed to try to say them in the original Hebrew, and the rabbi said, 'No, please repeat after me . . .' To Kitaj, it was obviously very important that he and Sandra were being married in a synagogue, and he, I imagined, had studied the Hebrew beforehand and memorized it. A drawer, lined with straw, was placed on the floor of the dais, and Kitaj stepped on the glass and broke it. I am getting the sequence of events all wrong.

Lucian Freud, whose white paper skullcap was too big and kept slipping off, stood at the edge of the dais, just outside the fringe of the canopy, and appeared to be unsure of himself, stepping from side to side, reaching as if to steady himself by putting his hands on chairbacks that were not there. His trousers appeared to be many sizes too big for him.

Stephen whispered to me, 'I can't stand being in the same place with Lucian. He is an evil man.'

After the ceremony, Kitaj and Sandra, arm in arm, walked all round the synagogue and out by the main doors, which swung in and out, in and out, clattering, behind them.

The men and the women mingled, hugging and kissing, then out to find Kitaj and Sandra waiting in the foyer of the synagogue to embrace and kiss their friends.

I said to Sandra, 'The fact is, marriage does sanctify a relationship. Relationships are impossible, but they are holy.'

'Impossible,' she said, 'but life without them would be so, so much less.'

'I love couples,' I said.

She said, 'You and Nikos should get married.'

Outside in the courtyard, I saw the impresario for artists Vera Russell, beautiful in a black hat with bright black birds' wings and a black veil over her face, and wearing, she told me, her father's riding coat with an astrakhan collar, which he had worn when horse riding in Russia before the Revolution.

John Golding, smiling, said to me, 'I wonder why I am the only abstract painter who's been invited.'

'Kitaj probably thinks he can convert you,' I said.

David H. was taking photographs.

A bus collected us. I sat next to John. We all got out at Langan's Bistro.

At my table were Gabriel Josipovici and his mother. Bottles of champagne were placed on each table, and waiters came round filling glasses in case the champagne in the bottles ran out.

Nikos sat a few tables away, but we were able to look across and smile at one another from time to time.

At about four o'clock, by which time Nikos had left to go back to work and there were very few people left, I walked home, thinking, over and over: I'm so lucky, I'm so lucky.

I wondered if Kitaj's dark night of the soul had had to do with Sandra not wanting to marry, which she then agreed to.

———

Lunch with Philip.

He said, 'I don't understand why I keep writing. Who understands? Who?'

———

Nikos and I went to Highgate Cemetery for the burial of Mario Dubsky.

Standing in the pit of the grave before Mario was buried, the art critic Bob Rosenblum gave a eulogy, then he climbed out and everyone there watched the gravemen bury Mario.

————

His sex life a total mystery to everyone, or so everyone I know says, Max Gordon has died from A.I.D.S.-related illnesses.

————

I have lived in London for longer than I have lived anywhere else, and my attachment is such that I want to be British, though I know I will never be English.

So I decided to apply for United Kingdom citizenship, though an anomaly, certainly, because as a Kingdom aren't the British subjects? I decided because my life has evolved in this country more than in America. I did not want to give up my American citizenship, but was told by someone at the American Embassy that I could have dual citizenship, which I thought of as a way of bringing together the two countries in my life.

A year or so after my application, I received through the post a form – OA5 – requesting an oath of allegiance, to be witnessed by a justice of the peace, a commissioner for oaths, a notary public, or some other authorized person.

I rang a barrister friend – Brian Green, QC – who lives in Montagu Square and who told me to come immediately to his house. He stressed: *immediately*. Thinking he must be going out with his wife the poet Yvonne Green for the evening and had little time, I rushed round. Both he and Yvonne greeted me warmly, brought me into the sitting room to sit in a deep, soft sofa. I had a choice of reading out either an oath or an affirmation, this last meant for those non-conformists who refused to take oaths, especially in God's name. Though I don't believe in God, I chose the 'Oath of Allegiance':

I, David Robert PLANTE, swear by Almighty God that, on becoming a British Citizen, I will be faithful and bear true

allegiance to her Majesty Queen Elizabeth the Second her
Heirs and Successors according to the law.

Brian insisted I read the oath out, read it out in a loud voice, which
I did, and then I handed the sheet of paper for him to sign, which
he did with a slight smile when he added the date. Handing the
sheet back to me, he said, 'Today is July the 4th.'

New York

Jennifer had a big opening at Paula Cooper Gallery. As she hadn't invited me, I wondered if I should go. (Should I write any of this down? Is it at all interesting to me or to anyone else?) But that was pride, my thinking I should have a special invitation from her – pride or something else – (How superficial my journal has been for a long while, skimming off, as it were, from the top layer without any attempt to go down deeper into another layer – pride or *something* else?). The fact is, I want special attention from Jennifer, want from her the recognition that I am, in my way, on a plane equal to hers (whatever that is), and on that plane – No, no, this isn't coming. I must go back to recounting, superficially, simply what happened.

Both Jan and Mark said I didn't need an invitation to the show, which I already knew. I knew, too, there was to be a party after the show in a new restaurant Jennifer has invested in – knew this from Helen McEachrane – oh, how can I account for all the interconnections? – which makes me realize that I don't write this journal for myself, for if I did, I wouldn't have to make all the connections. I said to Jan and Mark that I couldn't go to the opening in any case because I was having dinner with Mary Gordon. Helen said to me, 'That's *much* more glamorous than going to Jennifer's opening.'

Mary gave a reading that evening at a bookshop called Three Lives, run by feminist lesbians, and as she had asked me to come I had asked her to dinner afterwards.

I did go to Jennifer's opening first, about 6:30.

The taxi passed a big anti-Apartheid demonstration and I did think: here I am going to a gallery opening when I should tell the taxi driver to stop and let me out to join the demonstration.

In the gallery, I wandered about little boats, houses, picket fences and chain-link fences and people also, not recognizing anyone – but in came Jennifer. She was wearing a beautiful white dress with white shoes, the dress bulging a little from her five-month pregnancy. We embraced and kissed and she said, 'I hope you can come to the party afterwards.' Frowning, I said, 'I didn't know about it.' She frowned. 'I've been so busy,' she said. I said, 'I've already planned to have dinner with Mary Gordon.' 'Oh,' Jennifer said, 'invite her. I'd love to meet her. I'm reading her novel and I think it's fabulous.' I told her I'd *try* to come with Mary.

Dick Smith came in. Then Alex and Ada Katz. Then Mark and his friend David (they live together now in the Bank, and David paints pictures on fragments of shattered glass), then Julian, then Jan.

I spoke with Mathieu, who had just come back from Paris, and who looked very thin and sharp-edged, and who spoke in a sharp-edged manner, and who abruptly turned away from me to talk to someone else.

I left and walked from SoHo to the Village and the bookshop. As I approached, I saw a crowd of people on the pavement waiting to get in, a lesbian at the door keeping them out as the bookshop was filled to capacity, so I thought I'd have to say, 'I'm a friend of Mary,' but the lesbian smiled at me and said, 'I've been waiting for you,' and I had the sudden pleasure – what in America is the curious pleasure of being indulged as a celebrity? – of being recognized and treated in a special way, because I was brought through the crowd outside and the crowd inside, stepping among people sitting on the floor, to behind the sales counter to the shop's office where

Mary was sitting in an office chair, her reading material clasped in her hands.

She told me she had just come from a demonstration against Apartheid, where she was to speak, but when she got up onto the platform to give her speech she was told to step down because the black officials had to speak first, then when she, back on the platform, did give her ten-minute speech, she heard people asking one another, 'Who is this white woman?' Mary told this story with a look in her beautiful black eyes of pain and irony at the same time.

She gave her reading, the audience attentive.

After, she signed piles of books.

Then I said Jennifer had invited us to a party, and Mary said reluctantly that she would go, though she had hoped to spend the evening alone with me, but she left the going to me.

We got into a taxi to go to Avenue A and the restaurant Jennifer had invested in, called Hawaii Five-O.

I said to Mary that I wanted her to meet some of my closest friends, who made up a world, largely of artists.

I said, 'You see, I love Jennifer.'

Laughing, Mary said, 'David, your loving something is no guarantee that that person is loveable.'

As we entered the restaurant and I looked around, I felt, not that Jennifer and Mark and David and Jan and Julian and Dick and Alex would judge Mary, but that she would judge them, felt she had already judged them when she said, 'It looks too crowded.' 'I'll go ask Jennifer,' I said, and squeezed my way among tables to where Jennifer was sitting at a long table covered with what looked like the scrapings off many plates. She said sure there was room, she'd saved places at her table, and she made people move to make places for Mary and me. She told Mary how much she liked her novel, and they talked about pregnancies. Jennifer was being attentive to Mary, and I was pleased, but the noise of people talking in the narrow, stark, bare-brick space made it difficult for me to hear what they were saying across the table from each other, but I did hear

Jennifer tell Mary about her brother Jeff, who was going to have the operation to make him a she, and Mary told Jennifer about a transvestite she dated when she was in college, or so I thought I heard, the conversation turned from talking about pregnancies to talk about transsexuals and transvestites. I thought that Mary liked Jennifer. We ate tacos and drank marguerites.

Mathieu came over to the table and, crouching between Jennifer and me, sitting side by side, said, 'I think David should propose the toast.'

Turning to look at him her eyes narrowed, Jennifer said, 'No. I'll leave.'

He said, 'I think David should propose the toast and we'll see if you leave or not.'

Jennifer got up from her chair and went to another table, and Mathieu sat in her chair.

I said to Mary, 'They're always arguing.'

Mathieu said, 'She never does what I want.'

I thought I'd change the subject and asked him what he'd been doing lately, and he said, with a high-pitched groan, 'Trying to take care of my wife. She takes up all my time.'

Mary raised her head and looked away.

Mathieu left.

Mary talked with others at the table and I said I'd circulate for ten minutes to talk to old friends, Eric B. and Peter S. and, surprised to see her come from London for the opening, Doris, and I felt pleased to be among friends who do make up a world to me.

But I also worried that Mary would think: so *this* is the world in which David's intimate life resides!

As she and I were leaving, Wally Tworkov came hurrying towards us to talk to Mary, with whom, she said, she had a close mutual friend. Mary clasped her in her arms and said, 'You're the secretary of Ford Madox Ford!' Wally drew back and smiled and said, 'For five minutes.' 'But I've been wanting to meet you for so long,' Mary said; 'Ford is my absolutely favourite writer.' They talked, planned to meet again, and I felt, yes, that Mary was after all pleased to have come.

We walked to a little café up Avenue A. At a table, covered with paper on which one could draw with broken crayons supplied in a glass, Mary and I talked for an hour. We talked about moments of embarrassment when you recall you did something, said something that made you think you had been and were still a fool.

Mary said, 'It has to do with class.'

'Class?' I asked.

'Those moments of recollected embarrassment come to us because we're working class,' she said.

Providence

I am in a Holiday Inn, in Providence, with Mary Gordon, she having inspired me to come with her from New York to go to Mass at my parochial church, Notre Dame de Lourdes, as if she wanted me to resolve something in me about my past religion that needed my coming back to the church to do.

She woke me at six o'clock for early Mass. I don't know how she found out about the hour, but she did, and she drove up the hill to where the brick church steeple rises among tenement houses. The parish appeared deserted, and Mary parked in a side street where there were no other cars and we got out, and I immediately noted a hole in a stained-glass window, made as if by a thrown stone. I expected, and hoped, the door would be locked when Mary pulled at the handle, but it did swing open and we entered the foyer, where the linoleum tiles, brown and green, and the smell of floor wax were as I remembered from half a lifetime past. There was the rounded marble holy-water font, and the glass panels in the double doors forming, in white and purple, translucent crosses, and, beyond the doors, the main aisle of brown and green tiles leading into the nave.

Mass had begun, the priest facing the congregation of about five people. Mary went right to the first pew, and I followed her, and knelt with her for the consecration. She went to receive Communion while I remained kneeling, my face in my hands, and I kept my face in my hands when Mary returned, and I continued in that position until the end of the Mass.

I wanted to leave, but Mary said, 'We're going into the vestry.'
I had never been in the vestry. As devout as I'd been as a boy, I'd
never been an altar boy and had never viewed the parish priest as
a man I could have visited in the vestry after Mass. I had never
spoken to him outside of confession. I would have been as incapable of opening the door to the vestry, as Mary matter-of-factly did,
as I would have touched the tabernacle on the altar, sacred spaces.
Mary went in first. The priest, already divested, was putting on a
yellow baseball jacket over his black shirt with a clerical collar. He
seemed to have expected us and said, 'Come in.' Grey-haired, he
said he was about to retire.

When I gave my name he said he had buried my father and
mother.

He said he had to go, a baseball team of kids he coached was
expecting him. 'Stay and look around,' he said. And when Mary
asked him where she could get a couple of candles, he said, pointing to a cardboard box on a counter, 'Help yourselves.'

Dim grey light was showing through the windows of the church,
and the air was chilly. The little chapel with the baptismal font,
there where I was baptized, was used for storing cardboard boxes.
The brown and green floor tiles were cracked, and some were
unglued. Mary carried the candles, looking for a place to set them
and light them.

She said, 'This church looks like the butt end of something.'

I said, 'It is.'

Mary lit her candle from the only one lit, in a stand before the
crucified Christ, and I lit mine from hers. She knelt to pray and
I stood behind her, looking at Christ's white body hanging on the
black cross, blood running from his thorn-entangled head, from
his nailed hands and feet, from the lance wound in his side, from
his scourged flesh.

———

Mary told me that she had heard in New York that Jennifer has
given birth to a baby girl, Alice.

London

I had never known Stephen to weep, which I heard in his voice when he rang to say that Bryan has died.

He said, 'I loved him more than I have ever loved anyone else in all my life.'

Europe

Nikos has taken two months off from work for a long trip, by car, from London to Athens.

We are in Athens.

I would like to give an overview of everything we have seen. I'd like to be able to stand above our trip and see it, not only on a map, but as a map of everything we have done. This is impossible. I can only give accounts of the bits and pieces of what we have done.

I would like to be able to account for the differences and similarities among the countries we passed through in the car. Nikos said that might be done by describing the church steeples of the countries.

My longing is to make generalizations, but I can't, because I don't know enough.

I have to concentrate on details.

We've seen so much.

I asked Nikos what he recalls from our trip so far. He said, the countryside around Ham, where we spent the first night; Laon, where we stopped for an hour to visit the cathedral just when a chamber orchestra was playing and a boy's choir was singing and the priest from the pulpit raised his hands and said, '*Comme c'est belle la musique, c'est peut-être une prière*'; and the forests of the Ardennes, especially Beaulieu, where we stopped; and the Stanislas Square in Nancy where we spent our second night; and Colmar and the painting of *Our Lady of the Rose Bush* by Schongauer in the Dominican church (the museum of the Unterlinden was closed so we couldn't see the Grünewald Isenheim Altarpiece); and the Rhine; and Meersburg on Lake Constance, where we spent another night in a hotel called the Schiff, right on the lake, and there we drank marvellous white wine; and beyond Bregenz into the Austrian Tyrol; the crossing into Italy at the Reschen Pass and the drive down through the Italian Tyrol (which he didn't like so much because it was really German, not Italian); then the drive through the Veneto to Vicenza, where we stayed, and in the evening and the next morning walked about to study the Palladian buildings, and where we had our best meal; and then to Arezzo for the Piero *Discovery of the True Cross* and the drive to Città di Castello and from there to see the Piero *Madonna* at Monterchi and the *Resurrection* at Sansepolcro, which we had done a number of times when we had Il Molino, but which Nikos wanted to see again –

In a little Italian town, the name of which I've forgotten and where we stopped for lunch, we saw there was a festival in the piazza put on by *l'Unità*, the Communist newspaper, and we went to see. A slender taut aged woman in black, including a black kerchief tied tightly about her head, motioned us over to a trestle table on which was a roasted pig and bread and *fiaschi* of wine, and there we had our lunch. She asked us where we were from, and smiled when Nikos said Greece, and frowned when I said America. Music came from loudspeakers in a tree, and when the 'Internationale' came on the woman sang in Italian, and Nikos sang in Greek, but I did not know the English, and put my hands together as if praying to silently plead with the woman to forgive me. Tears were in my eyes seeing the old woman and Nikos singing the 'Internationale'.

I thought, as Stephen Spender from time to time has said: how can Nikos be happy in the capitalist world whose principles are not only in opposition to his Communist principles, but defeat his principles? I am most often unaware of this defeat in Nikos, because we live our daily lives, it seems, with no consciousness of overriding principles, but now I was vividly conscious. And conscious, too, that the little *Unità* festival was scruffy, and that the volume of the music from the loudspeakers was in excess of the number of people to hear it, though those who were there, as if in a chorus, did sing against their defeat, Nikos among them.

———

From Ancona, we took the ferry to Corfu. On Corfu, we stopped at a tavern for lunch – a stark building at the edge of the road, in a field, with a van pulled up under the corrugated-iron roof among the tables; bare bulbs dangled from wires. Three men were sitting at an oilcloth-covered table nearby; one was talking very loudly, sometimes shouting, and Nikos said he was a Communist shouting at the others for not being Communists. We were served our meze – meat balls and *tzatziki* and whole grilled anchovies – and while we ate the Communist stood and shouting more raised his jacket and raised his shirt to show the scars from torture when he was in a concentration camp for Communists on the island of Gyaros, where, Nikos said, Yannis Ritsos had been imprisoned. The man shouted: he was proud to be a worker; he shouted that capitalists were blinding men by sticking fingers in their eyes. Behind him, smoke was billowing out of a small shed, where the owner of the tavern was grilling lamb chops. The Communist, drunk, now shouted at one man who sat very still, but staring at him, then when he said something about a *viivlio*, though Nikos didn't understand what book, the drunken man Communist pushed the seated man, who stood, and they began to fight. The other men, one very fat, came out of the tavern to stop them. The – presumably – non-Communist stood back, tucking his shirt into his belt while the Communist, held back by two men, shouted insults at him, calling him a *putana*, then broke away from the men restraining him and slapped the non-Communist with his hand wide open across the face, and challenged him to a duel, to meet the next morning in their village square and fight until one of them won. The Communist said he would flatten

the non-Communist flatter than a transfer. The two men began
to fight again and again were separated. The tavern owner, looking towards us, said to the two men fighting that they shouldn't
in front of strangers. In the midst of all this, a large woman and
a girl walked about, with an air of ironic indifference, carrying
onions by the shoots in one hand and jugs of wine in the other.
After a while, the two fighting men calmed down and sat at separate tables, and as we were leaving the non-Communist got on his
motorbike and went off.

———

Athens is very hot and noisy, and we can't sleep. We are staying in
the flat of Nikos' mother, as it has been since she died.

From Corfu, we took the ferry to Igoumenitsa, then drove over
the dark mountains of Epirus to Ioannina, from where I remember passing a workshop in which men at a long workbench were
hammering out copper pots and dishes. We spent the night at
Dodona, then on over more high dark stark mountains of Epirus to
Meteora, where we had lunch, then to Kalabaka and the next day
through the plains of Thessaly, then over more mountains, passing
mountain villages and towns, to Lamia, and over more mountains
and through Amphissa to Corinth, where we spent the night in a
hotel on the beach, then the next morning to Nafpaktos, where
Cervantes lost an arm during the battle of Lepanto; then to Itea,
Delphi and Hosios Loukas and Thebes and finally to Athens.

Nikos had been to these places, but he couldn't remember when
and with whom; he couldn't remember anything about them.

———

To be aware. Oh yes, I am. I am aware of everything. Everything –
shop signs, a car tyre propped against a cement wall, a wooden box
of apricots, a plastic crate of *gasosa* bottles, a eucalyptus tree in the
wind, a wet *flokata* rug hanging over a balcony railing and dripping,
olive-oil tins, geraniums, a television set in a taverna, an oleander
bush, a kiosk selling newspapers in many languages – is an object of

awareness. And I have to ask myself: what awareness? What is the awareness that all the objects refer to?

As always, the terms I use I use confusedly. The term *awareness* has a deep and complicated history in Greece, and I, in Greece, am aware of that history, and, yes, it is a history that expanded beyond Greece into the whole of the Western world, and, expansive as it still is, is still the awareness with which, hardly aware that we do, we see, hear, touch, smell, taste, and which makes sense of what we see, hear, touch, smell, taste. I mean, Greek metaphysics.

And if I like to think I have a metaphysics of my own, which I do, I of course have one because of Greece. But when I ask myself, well, what do you mean by using the term *awareness*? I don't know what I mean, but I do know that, by some strange process of perception, details *do* make us aware, and our awareness made vivid *does* expand into something more general than the details. The irony is, I suppose, that the more vivid the details, the more aware I become of awareness, to which the details refer expansively. And, to me if to no one else, that expansive awareness is, ultimately, a universal awareness at its most idealistic to which, ultimately, my awareness refers.

At Hosios Loukas, oh, what awareness! Oh, the joy of the golden mosaiced space of awareness!

And the wonder: what is awareness itself, that magical, mysterious view of the world all around us?

The heat and noise of Athens make it very difficult to appreciate the city.

I remember Dodona, green, cool. There was no one in the wooden hut where we were supposed to buy tickets into the site of the ruins, and I noted that within the hut was a narrow bed covered by a kelim. Without tickets, we passed through the gates and into the site of ancient stone walls and pillars as porous as black sponges. A young man was cutting dry grass with a sickle and making bales, and others, on the far side of the ruins, were cutting the high grass with sickles. Nikos spoke to the young man, who identified the ruins and smiled and seemed very gentle. In that valley, with its clear green trees going up to the surrounding mountains, the tops with a little snow, I thought everyone must be gentle. There was a breeze, and from everywhere came the light, constant sound of sheep bells, like water gurgling in a stream. We climbed up to the top tier of the amphitheatre; the background of any play performed there would have been fields of clover, poplar trees, the mountains, the sky. In a field just beyond the ruins, farmers were hoeing the earth. We descended, walked on, deeper among the ruins, to the oracle's house, a square of large stone blocks, grass growing in the open square. I stood on a block of stone but couldn't step down into the square, because this was a pure place and I am impure.

We decided to spend the night in Dodona in a small hotel near the ancient site. Before dinner, we walked up into the foothills of the mountains to the village of Mantio, where the oracle ritualisti-cally came from. The village was falling apart, and what was new was made crudely with cement. There is so much rubble in all of Greece, and here there was garbage, broken bottles and rusted tins and plastic bags in a dry riverbed. Farmers came by on donkeys, and they all smiled and wished us good evening. In the village we sat at a café under a vine, with a view, below us, of the ancient theatre. An old man wearing a beret talked to Nikos, then the owner of the café; they said that no one under fifty lived in the village, all the young had left. The café owner took from his wallet the plastic identity card of a young man, his son. Studying ship-building in Bristol, England. As the old men and Nikos talked about the poverty of the area – the inhabitants there live off their sheep – an old woman walked by, bent over under a load of wood on her back, and with a spindle teasing out yarn from a hank of wool. The old man wearing the beret offered us some *tsipouro*, the spirit made from the lees of wine; Nikos then offered him *tsipouro*. With each drink we were given, on a little saucer, meze: sliced hard-boiled eggs on bread, sheep's cheese on bread, finely cut-up salad. The old man wearing the beret told us to come back, and he would kill and roast a lamb.

I knew that Nikos was happy, that he was in a world that he believes the world to believe in.

In the late evening, when we got back to the restaurant on the terrace, we found we were the only guests, and were served chicken grilled with oregano, tomato and cheese salad, home-baked bread, fresh yogurt, a local light wine.

Of course I hate my awareness, and wish I could give it up, or destroy it.

———

Athens cooler, and I feel better.

Of our trip, what keeps coming back to me:

We were driving up into the mountains from Nafpaktos, and, turning round a bend, saw, in a wood off the heat-glaring, pot-holed road, a fountain. We backed up, parked the car under a tree, and got out to drink from the fountain modelled on an ancient Greek fountain: a marble stoup in a wall, and overflowing from the stoup a gush of mountain water that fell into a little square pool, which itself overflowed through a trough to form a stream that flowed, about stones and the trunks of huge holm oak trees, into a wider stream that flowed down the side of the mountain. The stoup was green-brown with water algae. The water was cold and tasted as clear as it looked. The wall the fountain was set into had, like a little temple, a pediment with a keystone, and on the keystone was carved: '1969 TO NEPO TIΣ AΓAΠHΣ'. On either side were marble seats.

We decided to have lunch there, and I brought from the car the plastic bag of bread, cheese, tomatoes, and we put these on a marble seat.

But Nikos said that before we ate he wanted to clear up the area around the fountain. He began to collect together what had been thrown about: old newspapers, plastic cups, wads of toilet paper. I said, 'But it will be littered again once we leave.' He said, 'I want to do it.' I helped him. We even cleared the woods around the fountain and the stream, and, too, a pool that formed among the exposed roots of the biggest holm oak. We collected the debris into a pile by the fountain – including men's socks, broken children's toys – and with dry sticks to help the burning Nikos set fire to the heap. While the fire burned, sending smoke up into the branches, we had lunch.

After lunch, I said we should douse the fire and go on our way. Nikos said, 'I'd like to stay. I like it here.' He kept the fire going to burn all the rubbish down to ash. I sat on a marble seat and watched him.

———

To remember, if I will remember:

On the way to Hosios Loukas, we passed through a village called Distomo, at the entrance to which was a hand-painted sign in four languages: 'THIS LAND WAS MADE SACRED BY THE MASSACRE OF 218 INHABITANTS BY THE EVIL INVADERS OF HITLER'. The road to Distomo is one of the roads among three at the junction of which Oedipus killed his father.

To remember:

The cathedral at Kalabaka, Byzantine, with storks nesting in the detached campanile; all the frescoes were soot black, only the outlines of the saints with their haloes visible; a delicate crystal synthronon in the centre of the church, and a stove pipe across the nave.

Also at Kalabaka: the entire main street packed with men watching a football match on a coloured television set.

Also, in a yard, behind a wire fence, stacked slabs of marble.

At Dodona: the dark blocks of stone in the high grass.

In Metsovo: at an outside restaurant, a little girl carrying carefully, in both hands, a glass of water towards three men sitting at a metal table.

In the traffic of Trikala, a beautiful boy on a bicycle, carrying a large window frame.

Near Amphiarion, trees, houses, parked trucks covered in the dull red dust of bauxite from a nearby mine.

And from before Greece, on the ferry from Ancona: passing along the coast of Communist Albania, dark, without one lighted house.

———————

Nikos asked me if I would like to see where he will be buried. I said it would make me sad, but that, yes, I would go. He wants to be buried with his family. I do not want to be buried with my parents, though my brother Donald has told me that my burial space has been paid for and is waiting for me to lie forever with my mother and father, though I have not been to the grave since my mother's burial, and do not know where the cemetery is, except somewhere in Providence, a Catholic cemetery called Saint Anne's. I have no idea where my body will end up, and think now that I would like to be cremated and my ashes spread on the Aegean.

Nikos and I wore ties and jackets. We took a taxi, and looking out I wondered how I can characterize this city of Athens, which I thought must be in its details, as I am very bad at making generalizations. When we got out at a church near the cemetery, its bell was tolling, and from its steeple the Greek flag was flying at half-mast. Outside the church were many old women in absolute black, and along the pavement gypsies begging or selling candles and incense and charcoal for burning the incense. Nikos wanted to buy flowers, and went to a shop at the side of the cemetery – rather, what looked like a temporary stall put together with glass, thin rusting metal frames badly painted green, corrugated sheets of metal, cinder blocks badly cemented together so the cement slopped out of the cracks, wire, unpainted boards, sheets of clear plastic; the flowers, in plastic buckets and earthenware pots, were beautiful and fresh. With a big bunch of flowers we entered the gateway into the cemetery, all the marble blazing white in the sunlight. Many people, some standing about talking, some washing the marble slabs over the tombs. Tombs like small temples. Flowering judas trees alongside the paths, the tombs at either side, some tombs like small temples. The Stangos tomb had overgrown weeds growing from cracks, neglected. Angry, Nikos went to find the caretaker who is meant to keep the tomb in order, but came back, more angry, because he couldn't find the caretaker. He and I took off our jackets and rolled up our sleeves and pulled out weeds. Here his father and mother, his grandmother, and two aunts are buried. Nikos found a hose and attached it to a spigot and washed down the marble, washed out the marble containers at the foot of the tomb and placed flowers in each. The caretaker came, Nikos shouted at him, he shouted at Nikos, and went away. Nikos went for a priest, and was away for a long time while I arranged the flowers in the marble vases. The priest wore a high black cylindrical hat, a black soutane, and a white and silver stole; he said, rocking back and forth a little and mechanically, a prayer over the tomb. When he left, Nikos said, 'Let's go,' in the tone he uses when he says, as he often does, 'It's too late, too late for anything,' and, both of us silent, we slowly exited by the gate.

This is where Nikos would be buried.

———

We had lunch – fried aubergines and boiled courgettes and carrots and *scordalia* – and Nikos went to nap, I to follow in a little while.

My vision of history is so naïve that when I read of the foreigners in the court of, say, Alexius of Byzantium, I am amazed; it is as though I could only imagine Byzantium as entirely Byzantium, an historical entity that is self-referential. But had I been there in the court I might have met, say, an Englishman, an Egyptian, a Persian, even a Chinaman. It is the historical cross-references that excite me, and always have.

Now to join Nikos for a nap.

———

Back from a walk with Nikos to the top of Lykkabetus in the evening light. As we climbed, he described how Athens, starting in the 1950s, developed from a town to the immense city it now is.

He said, 'It was because of the Truman Doctrine. America gave Greece a huge loan after the civil war for reconstruction, and it's because of that that Greece is in the mess it is today.'

I asked, 'So you'd prefer that America hadn't given it?'

'Yes.'

'And do you think Russia wouldn't have taken over, maybe in a worse way than America?' I said. 'It's either America or Russia for all the less powerful countries. Can you name a country that isn't dominated by one or the other?'

He laughed. 'Switzerland,' he said.

At the top were many foreigners, some speaking strange languages.

I stayed outside but he entered a small white church where a service was being held. I saw that the priest was wearing a white cope, and saw Nikos going from icon to icon, making the sign of the cross. When he came out, he asked, 'Why didn't you want to come in?'

'It looked crowded and hot inside,' I said.

We walked down the high white rock.

He asked, as he often does, 'Why don't you join the Greek Church?'

'Would you want me to?'

'Well, it's the only true Church.'

'I thought the Roman Church was. But I can't join, because I'm not a believer.'

He knew this, so was ironically surprised. 'You don't believe?'

'No,' I answered.

'I do,' he said.

This surprised me.

'Don't you believe in the First Cause?' he asked.

I said, 'All my training in philosophy was based on the First Cause and its ultimate proof of the existence of God. You don't have to tell me about the First Cause, from Aristotle to Aquinas, which was, really, where my philosophical training stopped. But, no, I don't believe that the First Cause proves God exists. Still, still,

still – though I don't believe, something beyond my not believing makes me think that whatever we are we are because of something beyond us, out there where I suppose the great First Cause revolves around the world, revolves around us now.'

Nikos put his hand over my shoulders.

He often tells me I do believe.

As we descended, we came across a troop of soldiers, carrying rifles on their shoulders, ascending.

Acknowledgements

To my dear editor Anna Simpson for her devotion, and to my dear friend John Byrne for his advice.

Index

ALSO AVAILABLE BY DAVID PLANTE

BECOMING A LONDONER

A Diary

From previous lives in New York and Athens, David Plante and Nikos Stangos arrive in London as strangers to this new city and embark on a partnership that will endure for forty years. From the King's Road to Bloomsbury, connections appear to criss-cross through the air and the couple strike up friendships with Francis Bacon, Sonia Orwell, W. H. Auden and David Hockney, to name a few.

Plante has kept a diary of his life among the artistic elite for over half a century. Spanning the mid-sixties to the early eighties, this first volume of his memoirs reveals an intimate portrait of a relationship and a luminous evocation of a world of writers, poets, artists and thinkers.

'Absorbing, illuminating and hugely entertaining …
A vivid memorial to an entire era'
Times Literary Supplement

'Elegiac and often very funny … The treat of the year'
Spectator, Books of the Year

'The complexities of interconnected liberal literary and artistic life in 1960s and 1970s London are exposed in candid extracts from the extensive, sharply observant, drily witty diary that Plante has kept since 1966'
The Times, Books of the Year

ORDER YOUR COPY:
BY Phone: +44 (0) 1256 302 699; BY EMAIL: DIRECT@MACMILLAN.CO.UK
DELIVERY IS USUALLY 3–5 WORKING DAYS. FREE POSTAGE AND PACKAGING FOR ORDERS OVER £20.
ONLINE: WWW.BLOOMSBURY.COM/BOOKSHOP
PRICES AND AVAILABILITY SUBJECT TO CHANGE WITHOUT NOTICE.

BLOOMSBURY.COM/AUTHOR/ HTTP://WWW.BLOOMSBURY.COM/AUTHOR/DAVID-PLANTE/

BLOOMSBURY